Spice & Kosher:
Exotic Cuisine Of The Cochin Jews

Spice & Kosher

Exotic Cuisine of the Cochin Jews

Dr. Essie Sassoon
Bala Menon
Kenny Salem

TAMARIND TREE BOOKS
Toronto

Copyright © 2013 Bala Menon

All rights reserved. No part of this publication may be reproduced, stored in a retrieval system or transmitted in any form or by any means, electronic, mechanical, photocopying, recording or otherwise, without the prior written permission of the publisher. Inquiries should be addressed to:
        Tamarind Tree Books Inc.,
        14 Ferncastle Crescent,
        Brampton, Ontario. L7A 3P2, Canada.

Library and Archives Canada Cataloguing in Publication

Sassoon, Essie, 1936 -
Spice & Kosher: Exotic cuisine of the Cochin Jews /
Essie Sassoon, Bala Menon, Kenny Salem.

Includes bibliographical references and index.
ISBN 978-0-9919157-0-5

1. Sephardic cooking. 2. Jews - India - Malabar Coast - History.
3. Cookbooks. I. Menon, Bala II. Salem, Kenny III. Title.
IV. Title: Spice and kosher.

TX724.2.S47S28 2013   641.5'676   C2013-901738-0

To All Mothers

Contents

Acknowledgments		ix
Introduction		xi

Part I In Cochin, Kerala

Chapter 1.	Story of the Cochin Jews	3
Chapter 2.	Kerala Cuisine - Aromas, Colours & Flavours	9
Chapter 3.	How We Kept *Kosher* in Cochin	14
Chapter 4.	*Unu Nammukku* - Our Food (The Grace)	21

Part II Food Links Past & Present

Chapter 1.	So, What's For Breakfast?	27
Chapter 2.	Bounties From The Nets	38
Chapter 3.	Poultry In The Pot	58
Chapter 4.	*Kubbah*, You Adorable Dumplings!	70
Chapter 5.	The Lure Of The Pastels	75
Chapter 6.	Here's The Beef, Although It's Rare!	81
Chapter 7.	Lamb/Mutton	88
Chapter 8.	*Ris, Riso, Arrozo* or *Ari*, Rice is Nice!	93
Chapter 9.	Our Bread Basket	105
Chapter 10.	Our Vegetable Garden	111
Chapter 11.	Chutneys & Salads - Things to Relish!	126
Chapter 12.	Pickles & Preserves - Things in Jars!	137
Chapter 13.	Wine & Other Fine Drinks	143
Chapter 14.	In Plantain/Banana Country	154
Chapter 15.	Savouries, The Cochin Surprises!	158
Chapter 16.	Eating Brick & Mortar - The Charoset	163
Chapter 17.	Our Sweets are Sublime!	168

Part III An Ancient Treasure Chest

Chapter 1.	The Spice Story	191
Chapter 2.	Game-Changers in the Cochini Kitchen	196

Bibliography		202
Index		204

Acknowledgments

*"With all good wishes - May you succeed in your efforts
to tell the very important story!"*

This was what Dr. Barbara Johnson scribbled when she signed a copy of her acclaimed book *Ruby of Cochin: An Indian Jewish Woman Remembers*, in January 2011, at a York University event in Toronto, Canada.

It is an important story - about a microscopic community of Jews that lived in a remote corner of India called Cochin for two millennia. They practised their religion without fear or persecution and integrated with the social, political and economic life of the region, along with their Hindu, Christian and Muslim neighbours.

As Dr. Nathan Katz and Ellen Goldberg wrote in their *The Last Jews of Cochin: Jewish Identity in Hindu India*: "They acculturated without being assimilated and did not disappear like the Kaifeng Jews of China."

In their personal lives, there was great drama, beginning with high political and economic status in their early settlement of Cranganore, internecine violence, atrocities during the Portuguese era, clashes with the Moors, romance, diplomacy, high finance, international trade in spices and the anticlimactic 'sudden death' emigration to the Holy Land.

The food is part of the Cochin Jewish story. The mention of several emblematic foods of her community by Ruby Daniel in her book was the start of a project to collect this set of recipes, some of them hundreds of years old. Most of the dishes are still made the same way. Many visits to Kerala and Israel followed and several people helped along the way. We gratefully acknowledge their assistance.

Acknowledgments

Our thanks to:

- Dr. Nathan Katz, Bhagwan Mahavir Professor of Jain Studies and Professor of Religious Studies, Florida International University, Miami, Florida.
- Ellen Goldberg, editor/photographer, Miami, Florida.
- Dr. Barbara Johnson, Emerita Associate Professor of Anthropology, Ithaca College, New York. Visiting Scholar, Cornell University, New York.
- Dr. Shalva Weil, Hebrew University of Jerusalem, Israel.
- Dr. Ophira Gamliel, Hebrew University of Jerusalem, Israel.
- Dr. M.G.S. Narayanan, University of Calicut, Kozhikode, Kerala, India.
- Dr. Scaria Zakariya, Kalady, Kerala, India.
- Gila Rosenblatt, Aberdeen, New Jersey, United States.
- Ora Farchy, Houston, Texas, United States.
- Shlomo Mordechai, New York (N.Y.), United States.
- Bernadette Baum, New York (N.Y.), United States.
- Linda Hertzman, Vancouver, Canada.
- Rachel Roby, Petah Tikva, Israel.
- Bezallel Eliyahu & Batzion Bezallel, Moshav Kidroon, Israel.
- Shalom & Esther Nehemia, Moshav Nevatim, Israel.
- Pearly Simon, Haifa, Israel.
- Sippora (Venus) Lane, Tiberias, Israel.
- The late Sima Molly Muttath-Pal, Hadera, Israel.
- Matilda Davidson, Petah Tikva, Israel.
- Dr. Glennis Salem, Haifa, Israel.
- Yosef Hai family, Kfar Yuval, Israel.
- Yossi Oren, Moshav Taoz, Israel.
- Queenie Hallegua, Mattancherry, Kochi, Kerala, India.
- Reema Salem, Mattancherry, Kochi, Kerala, India.
- Sarah Cohen, Mattancherry, Kochi, Kerala, India.
- Elias (Babu) Josephai and family, Ernakulam, Kerala, India.
- Sam Abraham, Association of Kerala Jews, Ernakulam, India.
- Vicky Raj, Koder House, Fort Kochi, Kerala, India.
- Ajeeth Janardhanan, Executive Chef, CGH Earth, Brunton Boatyard, Kochi, Kerala, India.
- Daniel Dangoor, *The Scribe Magazine*, London, England.
- N.S. Madhavan, Retired IAS officer and writer, New Delhi, India.
- ... and many others in Israel and Kerala, India.

Introduction

The *Cochinim* (as the Jews from Cochin are called in Israel), like Jews across the world, love their food. Living for around 2,000 years on the lush, monsoon-swept Malabar coast in the southwestern corner of India, this close-knit, orthodox community stayed true to the dietary rules of the Bible, adapting the abundant and exotic local produce to develop some wonderful dishes.

Foremost among the culinary treasures the land yielded was the ubiquitous coconut; complementing it were the universally-loved pepper and spices like cardamom, cinnamon, ginger, turmeric, asafoetida, red and green chillies, coriander, fenugreek, fennel, assorted lentils, curry leaves and an astounding variety of vegetables and fruits.

All of us who love making, serving and enjoying good food, know that recipes do not demand total obedience. The kitchen is a place for creativity and recipes can be interpreted, ingredients altered and adapted to suit individual tastes and the produce available at hand.

Every Cochini Jewish kitchen was a place for gourmet cooking, with dishes that burst with flavour and health, tantalized and satiated generations. The Jewish housewife picked up ideas from friends, neighbours and acquaintances, tweaked them to conform to Jewish law and passed it down across generations, through daughters and daughters-in-law. Most recipes in this book are based on resources available in the Cochini Jewish kitchen around the middle of the 20th century, although not much has changed today. Cochin Jewish mothers were also reputed to be practical in the use of raw materials; they added, for instance, more potatoes in meat dishes to increase volume and feed larger families.

All these recipes adapt themselves to the modern kitchen with its electric blenders, ovens, refrigerators and microwaves. Printed or mimeographed records have been difficult to come by, although many Cochini women in Israel still remember being gifted these on their wedding days.

Ruby Daniel and Dr. Barbara Johnson mention some names of popular early 20th century Cochini dishes in their book *Ruby of Cochin: A Jewish Woman Remembers*.[1] We have tracked down all of them. Dr. Nathan Katz and Ellen Goldberg, who wrote the definitive anthropological book *The Last Jews of Cochin: Identity in a Hindu India*,[2] included some recipes collected during their stay in Cochin in the late 1980s.

Recipes in this book have been sourced from Cochin Jews in Mattancherry, Ernakulam and its suburbs in Kerala, India, various cities in Israel and from some who have settled in the United States and Canada.

Food evolves over the years and crosses geographical boundaries, but it is recognized that as long as you stick to a regional area, a time frame, basic ingredients and method of cooking, you can say that it is authentic to the community. Here, you will find many recipes that are common among the Jews, Hindus, Christians and Muslims who lived in proximity in small communities for centuries in the old Kingdom of Cochin; dependent on each other and transferring cooking styles and ideas to create easily identifiable but separate creations.

As Israeli researcher Ophira Gamliel points out: "Communities [in Kerala] may be differentiated by restrictions of food - vegetarian, non-vegetarian, *halal* or *kosher* defining each as Brahmin, non-Brahmin, Muslim or Jewish. But rice, coconut and curry leaves, the essential ingredients of the cuisine of all Kerala communities, define the cuisine of each community as typically Keralite."[3]

---

[1] Ruby (Rivka) Daniel was born in Mattancherry in the Kingdom of Cochin in 1912. In the book, co-authored by anthropologist Dr. Barbara Johnson of Ithaca College, New York, Ruby vividly describes the lives and stories of Jews in early 20th century Cochin. Ruby emigrated to Israel in 1951, where she lived on Kibbutz Neot Mordecai in the Upper Galilee, until her death in 2002.

[2] Dr. Nathan Katz and Ellen Goldberg from Florida lived on Synagogue Lane in Mattancherry, Cochin, 1986-1987, recording the history and rituals of the Paradesi Jews. They have been back several times since.

[3] Gamliel, Ophira, Dissertation, *Jewish Malayalam Women's Songs*, Part 1, page 132.

Several dishes, like the *dosa, idli, appam* and *puttu* continue to be made and eaten with relish in Cochini households/restaurants throughout Israel as is done in homes across Kerala. As mentioned earlier, one of the things that stood out for the Jewish community was *Kashrut*, the Jewish dietary laws.

Jewish cuisine owes its ingenuity to the prohibition of mixing meat and dairy, the ban on pork and fishes with no fins and scales (this means no seafood like shrimps and lobsters, scallops, crabs etc.). There are also other prohibitions, like not using certain cuts of meat, ensuring that food is not tainted with blood or is the result of hunting. In Cochin, the Jewish housewife discovered that coconut milk was a valued commodity, because it was the ideal alternative to milk to use with meat dishes. Kosher law also dictates that even soaps and powders for scouring utensils must not contain animal fat. This was easy in Cochin - because soaps were herbal and plant-based - and scouring agents were mainly wood ash and coir.

Writer Chitrita Banerjee, in her evocative book *Eating India: Exploring a Nation's Cuisine,* talks of how food in India has always been a matter of fusion - and one that is constantly evolving. She embarked on a search for vanishing cuisines and suggested that the 'gastronomic tradition of the Cochin Jews' was the one missing from the list of Indian cuisines that are now accepted and loved worldwide. As she explains: "...authenticity can only be preserved if people are motivated to study the community's history and present it to the world."[4]

This book attempts to fill that gap.

(*Note*: In 1996, the Kerala Government changed the name of Cochin to Kochi. In this book, however, we will refer to the city on most pages as Cochin (Queen of the Arabian Sea), as it was known throughout the years of Jewish settlement.)

---

[4] Banerjee, Chitrita, *Eating India: Exploring a Nation's Cuisine*, p. 236.

Part I
In Cochin, Kerala

Chapter 1

STORY OF THE COCHIN JEWS

Kerala's Jews or *Cochinim* make up one of the tiniest and most ancient of all Jewish communities in the Diaspora. They trace their history on the Malabar coast of India to 2,500 years ago, first landing on those pristine shores as sailors in the fleets of King Solomon to purchase spices, animals and precious metals.

The Old Testament mentions a number of materials imported from India into the Kingdom of Israel. We read in 3 Kings, 10:28:

"[…] And they came to Ophir and fetched from thence, gold, four hundred and twenty talents, and brought it to King Solomon". Again in 3 Kings 10:22, "For the King's navy once in three years went with the navy of Hiram by sea to Tharshish [believed to be the old name of Tharissapalli, near the harbour of Kollam or old Quilon] and brought from thence gold and silver, ivory (elephant tusks) and apes and peacocks".

Jewish historian Flavius Josephus, writing in the first century CE, explained in his *Antiquities of the Jews* that the trade mission of Solomon and Hiram to the land of Ophir was from the Red Sea port of Ezion-geber to 'Chryse' in the Indian Ocean (most probably in India). Ezion-geber is considered to be near the modern Israeli city of Eilat. [1]

Songs and oral traditions of the Cochin Jews tell of their early settlements in Malabar in places like Paloor and the port of Cranganore (today's city of Kodungalloor), soon after the destruction of the Second

---

[1] Flavius, Josephus. *The Antiquities of the Jews*. Chapter 6: 4, Project Gutenberg e-book, 2009.

Temple in 70 CE. They call this the 'First Diaspora'. One of the stories suggests they are descendants of Jews taken captive by Nebuchadnezzar in the 6th century BCE and came to India after being freed by Persian king Cyrus the Great.

Recorded history shows that Jews were present in Kerala in 849 CE. Hebrew names were engraved on copper plates granted by a Kerala Hindu King Ayyan Adikal Thiruvadikal of Venad (near modern-day Kollam or old Quilon) to Syrian Christian settlers, led by one Mar Sapir Iso, who were part of a trade guild called Manigramam. The Jews signed these Tharissapalli plates as witnesses, along with others who signed in the Pahlavi and Kufic languages. The plates were given on behalf of the Chera ruler Sthanu Ravi Varman.[2]

Copper Plates

In 1000 CE, the legendary Kerala emperor Cheraman Perumal Kulashekhara Bhaskara Ravi Varman, from his palace at Mahodayapuram in the Cranganore area, issued two copper plates to a Jewish merchant Issappu Irrappan (Joseph Rabban), believed to be of Yemeni descent. The plates conferred on the Jewish community 72 proprietary rights equivalent to those held by the Nairs, the then nobles of Malabar.[3]

This was during the 100-year war between the Kerala Cheras and the Imperial Cholas of the Tamil kingdoms and it is believed that the Jewish community contributed men and material (especially naval forces) to help the Chera emperor in the war efforts.[4] (During the 15th and 16th centuries, both the Zamorin of Calicut and the Raja of Cochin had Jewish regiments in their regular armed forces.)[5]

Replicas of these plates were presented to a delighted then-Israeli Prime Minister Shimon Peres on September 09, 1992, when he visited India[6] - a heart-warming piece of evidence that there was a safe haven for Jews in this little corner of India, centuries before the dream of Israel became a reality. The plates were presented by Kerala's tourism minister K.V. Thomas at a banquet in New Delhi, hosted by then Prime Minister Atal Behari Vajpayee.

---

[2] Aiyya, V. N. Nagom, *Travancore State Manual*, p. 244.
[3] Menon, Sreedhara A., *A Survey of Kerala History*, p. 45.
[4] M.G.S. Narayanan, *Cultural Symbiosis in Kerala*, Kerala Historical Society, Trivandrum, p .34.
[5] Mandelbaum G. David, *The Jewish Way of Life in Cochin*, pp. 423-460.
[6] http://www.hindu.com/2003/09/11stories/2003091108060400.htm

The original copper plates are preserved in the magnificent 460-year old Paradesi Synagogue in Cochin, the oldest functioning synagogue in the Commonwealth. (Israeli president Eizer Weizman visited the synagogue in January 1997, hailing Cochin as a "symbol of the persistence of Judaism and of *aliyah* ... I pay tribute to India for taking care of the Jews and their places of worship ...".)[7]

The Rev. Dr. Claudius Buchanan, a Scottish missionary who visited Cochin in 1806, deposited copies of these plates in the Public Library at the University of Cambridge.[8] He also deposited a copy of the Book of Moses, written on a 48-ft roll of soft leather, dyed red, which he 'hurriedly negotiated' and obtained from a synagogue in Ernakulam.

The copper plate inscriptions mention that several land rights and other honours were being given to the Jews in perpetuity "as long as the earth and the moon remain". Rabban was also made chief of a powerful trade guild called Anjuvannam. (Many early Western writers believed Anjuvannam to be a princely state.) Thus began the privileged existence of the Jews in Kerala. For almost five centuries, they thrived in their major settlement of Cranganore as traders and artisans.

Benjamin of Tudela recorded that "...throughout the island, including all the towns there, live several thousand Israelites. The Jews are good and benevolent. They know the law of Moses and the Prophets, and to a small extent the Talmud and Halacha..."[9] Another record is a tombstone in front of the Chennamangalam Synagogue with the date, in Hebrew characters, of the 28th of Kislev in the year corresponding to 1269 CE. It marks the death of one 'Sarah, Daughter of Israel'. The inscription, which is "perfectly decipherable is a quotation from Deuteronomy 32.4 and one that had not been recorded anywhere in the world."[10]

A cataclysmic flood in 1316 CE silted up the Cranganore harbour and trade moved to a new outlet that had opened to the sea towards the south, in a small town called Cochin. The Jews completely abandoned Cranganore by the middle of the 16th century after a horrific attack by the

---

[7] From video of Weizman's visit to the Paradesi Synagogue. In possession of Bala Menon.

[8] Buchanan, Claudius Rev., *The Works of Rev. Claudius Buchanan*, p. 133.

[9] Adler's Oxford Edition, 1907, pp. 63-65). Benjamin hailed from Pamplona in modern Spain.

[10] Mandelbaum, G. David, The Jewish Way of Life in Cochin, *Jewish Social Studies*, Vol. 1, No. 4 (Oct. 1939), pp 423-460. Indiana University Press: Stable URL: http://www.jstor.org/stable/4464305. Accessed: 25/04/2013 11:28.

Muslims in which their houses were burnt and scores slaughtered.[11] They spread out to small settlements like Chennamangalam, Mala, Palur, Paravur, Pulut, Madayi, Muttath, Tirutur and the biggest of them all Cochin, which had by then become the seat of the Perumbadappu Swaroopam dynasty that claimed descent from the ancient Cheraman Perumals.

11 CONGREGATIONS

There were Jews already living in Cochin before the exodus from Cranganore and they had a synagogue at Kochangadi and another across the bay in Ernakulam. A stone tablet from the destroyed Kochangadi synagogue is now embedded on a wall of the Paradesi synagogue.

By the 17th century, there were 11 congregations with their own synagogues – three in Mattancherry (Kadavumbhagam, Thekkumbhagam and Paradesi), two in Ernakulam (Kadavumbhagam and Thekkumbhagam - yes, same names!), one each in Chennamangalam, Mala, Palur, Muttam and Tirutur, and a splendid one in Paravur (at that time under the control of the King of Travancore).[12] Cochin Jewish songs also tell of a synagogue in a place called Southi (this has not yet been identified!)

Around this time, the Jewish population saw an influx with the arrival of those escaping persecution in Portugal and Spain. Most came as complete families and were received by the local Jews and the royal family.[13] The Raja of Cochin granted land to those who came from Cranganore and Europe to build homes and synagogues near royal palaces and retreats, absorbed them into the military and government and permitted them to flourish in agriculture, trade or any vocation they chose. (The Europeans, however, branched out from the original congregations and founded the Paradesi Synagogue in 1568.)

Many became palace courtiers and ambassadors. The Jews were loyal subjects and followed the advice of Prophet Jeremiah's *de facto* charter of the diaspora: "Build ye houses, and dwell in them; and plant gardens, and eat the fruit of them; and seek the peace of the city whither I have caused you to be carried away captives, and pray unto the Lord for it: for in the peace thereof shall ye have peace." (Jer. 29 : 4 and 7.)

---

[11] Zain al-Din Mabari, *Tohfut-ul-mujahideen*, cited by Katz & Goldberg, *Last Jews of Cochin*, p. 59.

[12] This was documented by a delegation of Jews from Amsterdam, led by Moses Pereyra de Paiva, that visited Cochin in 1685. Pereyra wrote about this visit in his *Nostesias os Judeos de Cochin* in 1687. (The synagogues of Palur, Muttam and Tirutur have disappeared - believed to have been abandoned or destroyed.)

[13] Sehgal, J.B., *The Jews of Cochin*, p. 21.

Across the Bay, in the little town of Ernakulam (then known as Anjikaimal) the Raja granted a large plot of land to another segment of Jewish traders to build a market and two synagogues. (Ernakulam has grown to become the main commercial hub of Kerala today and the market is a bustling area - with shops mostly owned by Muslims, but sporting Hebrew letters as shop numbers on the famous Jew Street.)

In his 1920 book *Jews of Asia*, Sidney Mendelssohn tellingly wrote: "While the Jews of Europe, from the 10th to the 16th centuries, were living under conditions, which, for a portion of the period, were stigmatized by Milman[14] as the 'Iron Age of Judaism', and while persecutions drove the scattered race in turn out of England, France, Spain, Portugal, Holland and Germany, as well as other less important regions, their brethren in the Far East, in the lands of the ... potentates of India, were living a life of peace and plenty, far away from the bigots, the robber kings, the conversionists, the Inquisitors, and the Crusaders."[15]

It is of interest to note here that in the late 18th century, Cochin was more important to the Jews than New York. Walter Fischel, a scholar of Oriental Jewry, wrote: "Cochin, one of the oldest Jewish settlements on Asian soil, had a much larger Jewish community than New York and surpassed it not only numerically, but also culturally. The Cochin Jewish community in 1792 had about 2000 Jews ... and 9 synagogues of considerable antiquity, while New York had only 72 Jewish families and only one synagogue."[16]

The close emotional and physical proximity with Kerala royalty continued until 1948 when the Kingdom of Cochin acceded to the newly-independent Indian Union; the Maharaja surrendered his political rights, and local politicians, representing pan-Indian parties, took control.

The birth of Israel in 1948, uncertainty over their status as one of the tiniest minorities in a newly independent and turbulent India, loss of special privileges in Kerala, sweeping land reforms that took away most of their vast rice and coconut plantations, led to mass emigration of the Cochin Jews to the Promised Land.

Today, there are several flourishing Cochini *moshavim* (settlements in Israel) - Nevatim and Shahar in the south, Aviezer, Mesilat Zion and Taoz

---

[14] Henry Hart Milman was an English clergyman who wrote the *History of the Jews* in 1829.

[15] Mendelssohn, Sidney, *The Jews of Asia*, Chapter VIII, p. 99.

[16] Walter Fischel - *From Cochin, India, to New York*, pp. 265-67, cited by Katz on page 102. *Harry Austrynn Wolfson Jubilee Volume.* Jerusalem: American Academy for Jewish Research, pp. 255-75.

near Jerusalem and Kfar Yuval in the far north. (Mesilat Zion boasts signs like Rehov Cochin and Rehov Malabar - *rehov* means street in Hebrew - dating to the early 1950s.) Sizeable numbers of Cochinis live in Binyamina, Petah Tikva, Rishon Le Zion, Ashdod, Jerusalem and Haifa. Moshav Nevatim also boasts a beautiful Cochini synagogue. The interior is a copy of the Kadavumbhagam synagogue of Ernakulam and the Holy Ark and the Torah scrolls were all brought from various synagogues in Cochin. A Cochin Heritage Museum has been set up near the synagogue.

Most Cochinis today work in the cities and in all professions in Israel, are intermarrying with other communities and recognized as a hardworking people with high self-esteem. Sociologists attribute this to the absence of a fear or siege complex, because in their centuries of life in Kerala, they did not face any discrimination or violence from the people among whom they lived. Many have also emigrated to North America.

After the establishment of Indo-Israeli diplomatic relations in 1992, Cochinis are renewing ties with their roots, travelling to Kerala to visit places associated with their ancestors and to see the synagogues, two of which have been turned into heritage museums. Some have bought valuable holiday properties in places where their parents/grandparents lived. Homes in Cochini *moshavs* all have satellite dishes beaming 24-hour Malayalam[17] channels into their living rooms.

(The history and traditions of the Cochin Jews have been documented in books and journals by scholars like Dr. Nathan Katz & Ellen Goldberg, Dr. Barbara Johnson, Prof. J. B. Sehgal, Prof. P. M. Jussay, Dr. Joan Roland, Dr. Shalva Weil and others. -*See Bibliography, page 202.*)

In Kochi itself, there are few Jews left. In Mattancherry, they number nine and there are 40 others around the Ernakulam area. There are no synagogue services, except at the Paradesi synagogue when Israeli tourists gather or when a Chabbad Rabbi visits from Mumbai.

As a former warden of the Paradesi synagogue, the late Samuel Hallegua, said: "There's nothing any of us can do to avert the end of Jewish life [in Cochin]. Perhaps, a day might come when someone here will start thinking that it all was a dream."[18] - *Bala Menon*

---

[17] Malayalam is the language of Kerala. The Cochinis speak a dialect called Judeo-Malayalam.
[18] Newton, Joshua, The Last Jews of Cochin, *The Jewish Journal*, July 5, 2001: Online: http://www.jewishjournal.com/travel/article/the_last_jews_of_kochi-20010706/

Chapter 2

Kerala Cuisine - Aromas, Colours & Flavours

Kerala cuisine is different from what the world generally considers fine Indian cuisine. It is a world apart from the rich, creamy curries and vigorous breads of north India. Blessed with abundant vegetables and fruits, gardens with spices that the world coveted for two millennia, a long coastline teeming with some of the finest edible fishes in the world, Kerala overflows with culinary creativity.

Aromas, colours, mystery flavours, the heat of chillies and spices cooled with coconut milk combine to make Kerala cuisine a kaleidoscopic adventure that keeps rolling through the day - everyday.

Ottawa chef Cameron Stauch is an enthusiast when it comes to Kerala food. As one who helped develop recipes for the Canadian film *Cooking With Stella*, Stauch says: "Indian food isn't just the restaurant food that we get in North America. There's so much diversity and variety that you couldn't taste all of India in a lifetime. You'd need many more lifetimes to taste everything."[1] About South Indian and Kerala food he says: "I really like [it]. I prefer it. I find it to be lighter food, fresher tasting." The film is mostly about Kerala and other southern Indian delicacies, because the

---

[1] Hum, Peter, A Chef's Passage To India; Cameron Stauch's experiences in Delhi helped inspire the film Cooking with Stella, *Calgary Herald*. Calgary, Alta.: Apr 11, 2010. p. C.

main character Stella is from Kerala. (Stauch is the author of the popular blog *http://www.indiaonmyplate.com/*).

Kerala, which was named as one of the *Ten Paradises of the World* and *Fifty Places of a Lifetime* in the 15th anniversary issue of the *National Geographic Traveler Magazine* in 2009[2], is a narrow strip of land in south-western India. It is also fondly called *God's Own Country.*

Bounded in the east by the magnificent Western Ghats/Sahyadri Mountains (the Benevolent Mountains) and in the west by the Arabian Sea/Indian Ocean, Kerala is endowed with great scenic beauty and is one of the richest states in India in terms of cash crops.

The highlands are covered with dense forests of valuable trees that include teak, rosewood and sandalwood, while the midlands are dotted with terraced plantations of tea, coffee, cardamom and pepper. In the foothills are estates of rubber, cashew and coconuts covering the entire length of the state. In the coastal areas and the hinterland are more coconut groves, interspersed with rice paddies, orchards of mango, banana, jack fruit, cashew, papaya and pineapples along with tree-lined canals and backwaters. Some 44 rivers crisscross the land, offering fresh water for vegetable gardens yielding every kind of tropical vegetable.

Kerala cuisine has been shaped by its maritime history. Judaism, Christianity and Islam came to the land along with the voyagers who landed on the coast to trade in spices or seeking to take control of their sources. They also contributed to the cuisine of Kerala.

The Arabs brought in fenugreek and fennel, the Portuguese chillies, tapioca and cashew. Keralites combined these with local spices in dishes already infused with the magic of curry leaves, tamarind pulp and coconut, creating a fragrant and piquant cooking style. Kerala's spice trade was for many centuries controlled by the Jewish community and they incorporated these spices into their cuisine.

The staple food of Kerala, however, is unpolished/parboiled rice - which takes on many incarnations throughout the day in Kerala kitchens. In Cochini Jewish homes in Israel and in Kerala, rice continues to be the main fare, with side dishes made according to ages-old recipes given in the following pages. Cochini Jewish cooking can be considered genuine classical cuisine, because recipes like the *pastel, ural, ispethi* and *chuttulli meen* have been in continuous use for hundreds of years.

[2] http://intelligenttravel.nationalgeographic.com/2009/09/17/50_places_of_a_lifetime_1/

•••••

In the early years of *aliyah,* it was difficult for the Cochinis, like Jews from around the world, to find the food of their choice in the New Land and they had to make do with unfamiliar products.

In a study by two Israeli doctors of the food consumption patterns of the early Cochinis, they found how the new arrivals were forced to adapt. They looked at 82 families from two unidentified villages near Jerusalem and pointed out how products like margarine and olives were foreign to them. From a rice-based diet, they were forced to consume mostly wheat-based meals, with cheese and margarine, instead of their preferred coconut oil and clarified butter.

The doctors reported: "The relatively high consumption of rice as well as the frequent use of bananas and certain spices… is reminiscent of food habits to which they had adhered to in India and which have been preserved in their new homeland. The extremely low consumption of meat, which falls much below the Israeli average, is in contrast to the level of fish consumption which may appear rather high in an agricultural population…"[3] The doctors were from the Laboratory of Nutrition, Department of Biochemistry, Hebrew University-Hadassah Medical School and the Department of Internal Medicine, Rothschild Hadassah-Hebrew University Hospital, Jerusalem, respectively.

'OLIVES ARE SHEEP DROPPINGS'

Israel was reeling under an austerity program at the time and food was rationed. Families received mainly Ashkenazi staples and these were foods the Cochinis hated. Rachel Sopher from Moshav Taoz recollects how her parents hated black olives. "They had never seen it. They called it sheep droppings…!"[4] There was margarine, which was unknown to the Cochinis who were brought up on rich coconut oil and clarified butter. However, they soon learned to barter these in the *kibbutzes* with European families in return for rice which was saved for Shabbat.

One of the definitive books about the Cochin Jews has been *The Last Jews of Cochin: Jewish Identity in Hindu India* by Dr. Nathan Katz and Ellen Goldberg. They first visited Cochin in 1984 and later lived in Jew Town,

---

[3] Guggenheim K, M.D. and Dreyfuss, F. M.D., "Food Habits and Food Consumption of Jews from Cochin in Israel", *American Journal of Clinical Nutrition*, Vol. 7, September-October 1959, p. 519.

[4] Quoted in *Ethnic Aroma*, The Jewish Agency for Israel. http://www.jewishagency.org/JewishAgency/English/Israel/Partnerships/Regions/Beitshemesh/Cookbook/Washington

(1986-87), embedding themselves into the Mattancherry Jewish community, studying their history, traditions and life-cycle rituals. They lived on Synagogue Lane in a huge, 400-year-old house with Raymond Salem (author Kenny Salem's uncle). Apart from the deep spirituality of the Cochin Jews, the Katzes also became enamoured with the food.

They arrived in Cochin during the Rosh Hashanah celebrations and observed all the festivals, until Hanukkah. "Kerala was always where spices were grown, so they had the freshest, most wonderful, pungent spicing in their food," says Katz. "I love Kerala food very much and what we experienced some 26 years ago is now part of our lifestyle here in Miami." The Katzes have travelled to Kerala many times since.

Fortunately for them, most of Kerala's spices are available at an Asian grocery near the campus of the Florida International University, where Dr. Katz is a professor of religious studies. "We also get curry leaves here, along with bitter gourd and drumsticks, vegetables we learned to love during our Cochin sojourn," Katz said.

"We have two mango trees in our compound here, along with banana and papaya, and sometimes make a mango chutney. For Shabbat and special occasions, there is always the famous Cochin Jewish chicken roast, a recipe we got from Glennis Salem, now in Haifa, Israel."

Ellen Goldberg adds: "Nathan is the Indian cook in our home and we also have green fish curry and the tamarind fish, for which we use salmon. Other favourites are the coconut rice, okra with fenugreek and the *hulba* sauce. It used to be great fun in Cochin. We used to go to the Chinese fishing nets at Fort Kochi and get fresh catch."

•••••

It is often said that our foods link our present lives with that of our ancestors; and it is not easy to explain why the smells of childhood last a lifetime and are able to ignite pleasant memories.

Ora Farchy, who was born and raised in Moshav Shahar in southern Israel and now lives in Houston where she is a Hebrew teacher, says: "I remember how hard it was for my parents to accept strange items like margarine and flour as food in the 1950s. They used to say: 'How can anybody eat these things?' It has been a long journey for us Cochinis. Although physical Cochin has receded from us when we consider concepts of time and space, the food has remained with us and, I think, will remain part of our consciousness and identity."

This sentiment is expressed plaintively by young Avithal Elias, a Cochini Jewish student at Technion - Israel Institute of Technology, Haifa. One of her recent posts on social media said: "I miss *puttu, idiyappam, appam, porotta, kadala kari, coconut chamanthi, fish curry, fish fry, unniyappam, murukku, banana chips, coconut curry stew, pachadi, kichidi, manga achaar, chambakka, chakkapazham, upillita pala sambahavangal, sadhya, palada payasam, dosa* ...I miss you My KOCHI !! Love U always."[5]

One of the community leaders at Moshav Nevatim in Israel, Itzhak Nehemia, who made *aliyah* when he was an infant, told sociologist Ashish Nandy: "We (still) like to live as if we were in Kerala."

Nandi tells us that when he visited Nevatim: "...indeed, Nehemia and his friends made it a point to serve us typical Malayali [*Malayali* from *Malayalam*, the language of Kerala] food and claim that the Malayali food the Cochin Jews prepared in Israel was better than that was available in Cochin."[6]

---

[5] Avithal, who was born in Kerala, is the daughter of Elias (Babu) Josephai, caretaker of the Kadavumbhagam Synagogue in Ernakulam. This magnificent *shul*, which is still in good condition, is not operational today. The dishes that Avithal has named are all everyday foods in Kerala. Most are included in this book.

[6] Nandi Ashish, *Time Warps*, p. 198.

Chapter 3

How We Kept Kosher In Cochin

- Dr. Essie Sassoon

"Since a healthy and whole body is in keeping with the service to G-d, since it is impossible to understand or know anything about G-d when one is sick, therefore one must distance himself from those things which ruin the body and instead should accustom himself to those things which cause the body to heal and mend..."
- Ramban, *The Mishnah Torah*, 4th chapter of *Hilchot Da'ot*.[1]

The food that we grew up with is the food we identify with. It is the same with food that we term Jewish. While the *cholent*, *kishke* and *gefilte* fish are considered true Jewish food by the Ashkenazi, it is very different for Sephardi, Mizrahi and those from far-flung, tiny communities.

In Cochin, where we grew up - and so did our ancestors for more than 2,000 years - it was fresh coconut milk-laced, highly spiced, aromatic dishes of tropical grains, vegetables, fruits and nuts and permitted meats that were quintessentially *kosher* and Jewish. For the Cochinis, these continue to be Jewish food.

Kosher is the Hebrew word which means 'fit'. *Kashrut* is the Hebrew word for keeping *kosher*. The Laws of *Kashrut* describe the kind of foods that Jews are permitted to eat or foods that are fit to eat and how it must

---

[1] Nahmanides (1194–c. 1270). Rabbi Moshe ben Nahman Girondi, known as Ramban, was a Kabbalist, rabbi, philosopher and physician from Girona, Catalonia in Spain.

be prepared and eaten. The *Kosher* laws were commanded by G_d to the children of Israel, given to Moses in the Sinai desert and then delivered to the people. These laws are found in *Leviticus 11* and *Deuteronomy 14* and were handed down through generations until it appeared in written form in the *Mishnah* and *Talmud*, along with various rulings by Rabbinical authorities.

In the Kingdom of Cochin and much earlier, throughout our 2,000-year joyful history on the Malabar coast, the observance of *kosher* laws has been absolute and a mark of our identity. For Cochini Jews, our food was Jewish because we adhered to the dietary laws as stated in the Hebrew Bible.

As observed by foreign scholars, the Jews of Cochin acculturated with the norms and rules of Kerala society without being assimilated into the dominant culture of the Hindus.[2]

Strict Observance

Protected by the rulers of Cochin and enjoying equal status with the then-dominant Namboodiri and Nair nobility, the Jews remained strict in their observance of food laws, earning respect from the wider community and the privilege of living without being disturbed in their religious and temporal lives.

"We are religious ... but not orthodox," the then head of the community, Sattoo Sabattai Koder, said during an interview in 1991. "Jews strictly observe the Shabbat and its customs as well as *Kashrut* (*Kosher* laws), and the major Jewish festivals.[3]

Only animals and fish that were edible according to Jewish law were eaten. Animals were slaughtered ritually with special knives. Meat and dairy products and the utensils used to cook them were kept apart. Blood was forbidden for consumption. All meat was washed clean and salted for half an hour and drained and washed again.

Gelatin was never used; instead, food starch and tapioca became the binding agents in Cochini Jewish cuisine. Eggs were examined after cracking them open to see if there was any trace of blood. If blood was found,

---

[2] Katz, Nathan & Goldberg, Ellen, *The Last Jews of Cochin*, 1995. The book is based on this recognition of identity, by the Jews themselves and the rulers and people of Kerala.

[3] Sahni Julie, *Indo-Jewish cuisine dates back 22 centuries*, The Gazette, Montreal, March 27, 1991. Syndicated from Los Angeles Times. http://proquest.umi.com.ezproxy.torontopubliclibrary.ca/pqdlink?did=1651 28271&Fmt=3&clientId =1525&RQT=309&VName=PQD

it was declared non-*kosher* and discarded. Internal organs, even chicken liver, were roasted on a wire mesh so that all blood was drained.

One of the major commandments of *kosher* law is: "You shall not boil a kid in the mothers milk". So meat and milk were never combined. In Cochin (and in Israel today), Cochini Jews strictly observe a waiting period of six hours after meat is consumed before ingesting a dairy product or anything containing milk.

All dishes accompanying meat are made with margarine or vegetable shortening/coconut oil instead of clarified butter/ghee. It must be noted that most middle-class Cochin Jewish families ate only fish and vegetables on weekdays while in Kerala.

No Community Shohets

Kosher chicken was eaten only on Fridays. There were two reasons for this bent towards vegetarianism: One, Kerala is part of the tropics and experiences intense heat and humidity; it made more sense to consume fresh fruits and vegetables and cooling dairy products like yogurt.

Two, towards the middle of the 20th century, there was a problem of getting ritually-slaughtered meat because there were no *shohets*. I remember only one *shohet* by the name of Yosef Hai, who made *aliyah* early and died in Israel. There was one Ezekal Roby who was a *shohet* and *moail* (one who performs *Brith Mela*). In later years, Jackie Cohen (known as Dickie) used to slaughter fowls for the community.

Chicken thus came to be eaten only for *Shabbat* with meat and lamb becoming rare on our menus. Beef was available to the community only when a Bene Israeli *shohet* was specially brought in from Bombay at the time of communal festivities, weddings or other special occasions. The slaughtered meat was at that time distributed to all households.

I remember how the Bombay *shohets* used to be housed in Queenie Hallegua's house, near the Paradesi Synagogue, occupying two rooms earmarked on the ground floor as servant's quarters. (Queenie still lives on Synagogue Lane.)

After the death of Jackie Cohen (Mattancherry matriarch Sarah Cohen's husband), Elias Joseph Hai of the Ernakulam congregation supplied fowls for some time but he had his flourishing flowers and aquarium business to run and stopped communal slaughtering.

Wine and dairy products like cheese were consumed only when made by members of the community. The wine for *kiddush* was made at home by the respective households.

Passover

In old Cochin, Passover dominated the religious life of the Jews and preparations for the festival began the day after *Purim*. There was an obsession with cleaning and scrubbing the house and every piece of furniture and utensils. Houses were whitewashed and even the wells were cleaned as the taboo of *chametz* (forbidden food) took on a dinosaur-like life of its own.

This Pesach Work of the Cochin Jews has been described in detail by Dr. Barbara Johnson in her dissertation *Shingly or Jewish Cranganore*.[4]

I remember how in all houses on Synagogue Lane, the dining room tables, which were made of antique teak wood, would be scrubbed clean. Boiling water would be poured over them before drying them out in the sun. Every nook and corner of the house was cleaned; wardrobes turned over; the pantry was the focus of attention and every article of *hamaz* (*chametz*) was thrown out.

If, for example, there was an unopened bottle of whiskey, it was either stored in a room called *hamaz muri* (*chametz* room) or it was sold to a non-Jew and bought back after Passover. The locked *hamaz muri* was opened only after Passover.

Most families had a separate room (*pessah-muri* in Malayalam) to store the Pesach utensils. Families that did not have this facility made the utensils *kosher* by holding them with tongs and immersing them in boiling water. Milk and meat must not be cooked in the same vessel in a 24-hour period. We believed that flavour from foods can remain within the confines of a room - so it was better to avoid prohibited foods altogether.

All edible articles, mainly spices and rice, were stored in this room. (Rice is not consumed by Ashkenazi and some Sephardic communities during Passover but the Cochin Jews have traditionally eaten it because it is not expressly forbidden.) Rice was purchased several days before Passover and examined meticulously about three or four times for the presence of wheat and then stored for Pesach. Rice flour and spices were powdered at home. (Any of the five grains - wheat, spelt, barley, oats, and rye - that come into contact with water for more than 18 minutes is con-

---

[4] Johnson, *Shingly or Jewish Cranganore in the traditions of the Cochin Jews*, MA thesis.

sidered *chametz*.) Everything was in accordance to the rules of *kosher*. Dr. Nathan Katz has observed: "The Cochin Jews developed Pesach customs influenced by Brahmin asceticism and Simchat Torah royalty symbols influenced by the local nobility that fitted nicely into the framework of *halakhah* (Jewish law)."[5]

"So important is 'Pesach work' to the Cochin community that, it is believed, if the woman makes even the slightest mistake in Passover preparations, the lives of her husband and children would be endangered."[6]

Until about 1990 or so, the Mattancherry Jews would rent a flour mill for a whole day; all the women would go and thoroughly clean the machinery to ensure that the community could get *kosher* flour.

When *matzah* was made in Cochin, the wheat was also powdered this way. From the 1990s, however, ready-made *matzah* began to come from Mumbai, courtesy of the Israeli consulate.

In Israel, the Cochin Jews do not eat *kitniyot* food, but we are allowed to consume rice during Passover. When we came to Israel this caused a lot of confusion and we had to consult Israeli religious authorities, who gave us permission to eat rice during Passover since it was our staple food.

The rice is bought one month before and checked for cracks through which *chametz* could have entered. This is a very complicated process. When shopping for Passover, each item we buy should be checked to see if they include *kitniyot*. Most products are marked in Hebrew - if it is *kitniyot* or is clean. I have a lot of difficulty in finding chocolate - which I always crave - that does not contain *kitniyot*. Even oil that is extracted from *kitniyot* is not used; we use oil made from walnuts or cotton seeds. See also page 104.

Making Of The 'Massa'

The culmination of Passover work, which lasted up to 30 days, was the making of the 'Massa' as the *matzah* was called. The *massa* is an unleavened bread and is mandatory for Jews to make it part of the Passover Seder (the ritual service and ceremonial meal) and is generally eaten throughout the eight-day festival. The making of the bread was a community affair, with all the women gathering in one house. The men mixed and kneaded the dough and the children ran with the dough balls to their mothers, who

---

[5] Katz &. Goldberg, "Asceticism and Caste in the Passover Observances of the Cochin Jews", *Journal of the Ameican Academy of Religion.* LVII/1

[6] *Ibid.*

flattened them with rolling pins and baked them on griddles in small kilns burning dried coconut husks. There was a lot of hymn-singing during the *matzah* work and it was a fun time for the community.

(The rolling pins had tiny, brass bells attached to them and the sounds fascinated the children.)

The Passover Seder Plate is a special plate containing six symbolic foods. The six items are:

1. *Maror*: Lettuce was used as the *maror* (bitter herb) in Cochin and continues to be used today in Israel.

2. *Charoset*: A sweet, brown, pebbly mixture, representing the mortar used by Jewish slaves to build the storehouses of Egypt.

3. *Karpas*: Celery dipped in vinegar (Sephardi custom).

4. *Z'roa*: A roasted shank bone, symbolizing the *korban Pesach* (Pesach sacrifice), a lamb offered in the Temple in Jerusalem and roasted for the meal on Seder night. In Cochin, a roast chicken wing (*kai oram* in Malayalam) was used.

5. *Beitzah*; A roasted egg, symbolizing the *korban chagigah* (festival sacrifice). In Cochin, we boiled the egg and this represented the holiday offering.

In Cochin, most families had silver *Seder* plates that were handed down from generation to generation. The Cochin Jews also kept a third bowl of wine on the Seder table, although I can't recollect its significance.

•••••

Kenny Salem adds:

Beef and lamb have been rarities on Cochini Jewish dining tables (in Cochin) since the 1950s. There were no *shohets* available and I recollect a wedding in the community when a *shohet* came down from Bombay in 1978 to do the ritual slaughtering of beef and lamb for the feast. (This was the last official Jew Town wedding - of Leslie Salem and Glennis Simon, both of whom now live in Haifa, Israel)

I remember my father Gumliel Salem telling me about a Jewish shohet by the name of Yosef Hai, who ran a *kosher* meat outlet near the Kadavumbhagam Synagogue on the far south of Synagogue Lane. However, after he left, the community has had only chicken and fish to choose as non-vegetarian dishes. Today, this chicken needs to be brought from

Mumbai, from Bene Israeli suppliers. Of course, in Israel, beef and lamb and new meats like turkey have become part of the everyday menu of the Cochin Jews.

Kosher Basics

The meat of all herbivores that have cloven hooves and 'chew the cud' are permitted. All others, including horse, pig, rabbit and carnivores are forbidden.

There are also a series of laws prescribing how the animal should be ritually slaughtered and be completely free of blood. There are also rules about which parts of the animal can be eaten. Animals that die of natural causes and those which are hunted are forbidden.

Reptiles, turtles, snails, insects of all kinds, frogs etc. are not fit for consumption.

Only fish with scales and fins are allowed to be eaten. All crustaceans like crab, lobsters, shrimp and creatures like shark and eel are forbidden.

Meat and milk must never be combined during a meal. Meat and dairy products must be kept apart and there should be a reasonable waiting period between their use. Separate utensils must be used for each.

Foods that do not fall into the categories of meat or dairy are called *parve* or neutral food and there is no bar on them being eaten along with meat or dairy preparations.

All fruits, vegetables and grains are *parve* (meaning neutral) foods, but it must be ensured that they are insect-free. If the foods are processed, they need *kosher* certification, meaning that no milk or meat have come into contact with them. Coffee and tea are *parve* if taken without milk or cream.

Fish and eggs are also considered *parve*, but must be blood-free.

All salt is *kosher*; what we call *kosher* salt is the crystalline variety used for *kashering* (to remove blood from meat).

Chapter 4

Unu Nammukku - Our Food (The Grace)

The mustard seeds jumped and crackled in the hot coconut oil as Batzion Bezallel sprinkled some fresh curry leaves over it. Two tablespoons of ground spices were already sizzling in the *wok* (called *cheena chatti* in Malayalam). A mouth-watering aroma floated around the kitchen and living room of her sprawling farmhouse in Moshav Kidroon.[1]

It's now time for the sliced shallots. These are special ones. In Kerala, they are called *cheriyya ulli*. Similar to pearl onions, small, red and round, these are the most flavourful in the onion family (it really belongs to the garlic family) and one of the main ingredients in the *Chuttulli Meen (See recipe on p. 44)* that Batzion is making today. The shallot paste is the ingredient that has given the name to the dish.

For the past two days, Batzion has been planning a menu for her daughter Bina, son-in-law and grandchildren, who are coming to visit from Vancouver. The *Chuttulli Meen* (Pan Fried Fish with Shallots) is a family favourite and one of the celebrated dishes born in the kitchens of the Jews of Cochin. Meanwhile, her husband, award-winning horticulturist Bezallel Eliyahu is on the *verandah* abutting the kitchen, smashing small green mangoes on a flat, black stone (*ammikallu*), the first step in making a succulent coconut and mango chutney. *(See recipe on p. 127.)*

---

[1] Kidroon is a prosperous *moshav* in central Israel, 30 km from Tel Aviv. Located in the Shephelah some 2 km east of Gedera, near the Tel Nof Airbase, it falls under the jurisdiction of Brenner Regional Council.

•••••

In the township of Aberdeen, New Jersey, Gila Rosenblatt is serving chicken for dinner. Although her children were born in Israel and her husband is of Ashkenazi origin, the family loves Cochin Jewish food. *Kozhi Pollichathu* is one of the favourites. The recipe was handed down to her by her mother who got it from her grandmother … in the small Kerala settlement of Chennamangalam.

"So many generations of Jews," says Gila, "and we use the same spices, the same measures, the same style of cooking and it tastes so wonderful every time I make it." The chicken has been cut and is boiling in the pot; now to add the rest of the ingredients … *(See recipe on p. 60.)*

••••

The summer months are bountiful for fishermen in the southern Indian state of Kerala. In Mattancherry, 91-year-old Sarah Cohen, the matriarch of the Cochin Jews, is looking at the king fish (*neymeen*) that has been bought by her reliable helper Taha, fresh off the nets in Fort Kochi, about eight km. away.

"This is great for making a lot of *meen undas* (fish balls)", says Sarah. Fish is now one of the staples for Jews in Kerala because there is no *shohet* in the community. For a couple of years, there was a Chabad Rabbi who helped the community but political shenanigans forced him out of the country.[2] "So it is fish for us," says Sarah as she supervises the cleaning of the fish in the backyard of her 420-year-old house, recently painted green and a popular halt for tourists visiting the fabled Paradesi Synagogue nearby. Sarah runs a small embroidery store, selling colourful *kippahs* and shawls. *(See recipe on p. 45.)*

•••••

Canada has its own celebrity Jewish chef of Cochini origin. Linda Hertzman is famous as the 'Spice Chef' of Vancouver, making a name for herself with innovative dishes based on ancient recipes from her hometown in India.[3] She runs a successful catering company Classic Ventures and also looks after a large *kosher* food business with husband Steve. Keen on experimenting with Western and Eastern fusion foods, Linda serves a specialty dish called Salmon Miso. *(See recipe on page 52.)*

---

[2] "Indian mission ends for a rabbi", *The Telegraph*, March 12, 201 http://www.telegraphindia.com/1120312/jsp/frontpage/story_15239298.jsp

[3] See blog: *http://jewsofcochin.blogspot.ca*. Also, *http://www.cjnews.com/index.php?q=node/90109*

•••••

This song is sung by Cochini Jewish women at the end of meals on festival days, after the singing of the Hebrew grace (*birkat ha-mazon*). The song has been set to different tunes and is sung in different styles, depending on the occasion.[4]

Hail the Lord who is giving us our food
this food that we are eating to our satisfaction

The One who reigns over the whole world
The One who feeds the entire universe
The One who nourishes all beings with a body
and who continues to feed them forever
Oh Lord, shower us with your abundance and generosity.

Unu nammukku Tharunnavane,
Undu niranju njan vasta vennam, vasta vennam.
Ullagil Nee vazhunna Thambiraney

Sarve ullage ellam Oottunavam, Oottunavan
Saiayaamavarku Ellaavarkum
nirthalum chaapiyaam kuravillathe, kuravillathe.
Niranja thirukayyil urakka venam
Thiruvellam aake nirayippannum, nirayippanum

As legendary American chef Julia Childs, who revolutionized the eating habits of Americans in the latter half of the 20th century, said in one of her television shows: "Train yourself to use your hands and fingers; they are wonderful instruments. Train yourself also to handle hot foods; this will save time. Keep your knives sharp. Above all, have fun." In her last book, *My Life in France,* she ends with this sentence: "... the pleasures of the table, and of life, are infinite – *toujours bon appétit!*"

In Hebrew, we say: *Be Te'avon - Enjoy!*

---

[4] Johnson, Barbara C. & Zacharia, Scaria, *Oh, Lovely Parrot!, Jewish Women's Songs from Kerala*, Track 31 on CD. The Jewish Music Research Centre, The Hebrew University of Jerusalem, 2004.

Part II

Food Links Past & Present

Chapter 1

So, What's For Breakfast?

For the Cochin Jews, like other Keralites, breakfast is mostly something made with rice. Apart from eggs, breakfast is generally vegetarian and involves the much-loved grain coming in different forms onto the morning plates, each outdoing the other in taste, in combination with an array of chutneys, stews, curries and dips.

It begins with a batter of rice and *urad dhal* (black grams)[1], which are ground together with a little water and left covered overnight. When the batter rises with the dawn, it is ready to be ladled into medium-sized iron griddles or flat saucepans, greased with coconut oil or clarified butter; to be made into blintz-like *dosas*, the smaller, spongy *uthappams*; or if steamed to take the shape of little rice cakes (*idlis*); press it through a mould and it becomes *idiyappam* or string hoppers. There are also *vellayppams* and *adas* in the rice treasure chest.

Throughout Kerala, in small tea shops, the favourite breakfast remains the famous *puttu* - created when fresh, grated coconut is added to powdered rice and steamed in small bamboo logs or coconut shells.

---

[1] *Urad Dhal* is known as black gram. In Kerala, this versatile lentil is called *uzhunnum parippu* and is available whole (black) or split and white with the skin removed. In many dishes, it takes the role of a spice, adding crunchiness. When the white split lentil is ground, it is the main ingredient in Kerala delicacies like *dosa, idli, vada* and *popadums*. Split, decorticated legumes (*Urad Dhal, Moong Dhal* and *Chana Dhal*) are also used like spices to make dishes such as *Rasam* and *Sambhar*.

Appam is one of Kerala's signature breakfast dishes. A fermented flatbread, made with rice and coconut, it originated in the homes of Jewish settlers in Cochin and was popularized across the state by the Syrian Christians. In some parts of neighbouring Tamil Nadu and in northern Sri Lanka, a similar dish is known as *Aappam*. There are many varieties of *appams* made in Cochini Jewish kitchens.

Appam
(Rice Fritters)

Makes 30 to 40 fritters.

4 cups rice flour	1 tsp salt
2 large eggs	1 3/4 cups water
1 1/2 tsp active yeast	1 tsp oil
2 tbsp sugar	1/2 cup oil for frying

Mix all ingredients (including 1 tsp oil) and set aside until batter rises (about 1 hour). Heat 1/2 cup of oil in frying pan until hot. Use a ladle to pour about 2 tbsp of batter into oil and fry until golden.

Turn fritter and remove from pan when second side is also browned. Use up all batter. Drain on paper towels.

Courtesy: Shlomo Mordechai, New York.

(Note: These fritters can also be cooked like pancakes in a deep round-bottomed pot, covered on low heat - *Gila Rosenblatt, Aberdeen, N.J.*)

Idiyappam
(String Hoppers)

Makes 25-30 hoppers.

Idiyappam is a favourite breakfast food of the Cochini Jews. It goes well with various savoury stews or plain with coconut milk and sugar.

1/2 kg - rice flour (Rosematta red rice flour & white rice flour mixed)	String hopper mould or idiyappam press (called Seva Nazhi in Malayalam. This is available in South Asian groceries).
2-3 cups boiling water	
1/2 tsp salt	

Dry roast the flour in a wok. In a bowl, mix the salt and flour well with a ladle. Add the water gradually and mix contents into pliable dough.

Put a little dough into the lightly oiled, string hopper mould and squeeze the lever onto string hopper mats in a circular fashion.

Place mats in a steamer and steam for about 5 minutes.

You can add grated coconut, cardamom powder and sugar with the *idiyappam* to get a delightful variation of the plain *idiyappam*. Serve with coconut milk and sugar or your choice of curries.

Paalappam or Vellayappam (Rice Crepes)

Makes 10-12 crepes.

These are similar to the *dosa*, but with spongy centres and lacier edges. These crepes are part of an array of breakfast rice dishes that goes well with eggs roasted in onion sauce or potatoes stewed in coconut milk or plain with sugar and milk.

2 cups rice flour
2 cups coconut milk
3/4 cup cooked rice
2 tsp yeast
1 tbsp sugar for fermentation
4 tbsp sugar for batter
3/4 cup coconut milk
Coconut oil
Salt to taste

Soak the rice in a covered bowl and leave for about four hours.

Dissolve the yeast and 1 tbsp sugar in 1/2 cup of tepid water. Keep aside. Grind the rice in batches along with three tbsp of cooked rice and a little water.

Add the yeast to the batter and leave overnight. Add 1/2 cup of coconut milk to make batter a little thinner. Add sugar and salt as needed. Stir well. Heat a griddle and lightly grease with coconut oil.

Pour a ladle of batter and spread it in a thin circle. Tap the edges of the batter with a piece of cloth dipped in oil. When cooked, the lacy edges of the appam will move away from the pan. Transfer with flat spatula onto serving dish.

Pongiya Appam
(Steamed Appam)

Makes 20-25 *appams*.

This is a popular breakfast item for the Cochin Jews and is similar to the *idlis* served across Southern India.

1 cup flour (in Cochin, only rice flour was used)	fresh coconut toddy was the raising agent)
2 cups semolina	3 1/2 cups water
3/4 cup sugar	1 cup grated coconut
1 1/2 tbsp yeast (in Cochin,	A pinch of salt

Combine the flour and semolina, along with the sugar, yeast, coconut, water and salt. Leave in a warm place to ferment for about three hours or until it rises. Pour the batter onto idly platters and steam for about 15 minutes. (Other suitable steamers can also be used.)

Optional: Place a piece of ripe banana/plantain and sprinkle nuts on top of batter before steaming.

• • • • •

As mentioned elsewhere, Moshav Nevatim, part of the Bnei Shimon Regional Council, is a settlement of the Cochin Jews in Israel. There are two popular restaurants on the *moshav*, serving authentic Cochin Jewish food to tourists going to Dimona and the Dead Sea. One is Miriam's Kitchen and the other is run by the Ephraim family.

Nehemia and his wife Miriam, who made *aliyah* more than 50 years ago from the Ernakulam congregation of Thekkumbhagam have been running Miriam's for about 14 years. Nehemia tells us that one of their most popular dishes is the *dosa* (a type of blintz), eaten with *chamanthi* (a tangy coconut chutney). There are also *idlis* (steamed rice cakes), a variety of chicken and beef dishes and the Cochin-Baghdadi *kubbah*.

At the Ephraim house, along with home-cooked food, guests can also hear stories from family members about Jewish life in Cochin in the early 20th century. The Ephraims can entertain groups from 4 to 40 people.

There are more than 50 varieties of *dosas* served across South India, ranging from the breakfast *dosa* to ones made by adding onions, buttermilk, wheat flour, grated coconut, spices, spinach, tofu or other fillings.

Everyday Breakfast Dosa Of The Cochin Jews (A Kind Of Blintz)

Maks 15-20 *dosas*, depending on thickness.

1 cup split black gram (urad dhal)	2 cups rice flour Salt to taste

Soak the split black gram in water for about three hours. Grind it with a little water to a smooth paste. Add 2 cups of rice flour. Add salt and let stand overnight for batter to rise.

Grease a hot griddle with coconut oil and spread the batter evenly in a circular shape - as thin as possible. Reduce heat.

Dab coconut oil on the edges of the *dosa*. Turn over with a flat spatula. When the edges turn crispy, transfer to a plate.

Sada Dosa (Plain Blintz)

Makes 12-15 *dosas*.

1 cup cooked rice	1/2 tsp fenugreek seeds
1 cup parboiled rice	1/2 tsp bicarbonate of soda
1/4 cup split black gram (white urad dhal)	1/2 cup yogurt
	10-12 tsp ghee or coconut oil

Wash the rice and split black gram. Add water and fenugreek seeds and let soak overnight.

Drain water and grind ingredients to make coarse paste.

Add salt, sufficient water and bicarbonate of soda and keep aside for some hours to let the batter rise. In a bowl, whisk the yogurt and add to the batter.

Heat an iron griddle or non-stick flat pan. Grease griddle and pour a ladle of batter. Spread thinly to form a circular shape.

Drizzle *ghee* or coconut oil at the edges. When it begins to crisp, turn over with a spatula. Transfer to plate after a couple of minutes.

The Masala Dosa

(This is the most beloved among *dosas* throughout India today)
Makes 10-15 *dosas*, depending on thickness.

1 cup plain rice	2 large potatoes, peeled and chopped
1 cup parboiled rice	12 cashew nuts,
1/4 cup white urad dhal	5 green chillies, chopped fine
1/2 tsp methi (fenugreek) seeds	1/2 cup coriander leaves, chopped
1/2 tsp soda bicarbonate	1 tsp urad dhal
1/2 cup yogurt	1/2 tsp cumin seed
10-12 tsp ghee or coconut oil, as preferred	1/2 tsp mustard seed
Water for grinding	Pinch of turmeric
	3 tbsp coconut oil
For masala:	Salt to taste
2 large onions, sliced thin	

Soak rice and dhal overnight in a large bowl of water. Drain and grind the rice and dhal to a rough paste. Add bicarbonate of soda, salt and some water. Let stay at room temperature for about 8 hours to allow batter to rise.

The Masala:
In a saucepan, heat some oil and splutter the mustard seeds. Lightly fry the green chillies and cashew nuts. Add potatoes, onions, cumin and cook until potatoes turn tender. Add turmeric, salt and coriander leaves and stir well.

The Dosa:
In a bowl, whisk the yogurt briskly and add to the batter.
Heat a tsp of *ghee* in an iron griddle and pour a ladle of batter. Spread evenly in a circular shape. Use a cheesecloth dipped in *ghee* to pat the edges of the batter. Let the edges sizzle and begin to crisp.
Ladle two tbsp of the potato and onion mixture in middle of *dosa*. Fold to cover *masala*. Remove with spatula when centre starts to crisp and brown.

PONGALAM
(A Dosa? No, It's Not A Dosa!)
(Spicy Crepes)

Makes 10-12 *pongalams*.

This batter-based dish, with some similarities to the *dosa/uthappa*, has been wrongly called 'Fongalam' in some newspapers and blogs, with butternut squash as the main component. Each community in Cochin made it with different ingredients. The Jews, however, did not use butternut squash and potatoes were rare in their *pongalams*. Also, butternut squash was not available in Cochin. Instead, grated carrots or grated cabbage went into the batter left over after making *idlis*; there was no way to refrigerate food in those days and the batter got sour to the right degree and became ideal for this dish. - Dr. Essie Sassoon.

2 cups of idli batter	2 green chillies, chopped fine
1 cup grated cabbage or carrots	2 dry red chillies, crushed
	1/2 tsp cumin seed
6 shallots, chopped fine	2 tbsp of grated coconut
1 sprig curry leaves	(optional)
1 small bunch coriander leaves	Salt to taste
1 tbsp chana dhal	Coconut oil for frying
1 tbsp urad dhal	

Heat 2 tbsp of coconut oil in a deep-bottomed pan and fry the *dhals*. Add the onions, chillies, cumin and curry leaves until onions begin to brown. (If you are using coconut, fry it along with the onions).

Add cabbage/carrot and fry for another 3 minutes. Mix all ingredients well into the batter. Heat 1 tsp of coconut oil in the same pan. Ladle about 3 tbsp of batter into the oil. Drizzle a little oil all around the batter and let the edges sizzle for two or three minutes.

Turn the *pongalam* over and cook until edges begin to crisp. Serve hot with coconut chutney.

Courtesy: Batzion Bezallel, Moshav Kidroon, Israel.

Polappam & Chikkiyathu
(Crepe With Stir-Fried Side Dish)

Makes 20 *polappams*.

The *polappam* is a type of crepe made with black gram and semolina and is a breakfast dish unique to the Jews of Cochin.

For Polappam:	2 large onions
1 cup black gram, soaked for about 8 hrs and then processed in a blender	1 cup grated coconut
	1 tsp mustard seeds
	3 green chillies, chopped fine
3 cups of semolina	1 small sprig curry leaves
	2 1/2" piece of ginger, chopped
For Chikkiyathu:	1/2 tsp turmeric
Two cups of pumpkin, skin removed and cut into cubes	4 tbsp coconut oil
	Salt to taste

Steam the semolina and process in blender along with the black gram, with water to get a batter-like consistency. Add salt and keep covered overnight.

Heat 2 tbsp oil in a skillet and fry the onions until they are translucent and begin to brown. Add the chillies, ginger and turmeric. Mix well.

Add the pumpkin pieces with 1/4 cup water; cover and cook for 10 to 15 minutes. Add the grated coconut. In another pan, heat the remaining oil and pop the mustard seeds. Add curry leaves and sizzle for 2 minutes. Pour over the pumpkin. Stir. In an iron griddle, use the batter to make crepes similar to the *dosa*. (See *dosa* recipe - p 31.)

Serve *polappam* with the *chikkiyathu*.

Optional: Hard, dried tuna (known as *Massa* in Cochin and available in plenty) can be grated and fried in coconut oil. This can be added to the cooked pumpkin, before taking pan off the stove. It adds an additional layer of flavour.

Courtesy: Pearly Simon, Haifa, Israel.

Cheratta Puttu
(Rice Steamed In Coconut Shell)

Makes 8 cones.

"A week before delivery, all the women of Jew Town gathered at the to-be-mother's house to make arrangements for the 'labour bed'.[2] A special treat at this gathering was a type of rice cake called *Cheratta Puttu* (*Cheratta* is coconut shell)."

Ruby Daniel describes the dish thus: "A kind of cake made with coconut mixed with rice flour and a little salt. It is poured into coconut shells with a few pieces of bananas on the top and cooked by steam. It is very tasty."[3]

1/2 kg coarse roasted rice flour (Rosematta rice preferred)
2 cups grated coconut
1 tbsp cumin seed
Approx. 2 1/2 cups water
Salt to taste
2 coconut shells (halved)

Dissolve 1 tsp salt in 1 cup of water. Slowly add this salted water, 1/2 cup grated coconut and cumin seeds to the rice flour and mix to a crumbly texture. Do not form dough. Place 2 tbsp of grated coconut in each half of the coconut shells, after piercing their 'eyes'. Add the crumbled rice flour. Top it with another 2 tbsp of grated coconut. Boil water in electric rice cooker or an *idli* cooker or other steamer.

Cover the steamer partition with a wet cloth and invert the coconut shells on the partition, Steam for 10- 15 minutes. Transfer the shells onto a plate and remove gently. *Puttu* is today made with bamboo or stainless steel cylinders steamed atop an aluminum pot to create a tubular shape. Modern-day versions of the *puttu* come stuffed with vegetables, meat, fish or fruit. Adding jaggery to the coconut is popular in northern Kerala. (These aluminum pots and steamers are available in Indian groceries.)

Puttu is a favourite breakfast dish in Kerala along with the *kadala kari*, a spicy stew made with black Bengal gram or steamed banana, as mentioned by Ruby Daniel. *Puttu* is also a popular item among the Tamils of northern Sri Lanka.

---

[2] Almost all children in Kerala in the years before the 1960's were born in their own homes, with the assistance of midwives.

[3] Daniel & Johnson, *Ruby of Cochin*. p. 175.

Upma or Uppumavu
(Fluffed, Spiced Semolina)

Serves 6.

The *upma* is an excellent porridge-like breakfast dish, easy to prepare, filling and nutritious. Vegetables like peas, carrots, potatoes, cauliflower, cabbage, tomatoes, capsicum (bell peppers) and fried peanuts or cashews can be added to make variants of this dish. It can be eaten alone or with any curry, steamed bananas or just a sprinkling of sugar.

2 cups semolina (sooji)
1 large onion, chopped fine
1" ginger, chopped fine
4 green chillies, chopped
3 dried red chillies, crushed
1/2 cup grated coconut
1 tsp black gram (urad dhal or split peas)
1/2 tsp mustard seeds
1 sprig curry leaves
6 tbsp clarified butter or vegetable oil
Salt, as needed
Water

Lightly roast the semolina in a non-stick pan. Stir continuously so that it does not brown. Remove from heat and keep aside. Heat the clarified butter or oil in another pan and splutter mustard seeds. (Clarified butter enhances the aroma and taste.)

Add onions, chillies and curry leaves and sauté until onions become translucent. (If you want the *upma* to have a light yellow colour, add a pinch of turmeric). Add ginger, *urad dhal* and fry for 2 more minutes. Add 2 cups of water, salt and let boil. Reduce heat. Add the roasted semolina, stirring slowly to prevent clumping. Sprinkle coconut flakes and mix. Cover the pan and cook on low heat for about 5 minutes. The semolina will absorb all the water and turn a little fluffy, much like couscous. Pour a few tablespoons of water if it seems dry and heat for 2 more minutes.

Idlis
(Soft, Steamed Rice Cakes)

Makes 18-20 *idlis*.

The *idli* is an ancient south Indian preparation dating back to more than 1000 years. The scholar-king Someshwara III (1127-39) of the Chalukya dynasty who ruled over regions covering today's Karnataka state and bordering Malabar, mentions the *idli* recipe in his Sanskrit encyclopedia, '*Manasollasa*', written in 1130 A.D.[4]

1 cup urad dhal	1/2 cup cooked rice
3 cups Basmati rice or any rice	Salt to taste
1 tsp fenugreek seeds	

Soak *urad dhal* and fenugreek seeds in one bowl and rice in a separate bowl for about 5 hours. Drain and grind *urad dhal* and fenugreek seeds with water. When half done, add rice & salt and grind again. Add water as needed. Add cooked rice and grind again to a coarse paste. Keep covered for 12 hours to allow for fermentation. Stir the batter and ladle into lightly greased *idli* mould. Steam for ten minutes in a pressure cooker or steamer.

KALLAPPAM
(COCONUT TODDY PANCAKE)

Makes 12 pancakes.

Kallu means coconut toddy in Malayalam, and *Kallapam* is a popular rice pancake, made using *Kallu* as the rising agent. It tastes similar to the lacy-edged *Paalappam*. In Israel, yeast is used instead of toddy. Goes well with meat or vegetable stews.

2 cups rice	2 tsp sugar
1 cup cooked rice	1/2 glass of fresh toddy
1 1/2 cups grated coconut	(or 1/2 tsp yeast)
6 shallots	Pinch of salt
1 tsp cumin seeds	

Combine sugar and yeast in 1/4 cup warm water and keep aside for 5-10 minutes. It should rise to twice its volume. Grind rice, grated coconut, shallots and cumin with a little water to form smooth batter. Add yeast mixture or fresh toddy and stir well. Keep overnight for fermentation. Make Kallappam like the *dosa* on a heated iron griddle or heavy skillet, dabbing the edges with coconut oil or clarified butter/ghee. The centres remain fluffed and spongy.

---

[4] Achaya, K. T. *Indian Food: A Historical Companion.* Oxford University Press, New York, 1994, p. 90.

Chapter 2

Bounties From The Nets

The people of Kerala have a choice between *kadal meen* and *puzha meen* (fishes caught in the ocean and from the 44 rivers, lakes, backwaters and canals that crisscross the state). In Cochin itself, the catch from the Arabian Sea yields a variety of fish - from sardines (*mathi/chaala*), mackerel (*ayla*) and pomfret (*avoli*) to several types of bigger fish like seer, kingfish (called *ney meen* or *aikura*) and tuna (*choora*). Barracuda (*seelavu*) and sharks (*sravu* - which are not *kosher*) are caught in quantities, along with valuable prawns/shrimps (*chemmeen* - also not *kosher*).

There is a fish called *kora*, a type of grouper which is a prized product. (Once upon a time, it used to be called Jewfish, because it was considered a clean fish to eat. For commercial purposes, however, and because the name was considered offensive, it is today called 'dufish' in the US and elsewhere.)

The Jews of Kerala have traditionally been avid fish eaters. Their ancient settlement in Kodungalloor (Shingly) was on the banks of the fabled Periyar river, which teems with marine life. Today, the desirable mullet (*thirutha*) is mainly caught in the Chinese fishing nets at the Kochi harbour mouth where the Periyar empties into the Arabian Sea.[1]

---

[1] The giant cantilever nets are believed to have been brought to Cochin during the time of Kublai Khan by explorer Zheng He (in the mid-13th century).

In Kerala, fish is cooked in different ways in different homes, leading to scores of recipes - with small changes in the ingredients - sometimes with the same name.

Noted Malayalam writer N.S. Madhavan, wrote about this abundant fish resources in the online edition of the popular *Outlook* magazine.

"My memories of succulent prawns take me back to the late Cohen, one of the last of Kochi's Jewish community, who also performed duties as the priest at Kochi's synagogue. He owned a fishing boat, which he gave on hire. Along with rent, he was also entitled to a customary portion from the day's catch. If it was prawns, which is not *kosher*, he would distribute it among friends.

"My father was his colleague and a dear friend; we cherished the deep sea bounty with gratitude to Cohen Sir. Fish cooked in a green gravy of ground coconut and coriander leaves is what I faintly remember of the Kochi Jewish fish curry. There aren't many people left now to ask for the recipe."[2]

Madhavan here was referring to Jackie Cohen, who was once caretaker of the Paradesi synagogue. However, Jackie Cohen was only a weekend fisherman who waited patiently with his single rod fishing line at the Mattancherry jetty. The Cochin Jew who owned the fishing boat was Isaac Hallegua. Prawns or *chemmeen* is a valuable product for fishermen and for Isaac Hallegua, any haul of prawns meant good money on that day. However, Hallegua made it a point to distribute a part of the prawn catch free to people close to the Jewish community.

Cochin Jewish Green Fish Curry

Serves 6.

Coriander, known as *malli* in Malayalam and *dhaniya* in Hindi is grown throughout India and the fresh leaves and seeds are part of every regional cuisine in the subcontinent. In the Western world, it goes by its Spanish name of *cilantro*.

The leaves have a slightly citrus flavour, while the seeds are warm and nutty to taste and are roasted and powdered to become an elemental in-

---

[2] Madhavan, N.S., Those Mean Papas, The sea, the fresh catch, the Kerala fish curry, from Kochi to Kozhikode, *Outlook Magazine*, January 09, 2012. N.S. Madhavan is author of the award-winning *Litanies of Dutch Battery* and other works. Now retired, he was an officer of the Indian Administrative Service in its Bihar cadre. http://www.outlookindia.com/article.aspx?279394. Excerpt reprinted with permission.

gredient of the Indian curry powder. The leaves add color, a fresh flavour and delightful aroma to hot dishes. Coriander is also sometimes referred to as Chinese parsley or Mexican parsley.

This dish is very popular during Pesach (Passover).

> 1 kg firm white fish fillet (seer fish, tuna, halibut, tilapia. In Kerala, seer fish - neymeen or aikoora - is favoured).
> 1 cup grated coconut
> 1 cup chopped coriander
> 1 tsp red chilli powder
> 4 green chillies - chopped fine
>
> 3/4 tsp turmeric
> 1 tbsp cumin
> 2 tbsp vegetable oil
> 2 onions, finely sliced
> 3 cloves of garlic, chopped fine
> 2 cups water
> Salt and pepper to taste
> 1 1/2- tbsp coconut oil

Add coconut, coriander, chilli powder, turmeric and cumin to 1 cup of water in a food processor. Blend ingredients until it turns into a smooth paste. Fry the onion in vegetable oil in a skillet over medium heat, until the slices turn golden brown.

Add the chopped garlic, add 1/2 cup of water and the coconut-based paste. Sprinkle salt and pepper over the mixture. Bring it to a boil. Let the mixture simmer until it begins to thicken.

Pour 1/2 cup of water and slowly slide the fillets into skillet. Bring it to a boil on medium heat, then cover the pan partly to let steam escape and simmer again on low heat. Occasionally, lift pan and ladle sauce onto the fillets. Cook until fillets become flaky. This should take around 12 to 15 minutes. Garnish with chopped coriander and drizzle the coconut oil over the dish.

Courtesy: Queenie Hallegua, Mattancherry, Kerala, India.

•••••

A Tip From The Past:

"When fish is to be boiled, it should be rubbed lightly over with salt and set on the fire in a saucepan or fish-kettle sufficiently large, in hard cold water, with a little salt. A spoonful or two of vinegar is sometimes added, which has the effect of increasing its firmness.

"Fish for broiling should be rubbed over with vinegar, well dried in a cloth and floured. The fire must be clear and free from smoke, the gridiron made quite hot, and the bars buttered before the fish is put on it. Fish to be fried should be rubbed in with salt, dried, rolled in a cloth and placed for a few minutes before the fire previous to being put in the pan."[3]

· · · · ·

Green Fish Curry In Coconut Milk

Serves 6.
This is another version of the Green Fish Curry.[4]
In this recipe, coconut milk is used instead of grated coconut and there is also mustard, ginger, cardamom and curry powder added. The sauce is richer and thicker.

1 kg firm fish fillets (seer fish/ tilapia, salmon)
1 1/2 cups thick coconut milk
1 large onion, chopped fine
4 shallots, chopped
2" ginger, sliced fine
6 green chillies, sliced fine
6 cardamom pods, skinned & crushed
3 cloves of garlic

1 1/2 tsp coriander powder
1 tsp curry powder (garam masala or fish masala)
1 tsp mustard seeds
1 sprig curry leaves
1 large bunch coriander
2 tsp lemon zest (optional)
3 tbsp coconut oil
Salt and pepper to taste

In a large pan heat the coconut oil and splutter the mustard seeds. Add cardamom and shallots and fry until shallots turn brown.

Use a food processor to blend the chopped onion, garlic, coriander powder and ginger with 3/4 cup of coconut milk into a paste. Add spice paste to pan with the green chillies and some water and let cook for about 15 minutes. Slide the fillets into the pan. Add curry leaves, pepper, curry powder, coconut milk and cook on low heat. Stir the gravy. Remove from heat when fish is flaky. Garnish with fresh coriander/zest.

---

[3] Montefiore, Cohen Judith. *The Jewish Manual*, Chapter III, p. 22.

[4] A Cochin Jewish fish curry and coconut rice were featured items at UK's largest Jewish food festival in Golders Green in May, 2013. The fourth edition of the annual festival was held at the London Jewish Cultural Centre, in Ivy House. The Cochin dishes were demonstrated by Nikita Gulhane from the Spice Monkey cooking school of London. See:http://www.times-series.co.uk/news/10431441._Fantastic__Jewish_food_festival_attracts_hundreds_of_visitors/ Note: There were no recipe details given.

Cochin Fish Curry with Pomfrets

Serves 4.

Pomfrets, a favourite fish in Kerala, are perciform fishes belonging to the family *Bramidae*. They are found in abundance off the Kerala coast, the Atlantic, Indian and Pacific Oceans. The largest of the species, the Atlantic pomfret, Brama brama, grows up to 3.5 ft long.

In Kerala, the fish available in markets is about 8" long and 6" inches wide. The pomfret is also known as *pamflet*, a word which comes from the Portuguese *pampo*, referring to similar fish like the blue butterfish. The fish is excellent for frying.

2 large pomfrets
1 large bunch of coriander (cilantro)
5 green chillies, chopped fine
1 lemon
2 tbsp grated coconut
1 large onion
2 tsp garlic powder or 5 cloves of garlic, chopped fine
Salt to taste
1 cup water
1/2 cup oil

Clean and wash the pomfret. Make slits across the middle on both sides. Coat with salt and juice of half the lemon. Chop the onion and garlic and mash them to a paste. Grind coriander, three green chillies and grated coconut into a paste.

Heat oil in a wok and fry the fish individually. Remove from wok and keep aside. In the same oil, add onion and garlic and fry until browned. Add one cup of water into wok. Let boil. Slide the fried pomfret into wok. Reduce heat. Add salt and coriander paste and bring to boil again. Remove from heat and add rest of the lemon juice and chopped green chillies. A sprinkling of ground pepper is optional.

The pomfrets can also be cut into small steaks and fried.

Meen Varuthu Vechathu
(Fish Fillets In Vegetable Sauce)

Serves 10.

This is one of the few dishes made by the Cochinis which combine fish and vegetables to create an unusual taste experience. The baked fish absorbs the flavours of sweet potato and spices that renders it very juicy.

1-2 kg fish cut into strips or filleted
Spices for the fish:
1 tsp turmeric
1/2 tsp hot red pepper powder
2 tsp sweet paprika
1 tsp salt
1 tbsp oil

Soak the fish in water with 1 tsp turmeric powder, 3 tbsp vinegar, 2 tsp salt for about 30 minutes and rinse. Mix all the spices together and rub the fish with it. Bake the fish in the oven till done.

For The Vegetable Sauce:

1 eggplant, cut to small slices
2 potatoes, peeled and sliced
1/4 kg okra
1 sweet potato, peeled and sliced
1 large onion, diced
8 cloves of garlic, chopped fine
1" ginger, chopped fine
2 green chillies, chopped fine

Sprinkle salt on eggplant pieces and squeeze out the water. Combine the vegetables, sprinkle some salt and bake in oven until they are done.

Sauté the onions and garlic till cooked and add ginger and pepper. Add 2 cups of water. Add the following spices: 1/2 tsp turmeric, 2 tsp ground coriander, 1/2 tsp hot red pepper powder, 1 tsp sugar, 4 tbsp vinegar and salt according to taste.

Boil the sauce till the spices and vinegar are cooked. Add 1 cup coconut milk and 2 tbsp of ground coconut, and continue cooking.

Add the baked vegetables and cook till the vegetables absorb the spices. Add the baked fish to the sauce, mix gently, let come to boil. Switch off heat and leave it covered to let the vegetables and fish absorb a lot of the sauce.

Courtesy: Gila Rosenblatt, Aberdeen, New Jersey, United States.

CHUTTULLI MEEN
(FRIED/GRILLED FISH WITH ROASTED SHALLOT SAUCE)

Serves 5.

The sweet flavour of shallots and the piquant blend of spices come together with flaky fish, to create this celebrated dish, an original recipe of the Cochin Jews. The dish has now crossed over to other communities and has been featured on BBC Television and several Indian and international networks. It is usually served with stuffed or grilled potatoes or okra cooked in coconut cream (*See recipe on p.117*).

1 kg of firm fish - (mullet, bass, trout fillets)	3 tsp coriander powder
10 shallots (or pearl onions)	4 green chillies - chopped fine
2 sprigs curry leaves	2" ginger, chopped fine
1 tsp pepper	4 cloves garlic, chopped
1 tsp cumin powder	2 tbsp lemon juice
5 cardamom pods, husked and crushed	1 bunch coriander - chopped fine
	2-3 tbs oil (coconut oil preferred)
	Salt to taste

Clean and pat dry the fillets and keep aside. Heat coconut oil in a frying pan and roast the shallots, curry leaves, chillies, pepper, cumin, cardamom and coriander seeds on medium heat. Let the shallots turn brown.

Add the salt and lemon juice and grind together to make a rough paste. Rub the paste on both sides of the fillets.

Fry the fillets in a skillet, basting often with coconut oil till the fish browns and the skin crisps. Garnish with coriander and wedges of lemon. (Instead of pan frying, the fish can also be grilled on charcoal for a variant of the dish.)

Courtesy: Batzion Bezallel, Moshav Kidroon, Israel.

Meen Unda Kari
(Cochin Jewish Fish Kofta Curry)

Makes 25 *undas*.

Fish fillet is crumbled, mixed with spices and fried to make delightful dumplings which are then immersed in a spicy sauce in this original dish from Cochin. The tamarind extract or the lemon juice adds the sourness to offset the strength of cardamom, cinnamon and coriander.

1 kg firm, white fish fillets	1/2" inch cinnamon
(sea bass/mullet/king fish etc)	1 tsp curry powder
3 large tomatoes diced	1/2 tsp cardamom powder
2 or 3 pieces tamarind	2 onions, chopped fine
(soaked in water/squeezed	1 onion, chopped rough
for the juice) or 2 tsps lemon juice	1 tsp cumin powder
3 tbsp all purpose flour	1 tsp mustard seeds
2 tbsp rice flour	1 tsp coriander powder
1" ginger, chopped fine	10 green chillies/chopped fine
1/2 tsp fennel seeds	1 large bunch coriander
6 pods garlic, crushed	2 tsp red chilli powder
2 cloves	1 tsp sugar
1/2 tsp turmeric	3 tbsp oil
1 tsp ground pepper	Salt as needed

Wash and clean fish. Boil and crumble. Blend chopped onions, some coriander leaves, 5 green chillies and ground fennel seeds into a paste.

In a wok, fry the chopped onions, garlic, along with tomato and rest of the spices. Splutter the mustard seeds. Add the onion and coriander paste, remaining chillies and salt and sauté for a couple of minutes.

Add 3 cups of water, lemon juice or tamarind water and cook for 20 minutes over low fire until the sauce begin to thicken.

Knead the crumbled fish along with the rice and all-purpose flour, salt and curry powder into a smooth mixture. Form into small balls.

In a large saucepan, fry the fish balls until golden brown. Add the fish balls into the sauce in the skillet, reduce heat and simmer for about 10 minutes. Garnish with whole coriander leaves.

Courtesy: Reema Salem, Mattancherry, Kerala, India.

Meen Undas (Fish Balls)
Cochin Fish Patties/Cutlets

Makes about 30 cutlets.

Ora Farchy's mother Rebecca made these mouth-watering fish balls (or flat croquettes) in Moshav Shahar in Israel in the 1950's, and before that in Chennamangalam - where she got the recipe from her mother Sarah.[5] Today, this chopped fish with mashed potatoes, coated with bread crumbs and then deep fried in oil is a favourite party-time snack all across Kerala. In Israel, half a cup of finely chopped olives is also added to the mix.

(Note of interest: The Central Institute of Fisheries Technology in Cochin, which began operations in 1957 claims on their website that 'fish cutlets' were one of many products developed by the institute).

1 kg firm fish fillets (tuna or any firm fish is fine)
1 bunch coriander, chopped fine
2 large onions, chopped fine
4 green chillies chopped fine
5 tsp finely chopped ginger
3 potatoes, cooked and mashed
5 cloves of garlic, chopped fine
1/2 tsp turmeric
2 tsp pepper
1 tsp red chilli powder
1/4 tsp cloves ground
Coriander and cinnamon powder to taste
1-2 tsp lemon juice
4 eggs
Bread crumbs, powdered
Salt to taste
Oil to fry

Cook fish & crumble; add salt and turmeric and mix well. Fry chopped onions in oil in a shallow pan until golden brown. Add chillies and other spices. Mix paste, along with the mashed potatoes into cooked, ground fish. Squeeze the juice of lemons into mix.

Shape mixture into flat rounds or oval forms, dip in beaten eggs, roll in bread crumbs and refrigerate for about three to four hours. In a wok, deep fry the cutlets over medium heat.

Optional: You can also prepare a tomato sauce and add the fried fish patties and simmer for 30 minutes on a low heat.

Courtesy: Ora Farchy, Houston, Texas.

---

[5] See Rebecca's charoset recipe on p. 167.

Ora's mother Rebecca passed away in December, 2012. She was the last of the older generation among the Cochinis in Moshav Shahar, Israel. Ora had this to tell us: "A lot of wisdom and knowledge about the unique way of life of Cochin Jews and their traditions have gone away with her. It is very sad."

Chaala And Koorka Salad (Sardines & Chinese Potato Salad)

Serves 6.

Dr. Usha Mohan of Bengaluru, India, remembers her mother the late Dr. Esther Salem (Minoo) of Jew Town in Mattancherry, making a delicious salad with fish and Chinese potatoes.[6] "Sardines or anchovies (*netholi/uzhuva* in Malayalam) were the fishes of choice," says Dr. Mohan, "because they had the oily flavour that blended well with the coconut."

The salad can also be made with other meatier fishes, filleted or chopped with the bones removed.

1/4 kg sardines
1/4 kg Chinese potatoes
1/2 cup coconut oil
1 cup coconut milk
1/2 tsp mustard seeds
1 sprig curry leaves

4 cloves garlic
1" piece ginger
1/4 tsp turmeric
2 green chillies, chopped
Salt and vinegar to taste

In a wok, heat coconut oil and fry the cleaned sardines (*chaala*) until crisp. Skin and cook the *koorka* in a bowl of water on medium heat until it softens.

In a deep pan, heat some coconut oil and splutter the mustard seeds. Add curry leaves, chopped garlic and ginger, turmeric, green chillies and sizzle for about two minutes or so until the raw smell of the garlic is gone. Add coconut milk, salt and vinegar to taste.

Let simmer for a while and turn off the flame. Add the fried sardines and *koorka* and raw, chopped onions. Mix well.

Courtesy: Dr. Usha Mohan, Bengaluru, Karnataka, India.

---

[6] See note about *koorka* or Chinese potatoes on p. 64.

Fish Salad With Tomatoes And Coconut Milk

Another version of a Cochin Jewish fish salad calls for tomatoes and coconut milk, without the potatoes.

After the fish is fried, pour a cup of coconut milk over the fish. Add half a cup of raw, chopped onions and half a cup of raw chopped tomatoes and a pinch of salt. Mix gently to prevent fish from flaking. Let the fish soak for a couple of hours, absorbing the coconut, tomato and onion flavours. Garnish with coriander leaves.

Cochin Jewish Fish Curry With Coconut Milk

Serves 8.

Coconut oil and coconut milk combine with the various spices to make this a very seductive dish. One serving is never enough!

1 kg fresh, firm-fleshed fish
1 cup thick coconut milk
2 onions, chopped fine
4 garlic cloves, chopped fine
1" ginger, chopped fine
1 or 2 red dried chillies, crushed
2 tbsp coriander powder
1 tsp cumin powder
1/2 tsp turmeric
1 tsp ground pepper
3 tbsp coconut oil
Tamarind water (squeezed from a ping-pong sized ball of pulp in a little water)
1 large bunch coriander leaves
Salt to taste

Clean, slice fish to desired fillet size. Heat 3 tbsp of coconut oil in a deep saucepan. Add the onions, garlic, green chillies and ginger and sauté until onions begin to brown.

Add the coriander powder, cumin power, crushed red chillies, turmeric, pepper, tamarind extract, salt and cook another 2-3 minutes. Add 1 cup of water and bring the mixture to boil. Slide in the fish fillets and cook for about 5 minutes on medium heat.

Pour the coconut milk over the fish and simmer on low heat for another 10 minutes. Do not boil. Remove from heat and sprinkle coriander leaves over dish.

MEEN PEERA OR MEEN PATTICHATHU
(COCONUT-LACED FISH)

Serves 4

This fish dish is a perennial favourite - it is delicious and easy to make. The fish used is mostly anchovies (*netholi* or *uzhuva*) and there is liberal use of grated coconut. (If you prefer not to deal with fish bones, you can use sliced white fish fillets).

1/2 kg anchovies, heads cut and cleaned or white fish fillets, sliced into 1" pieces
2 tbsp coconut oil
1 1/2 tsp mustard seed
3 cloves garlic, chopped fine
8 shallots, chopped fine
6 green chillies, chopped fine
1" piece of ginger, grated

1/4 tsp turmeric
3 pieces kudampuli (gambooge)
1/2 tsp chilli powder
1 tsp turmeric
1 sprig curry leaves
1/2 cup water
3/4 cup grated coconut
Salt to taste

In a processor, coarsely blend the grated coconut, shallots, garlic, ginger and chillies. Heat the coconut oil in a skillet. Pop mustard seeds, reduce heat and add coconut paste, cooking on low heat until browned.

Add the curry leaves, turmeric, *kudampuli*, salt and water. Cook for about a minute and slide the fish in, coating the fish with skillet mixture. Cover and simmer for 10 minutes or until fish is done. Drizzle a tsp of coconut oil over the dish. (Pieces of raw mango can be used as the souring agent instead of the *kudampuli*.)

Courtesy: Sippora Lane, Tiberias, Israel.

FISH, EGGPLANT AND
COCONUT MILK CASSEROLE

Serves 8.

This is a dish best served cold - the fish will soak up the coconut milk, lemon juice and the heat of the chillies.

1 kg of firm, white fish fillets, cut into 2" pieces

2 large onions, sliced thin
1 eggplant cut in thin slices

2 cups coconut milk
5 green chillies, sliced lengthwise
1 1/2 tsp chopped mint leaves
1 1/2 tsp chopped dill
1 small bunch of coriander leaves, chopped fine
6 tbsp coconut oil
Salt to taste

Heat coconut oil in skillet and fry fish fillets until browned on both sides. Remove with slotted spoon. Slide eggplant slices into pan and fry until they begin to crisp. Add the dill, coriander, mint, onion and fry for about 2 minutes. In a deep-bottomed dish, layer the eggplant mixture with fried fish. Add coconut milk and salt. Pour into dish. Chill for some hours before serving. Garnish with chopped coriander.

Meen Varuthathu (Fried Fish)

Serves 8.

1 kg fillets of any firm fish
4 cloves garlic, mashed
1" ginger, grated fine
1 tsp tamarind paste
1/2 tsp turmeric
1 tsp red chilli powder
1/2 tsp ground pepper
3 to 4 tbsp lemon juice
1/2 bunch coriander, chopped fine
Oil for deep frying
3-4 tbsp all-purpose flour

In a large bowl, combine all ingredients with the lemon juice.

Add fish fillets. Stir in the coriander leaves. Let the well-coated fish marinate in the refrigerator for about six hours.

Heat oil in a deep frying pan. Pat fish fillets in flour and fry in batches, turning them over, until they turn golden brown.

Variant: Instead of frying, opt for baking in an oven preheated to 350 degrees for about 15 minutes or until done.

Courtesy: Ora Farchy, Houston, Texas.

Meen Pollichathu
(Fried Fish In Coconut Milk & Tomato Sauce)

Serves 8.

The fish for this delectable dish is marinated and fried as mentioned in the previous recipe.

For the sauce:
2 large onions, chopped fine
2 green chillies, chopped
A few curry leaves
2 large tomatoes, chopped
1 tsp turmeric
1 tsp red chilli powder
2 tsp coriander powder

1 tsp garlic powder
1" ginger, chopped fine
1 tbsp vinegar
1 tsp sugar
1 cup coconut milk
3 tbsp coconut oil
Salt to taste

Heat the coconut oil in a frying pan and sauté onions along with curry leaves, ginger, green chillies and garlic powder until the onions begin to brown. Add red chilli powder and coriander powder and mix well until the oil starts to separate. Add vinegar and chopped tomatoes and cook for a few minutes until all ingredients look blended. Add coconut milk and stir well. Gently slide the fried pieces of fish into the gravy, let simmer for about three minutes and take off heat.

•••••

'Spice Chef' Of Vancouver

Linda Hertzman (née Salem) is a Cochini Jew who has made a name for herself in the catering business in Vancouver, Canada. Known as the *Spice Chef*, "she routinely wows Vancouver's Jewish Community with exceptional food that goes far beyond general Ashkenazi fare".[1]

Linda grew up in Cochin's Jew Town in Mattancherry and made *aliyah* in 1983 - but came to Toronto soon after getting married. Although she had a degree in psychology, her first love was cooking and so completed courses in food service and restaurant management from George Brown College and Seneca in Toronto. Her family's first venture was the Raisins,

---

[1] Cramer, Lauren, Chef influenced by spices of Native India, *The Canadian Jewish News*, May 24, 2012. http://www.cjnews.com/index.php?q=node/90109

Almonds & More kosher food store in Toronto. The Hertzmans later moved to Vancouver with their three children - where they purchased a restaurant and called it Aviv's Kosher Meats, with Linda working in the kitchen and then branching out into catering.

She now runs a company called Classic Impressions, specializing in gourmet *kosher* cuisine for any occasion, from "elaborate *b'nei mitzvah* receptions to intimate brisses, luncheons, weddings and everything in-between... Our reputation is for food that lingers in memory long after the last forkful has been consumed." Her Toronto-born husband Steve manages the Kosher Food Warehouse in Vancouver.

Linda says: ""I put a lot of Cochini fusion into my dishes, making items like *kubbah* dumplings with meat fillings and pastels, similar to blintzes but more savoury. I love playing around with flavours, trying out different things...." She also makes *hamin*, the traditional Cochini cholent or *kofta kababs* and fish with a mix of other Sephardi/Mizrahi flavours. "It's all about themes these days," says Linda. "We'll still have salmon on the menu, but it's more likely to be *miso salmon* rather than lemon pepper."

Salmon Miso

Makes 6 portions.

(Miso is a fermented bean paste and is a traditional Japanese seasoning. Made with rice, barley or wheat and soya beans combined with salt and a yeast mold called *koji*, it is a concentrated, savoury food additive. The mixture, which is aged sometimes for up to three years, can be used in sauces and spreads and in meat and vegetable pickles, dips and casseroles.)

1 kg salmon fillets
1 cup miso paste
1/2 cup brown sugar or honey
2 tsp sesame oil
2 tsp fresh, minced ginger
2 tsp fresh minced garlic
1/4 cup rice vinegar

Add all ingredients in a large skillet in about 1" of water and bring mixture up to boil. Let cool. Marinate the salmon in the mixture for up to 24 hours. Preheat oven to 400 degrees F (200 degrees C). Bake the salmon until the fillets are cooked. Alternately, grill them. Serve with sticky rice.

Meen Inji Ulli
(Fish With Ginger, Coconut & Onion Paste)

Serves 3.

Similar to the *Chuttulli Meen* (*page 44*), this dish is a unique creation of the Cochin Jews. Ginger and onion dominate, while the grated coconut and coconut oil allows for an engaging fragrance.

6 pieces, any fish of choice, washed cleaned (if they are not fillets, they should be scored)
1 cup grated coconut or
1 cup dried coconut (copra), powdered
1 large onion, chopped

2" piece of ginger, chopped
2 green chillies, chopped
1 small sprig curry leaves
1 small bunch coriander leaves
3 tsp vinegar
1/2 cup coconut oil
Salt to taste

The marinade:
1/4 tsp turmeric
1 tbsp red chilli powder
1 tsp garlic powder

1 tbsp vinegar
Salt to taste

Combine all ingredients to make a paste (add a little water if it is too thick). Marinate fish with paste and keep aside for about two hours.

In a skillet, heat the coconut oil and deep fry the fish. Take out with slotted spoon and transfer to serving dishes. In a food processor, blend the coconut, onion, ginger, chillies, curry leaves, vinegar, coriander leaves and salt to make a thick paste. Arrange the fried fish and use the coconut paste as a spread over the fish. Serve hot.

Simple Sardine Curry

Serves 6.

This version of fish curry uses the *kudampuli* (Garcinia cambogia or the Malabar tamarind) for a refreshing sourness that enhances the flavours of everything else that goes into the dish. The dried *kudampuli* is purplish black in colour; and sardines are the most abundant fish available across Kerala.

1/2 kg sardines
1/4 cup pearl onion or shallots, chopped
3 to 4 pieces, dried kudampuli
1/2 cup grated coconut
2 tbsp coriander powder
1 1/2 tbsp red chilli powder
1 tbsp ginger, chopped fine
1/2 tsp turmeric
3 green chillies, sliced
1 sprig curry leaves
2 tbsp coconut oil
Salt to taste

Grind the coconut with a little water to make a smooth paste. Soak the *kudampuli* in 1/2 cup of water for about 10 minutes. Drain and soak the *kudampuli* again for another 10 minutes.

Immerse the cleaned sardines in water in a heavy saucepan. Add the *kudampuli* (with its water), coconut paste, coriander powder, chilli powder, ginger, green chillies and turmeric. Mix well. Cook covered on medium heat for about 8 to 10 minutes. Add salt to taste. In another shallow pan, heat the oil and sauté the shallots and curry leaves till they turn fragrant and brown. Add to fish curry. This curry is ideal with hot rice or a variety of breads.

Cochin Fish Curry With Coconut Milk & Shallots

Serves 8.

This fish dish with its rich and thick gravy goes well with all types of breads.

1 kg firm fish fillets
15 shallots, chopped coarse
4 large tomatoes, chopped
5 cloves garlic, chopped fine
5 green chillies, chopped
1 tsp cumin seeds
2 tbsp coriander seeds
1/2 tsp turmeric powder
1 tsp cardamom powder
1 cup coconut milk
1 sprig curry leaves
4 tbsp coconut oil
Salt to taste
1 large bunch coriander leaves, chopped fine

Grind garlic, green chillies, cumin and coriander seeds with 1/4 cup coconut milk to a smooth paste. Heat 2 tbsp coconut oil in a large skillet and sauté the shallots, along with turmeric, until they turn translucent.

Add the coconut-coriander paste, mix well and fry on medium heat for about five minutes. Add the fish fillets, 1 cup of water and cook covered for another five minutes. Add the remaining coconut milk, reduce heat and let simmer until the sauce thickens and fillets turn flaky.

In another shallow pan, heat the remaining oil and fry the curry leaves. Add the chopped tomatoes and stir fry until they turn mushy. Take off stove and spread over the fish.

Cochin Tuna Salad

Ajeeth Janardhanan, Executive Chef at the famed Brunton Boatyard hotel in Fort Kochi, is an aficionado of Cochin Jewish cuisine. He regularly presents Jewish dishes on 'theme' nights at the hotel's many restaurants. This is how he makes his popular tuna salad.

To preserve the Tuna:
1 kg tuna - filleted
Water- to cover the tuna
100 gms - bay leaves

80 gm salt- for every litre of water added
Sunflower or virgin olive oil

Layer the bottom of the pan with half the bay leaves. Put the fish down in a single layer on top of the bay leaf. Cover with the rest of the bay leaf. Add the water and salt by measure. Allow to cook for 25 minutes and cool in the water itself. Drain the fish and allow the fish to rest for some time. Take a sanitized, dry vessel with lid. Put the fish and cover with the oil.

This fish can now be used for months on end for sandwiches, salads or eaten as is. Be careful to take out the fish with a dry and sanitized spoon or ladle.

For the salad:
20 gm ash gourd
20 gm snake gourd
20 gm ridge gourd
20 gm yellow pumpkin
5gms sliced shallots

For the dressing:
10 ml oil from the preserved fish
3 gm chopped garlic
2 whole red chillies
5 ml lemon juice

Cut the vegetables lengthwise and blanch in water. Slice the shallots into thin rounds. Heat the oil and add the garlic and whole red chillies.

Cool the oil and whisk the lemon juice into it. Break the tuna into flakes and gently mix it with the vegetables and sliced shallots. If you have lettuce, spread it on a plate and put the mixture on top and drizzle the dressing over it.

(Chef's note: The vegetables need to be shocked after blanching by rinsing them in chilled water to help maintain colour, crunchiness and nutrients.)

Courtesy: Ajeeth Janardhanan, Brunton Boatyard, Cochin.

•••••

"The curry we usually ate on Saturday night was eggs cooked in sauce and dried salted fish fried, as we must have hot meal and there is no time to cook meat. We had to cook quickly after dark on Saturday, as we couldn't light a fire during the Shabbat. There was a woman selling the salted fish, who lived on the other side of the Misro Palli and I had to go and buy the fish from her".[2]

Ruby Daniels lived in the middle of Synagogue Lane, halfway between the Paradesi Synagogue to the south and Kadavumbagham Synagogue to the north. The Misro Palli was an open area off Synagogue Lane and is believed to have once been a *midrash* or school (hence the name Misro). Palli means place of worship, but there never was any place of worship there. - Kenny Salem.

Unakka Meen Varuthathu (Fried Salted Fish)

Serves 6.

The dried fish that Ruby talked about were the *kozhuva*, *mullan* and the *manthal* (in Malayalam), the most popular among dried, salted fish used in households throughout Kerala. The *kozhuva*, also called *netholi* or *podimeen*, is known to us as anchovies. The *mullan* is a small, bony fish which we call 'silver belly fish' or 'pony fish' or 'tooth pony'. The *manthal*, also called *nangu*, is known as the Malabar sole. The *kozhuva* is the most popular and many Cochinis take packets of this dried fish to Israel whenever they visit Kerala. They can be prepared as a quick snack.

[2] Daniel & Johnson, *Ruby of Cochin*, pg 32.

1/4 kg anchovies or tooth pony
or Malabar sole
6-8 shallots, chopped
1" ginger, chopped
2-3 garlic cloves, chopped
3-4 green chillies, slit lengthwise
2 tbsp red chilli powder
1/2 tsp turmeric powder
Coconut oil for deep frying
No salt is needed

Wash the fish well, at least three or four times, to get rid of the excess salt. Soak in water with chopped lemon (this will remove the smell). Cut off tail and head of fish. Grind the shallots, garlic, chilli powder and turmeric powder into a coarse paste. Marinate fish in paste for about an hour. In a heavy frying plan, heat coconut oil and fry the green chillies and curry leaves. Take it out of pan with slotted spoon. Keep aside. In the same pan, deep fry the fish in batches on medium heat, turning over until they are dark brown and crisp. Garnish with the slit chillies and curry leaves.

NANGU/MANTHAL KARI
(DRIED MALABAR SOLE CURRY)

Serve 10.

1 kg dried, salted Malabar sole
8 shallots, chopped
1 tomato, chopped fine
6 cloves of garlic, chopped
1/2 mango, chopped fine/or
tamarind extract/gambooge
1/2 cup grated coconut
4 green chillies, halved and slit
2 tsp red chilli powder
1 tsp cumin powder
1/ tsp turmeric powder
1" ginger, grated
1 sprig curry leaves
3 tbsp coconut oil

Grind the grated coconut, red chilli powder, turmeric and cumin with a little water to make a paste. Wash fish and soak in cold water for about an hour to let the salt leech out. Drain. Rub the coconut paste on the sides of fish and set aside for about an hour.

Heat 2 tbsp coconut oil in a deep pan on low heat. Add shallots, ginger, garlic and green chillies and sauté until onions turn translucent. Add curry leaves, tomato and mango pieces (or tamarind extract/*gambooge*). Stir fry. Add fish along with 2-3 cups of water and let come to boil. Simmer for 10 minutes to allow excess water to evaporate. Drizzle a tbsp of coconut oil and mix well.

Chapter 3

POULTRY IN THE POT

In North America, a roast means a chunk of beef or pork roasted in an oven for a couple of hours or more if it is slow cooked. In Kerala, however, a roast means cubed pieces of chicken or beef cooked on a stove in a deep pot with a flavorful combination of onions, spices and chillies. Most often, the meat is pan fried or deep fried before it goes into the pot to soak up the spices. A garnish of either fried green chillies, slit lengthwise, or freshly chopped coriander leaves adds colour and tartness. The Cochin Jewish chicken roast is one of the favourites of the Katz family in Miami, Florida. They got this recipe from Dr. Glennis Salem of Mattancherry, who now lives and practices in Haifa, Israel.

COCHIN JEWISH CHICKEN ROAST WITH THICK, BROWN ONION SAUCE

1 kg chicken, cut into pieces
3 large onions, chopped
8 shallots, ground to a paste
2 large tomatoes, chopped
2 pieces ginger 2", grated
3-4 green chillies, slit lengthwise
1 tsp dried red chilli powder
1 tbsp cayenne pepper
10 garlic cloves, smashed
10 whole cloves
4 tbsp coriander powder
1/4 teaspoon fennel powder,
8 cardamom pods, husked, crushed
1/4 tsp turmeric powder
1 sprig curry leaves
1 cup coconut milk (optional)
Coconut oil for frying
Salt to taste

Serves 6.

In a large bowl, combine chicken pieces with chilli powder, coriander powder, turmeric and salt. Cover and set aside for about 3 hours to let the chicken absorb the spices.

Heat coconut oil in a deep-bottomed frying pan and deep fry the chicken pieces. With a slotted ladle, take out the fried chicken and keep aside. In the same pan, sauté onions until brown. Add the green chillies, ginger, shallot paste, fennel, cloves, garlic, cayenne pepper, cardamom and curry leaves and fry for about three minutes. Add 1 cup of water, slide in the fried chicken pieces and tomatoes and bring to a boil, about 10 minutes. Reduce heat and let simmer until gravy thickens.

(Optional: Add the coconut milk and let simmer for five minutes for a creamier gravy. Don't bring it to boil or the milk will curdle.)

Chicken In Cashew Nut Sauce

Serves 6.

This dish is a fancy variant of the previous Chicken Roast recipe.

1 kg boneless chicken, cubed
3 large onions, chopped fine
2 tomatoes, chopped
4 large onions, thinly sliced
25 cashew nuts
Juice of one lemon
12 cloves of garlic, chopped
2 pieces of ginger 2", grated
1/2 tsp cumin seeds
2 tsp red chilli powder
1/4 tsp turmeric powder
1 tsp mustard seeds
1/2 cup chopped coriander leaves
Salt to taste
Coconut oil

Grind onions, ginger, garlic, cumin, chilli powder and turmeric into a smooth paste. Immerse cashew nuts in a bowl of water for an hour. Drain. Grind nuts to a paste with 3 tbsp of water. Keep aside. In a deep saucepan, heat the oil and pop mustard seeds. Add sliced onion and fry until they turn translucent. Slide in the chicken pieces and add salt to taste. Add the chopped tomatoes and the onion and garlic paste. Add a cup of water and bring the mixture to a boil. When chicken is done, add the cashew nut paste and lemon juice. When mixture begins to bubble, reduce heat and simmer for about five minutes. Garnish with chopped coriander leaves.

Kozhi Pollichathu
(Chicken In Thick Gravy)

Serves 10-12

2 kg chicken, cut into desired pieces
6 cloves garlic, chopped fine
3 onions, chopped rough
2" ginger, chopped fine
3 tbsp oil
4 tbsp vinegar
2 tsp red chilli powder
1 tsp black pepper
4 tbsp coriander powder
1 bunch coriander for garnish
Salt to taste

Grind chilli powder, pepper and coriander powder with oil and vinegar. Marinate chicken in the spice mix. Leave covered in refrigerator for about three hours. Cook chicken in a little water on medium heat for about an hour and add onions, ginger, and garlic when about 10 minutes are left. Let gravy thicken. Garnish with fresh coriander leaves.

Courtesy: Gila Rosenblatt, Aberdeen, New Jersey, United States.

Kozhi Varuthu Arachathu
(Chicken In Rich, Fried Coconut Sauce)

Serves 6.

1 chicken, cut into cubes
4 onions, chopped
4 green chillies, chopped
1 small sprig curry leaves
6-8 cloves of garlic, crushed
2 1/2" pieces ginger, chopped
1/2 tsp turmeric powder
1 1/2 tbsp red chilli powder
4 tsp coriander powder (lightly fried)
1 tbsp garam masala
1 cup grated/desiccated coconut
1/2 cup coconut oil
2 tbsp vinegar (optional)
Salt to taste

In a dry wok, stir fry the coconut on medium heat till it browns. Let cool and grind to a powder in a processor. Heat coconut oil in a deep saucepan and sauté onions along with garlic, green chillies, curry leaves and ginger until onions start to curl and brown.

Add turmeric, chilli powder and coriander powder. Mix well till the oil starts to separate. Add the chicken pieces along with one cup of water and stir. Add salt to taste. Cover the pan and cook on low fire for 15 minutes. If the gravy is thin, cook uncovered for another 5 minutes. Add the *garam masala* mix and the fried coconut and mix well.

(Optional: Add 2 tbsp of vinegar before taking pan off the fire.)
Courtesy: Rachel Roby, Petah Tikva, Israel.

COCHIN JEWISH CHICKEN CURRY (NOW PART OF ISRAELI CUISINE)

The Israeli Embassy in Washington DC., contributed this recipe to the Jewish Virtual Library of the American Jewish Co-operative Enterprise. (AICE, established in 1993 as a nonprofit and nonpartisan organization, 'provides educational materials, promote scholarship etc.').

The article says: "After its independence, Israel discovered a new Jewish community, the Cochin Jews of India..... One of their principal dishes is chicken curry which has now been incorporated into Israeli cuisine".[1]

(The recipe is being included here for record.)

It needs to be pointed out, however, that the Cochin Jewish community was not 'discovered' by Israel. They were in existence for more than 2000 years and were well-known to international Jewish and Christian scholars in Europe from around 1000 CE.

Cochin Jews were part of the International Zionist movement, long before Israel came into being and Cochin leader Napthali Raby wrote to Theodore Herzel in 1901, promising financial and other support of his community. Also, apples and olive oil, mentioned in the recipe, were seldom used by the Cochinis, because they were not available in Kerala.

2 lb chicken
4 large tomatoes
2 apples
1-1/2 cups flour
1/2 cup water
3 tbsp olive oil
2 garlic cloves
2 tbsp sugar

5 large onions
1-1/2 tsp salt, pepper
2 tbsp grated coconut (optional)
1 cup chopped parsley
1 tsp ginger, ground
1 (or more) tbsp curry powder
3 cups clear broth or coconut milk

[1] *Jewish Virtual Library* - http://www.jewishvirtuallibrary.org/jsource/Food/Chickencurry.html

Cut chicken into serving pieces and fry in 1 tbsp oil until lightly browned. Add water and simmer for 20 minutes until chicken pieces are tender. Drain and put aside. Add onions, garlic, tomatoes, parsley and apples (all diced) to the frying pan and sauté over medium heat (for about 2 minutes or until the rawness of ingredients disappears).

Add sugar, ginger and curry powder. Sprinkle with flour and pour in clear broth or coconut milk. Add coconut and chicken and sauté for an additional 10 minutes over medium heat. Serve hot with rice.

Source: Embassy of Israel.

© Copyright American-Israeli Cooperative Enterprise, Reprinted with permission.

MINTY CARROT CHICKEN

Serves 6.

A version of this simple Cochin Jewish recipe was published in *The Book of Jewish Food*, by food writer Claudia Roden (Knopf, 1996), attributing it to Queenie Hallegua of Cochin. In a variant of this dish, carrot is used along with potato to add bulk to dish... Sometimes the carrot is finely grated, thickening the gravy considerably.

1 kg chicken, cut into pieces	*2" ginger, chopped fine*
1/2 kg carrots, halved and cut into lengthwise slices or rounds	*1 tsp turmeric*
	3/4 cup mint leaves, chopped fine
3 large onions, chopped	
3 cloves of garlic, chopped	*4 tbsp coconut oil*
4 green chillies, chopped fine or sliced lengthwise	*Salt to taste*

In a heavy skillet, heat the coconut oil and fry the onions until brown. Add garlic, ginger, turmeric and chillies and mix well. Add the chicken pieces and cook for about 15 minutes.

Add the carrots along with 2 cups of water and salt and cook for another 20 minutes. Add the chopped mint and simmer until gravy reaches desired consistency. Drizzle a tbsp of coconut oil over the gravy. Serve hot over rice or with breads.

Courtesy: Reema Salem, Mattancherry, Cochin, India.

Kozhi Puzhungiathu
(Chicken With Vegetables)

Serves 6.

1 kg chicken, cut to desired sizes
250 gms string beans
200 gms squash, chopped
2 tomatoes, chopped coarse
3 cloves garlic, chopped fine
2 onions, chopped coarse
2 tbsp coconut or vegetable oil
1/2 tsp pepper
1/2 tsp turmeric
1 cup chicken stock

In a deep skillet, heat coconut oil. Fry garlic, onion and spices until onions are browned. Add chicken pieces along with the beans, squash and tomato. Mix well. Add stock and cook for 30 minutes, partially covered on medium heat or until chicken is done.

Courtesy: Gila Rosenblatt, Aberdeen, New Jersey.

Cochini Spicy Chicken

Serves 6.

1 kg chicken
2-3 tsp vegetable oil
1 large onion, chopped rough
3 cloves garlic, chopped
1" ginger, grated
1 bunch coriander, chopped fine
1/4 tsp sugar
1/2 tsp pepper
1/2 tsp paprika
1/4 tsp cumin powder
1/2 tsp red chilli powder
2 green chillies, chopped fine
3 tsp tomato paste
1/4 tsp turmeric powder
1/2 tsp coriander powder

Clean chicken and cut into ten to twelve pieces. In a deep pot, heat vegetable oil. Add the chicken and fry, turning the pieces over and over until they begin to brown. Add onion, garlic, ginger and coriander. Sauté until the onions begin to glaze over. Add sugar, tomato paste, turmeric, coriander powder, pepper, paprika, cumin, green and red chillies.

Add 3/4 cups of water and cook on low heat for another 30-40 minutes until the chicken is well cooked and the sauce thickens.

Courtesy: Ora Farchy, Houston, Texas.

Kurkirachi
(Chicken With Chinese Potatoes)

Koorka is a small, hairy tuber belonging to the mint family of plants (*Lamiaceae*) and is native to tropical Africa. Botanists call this herbaceous perennial *Plectranthus rotundifolius* or *Solenostemon rotundifolius*.

It is cultivated extensively throughout South Asia and is in plentiful supply in Kerala where it has become a much-loved part of the local cuisine. In the West, it is called Chinese potato (nobody knows why!), Coleus potato, Hausa potato, country potato or native potato.

While the Syrian Christians and Hindus use the *koorka* mainly with beef (from the local water buffalo/oxen) or as a stir-fried, stand-alone side dish, the Cochin Jews used only chicken to make this delectable, earthy-tasting dish. One reason offered by an Ernakulam Jewish family was the difficulty of obtaining *kosher* beef in Kerala.

The *koorka* has a tough skin and it was youngsters in the family who were given the task of putting the tubers in a gunny bag and beating it on the floor. This allows the skin to peel off easily.

The aroma of the skinned tuber is akin to the smell rising from the Kerala soil after a heavy rainfall. Fresh and invigorating! Soaking the *koorka* in water for a while also helps when scraping the skin off with a knife.

Sarah Cohen of Mattancherry was quoted in a magazine *Live Encounters*, mentioning this dish as one of the community's favourite recipes.[2]

Serves 6-8.

1 kg chicken, cut into pieces
20 koorka, peeled, cut into small cubes
2 onions, chopped
2 or 3 fresh green or red dry chillies
8-10 shallots, chopped

1 sprig curry leaves
2 tsp of ginger, chopped
3 cloves garlic, chopped
1/2 tsp turmeric
3 tbsp coconut oil or other vegetable oil
Salt and pepper to taste

In a deep skillet, heat the oil and fry the onions, shallots, garlic, chillies, turmeric and curry leaves for a few minutes. Add the chicken and 1 cup

[2] Ulyseas, Mark. Jews in God's Own Country. Special Report, *Live Encounters*, September, 2011. - http://issuu.com/liveencounters/docs/september2011

of water and continue cooking till the chicken is half done. Stir. Add potatoes, close the lid and cook on medium heat until chicken is well done and the liquid is mostly absorbed. Open the lid and let the curry dry.

Courtesy: Matilda Davidson, Petah Tikva, Israel.

Mulagirachi
(Jewish Capsicum Chicken)

Serves 6.

Bell pepper or capsicum was not readily available in Cochin until the late 20th century. So chicken with capsicum is a newcomer to the Cochini menu list. In Kerala, this spicy dish is served in several restaurants in Cochin as Jewish Capsicum Chicken (following the recipe from Menorah in Koder House, Fort Cochin). The same ingredients and the same method are also used to cook mutton/lamb.

1 kg chicken, cut into desired pieces
2 large onions, chopped rough
2 large tomatoes, chopped
3 green bell peppers, julienned
4 cloves garlic, chopped
4 tbsp tomato paste
2 tsp dry red chilli powder
12 peppercorns
4 tbsp coconut oil
1 bunch coriander, chopped

Salt to taste
To make marinade:
4 tbsp coconut milk
3 tsp coriander powder
2 tsp chopped ginger
3 cloves garlic, crushed
1 tsp cumin powder
1 tsp red chilli powder
1/2 tsp turmeric powder
1 tsp pepper
Salt to taste

Coat chicken with the marinating ingredients and coconut milk. Chill in refrigerator for about 3 hours. In a deep skillet, heat 2 tbsp of oil. Add onions, garlic and peppercorns and sauté until the onions turn brown. Add bell peppers, tomatoes and chilli powder and sauté about five minutes. Slide the marinated chicken gently into skillet along with 1/2 cup of water. Add the remaining 2 tbsp of oil. Cook covered over medium heat until chicken becomes tender. Add the tomato paste. Stir well and cook for another 3 minutes. Garnish with coriander leaves.

Courtesy: Vicky Raj, Koder House, Fort Kochi, Kerala, India.

Erachi Olathiathu
(Dry Chilli Chicken Roast)

Serves 6.

1 kg boneless chicken, cut into bite-size cubes
4 large onions, chopped fine
4 green chillies, chopped fine
1 small sprig curry leaves
4 cloves of garlic, chopped
2 1/2" inch piece of ginger, grated fine
1/2 tsp turmeric
3 tbsp red chilli powder
2 tbsp garam masala
6 tbsp coconut oil
Salt to taste
2 tbsp vinegar - optional

In a deep saucepan, heat coconut oil and fry the onions, curry leaves, garlic, ginger and green chillies for a few minutes. When the onions begin to glaze, add the turmeric and chilli powder. Add salt to taste and mix well. When the oil starts to separate, add the chicken pieces. Stir to let the pieces get coated with the onion mixture. (Note: no water is to be added.)

Reduce heat, cover saucepan and cook for 30 minutes, turning over chicken pieces once or twice. Stir in the *garam masala**. Take pan off the stove after a minute. The gravy should be very thick or even dry, according to your taste. (**See garam masala recipe on p. 201.*)

(Optional: Add two tbsp of vinegar when sliding chicken pieces into the saucepan.)

Courtesy: Rachel Roby, Petah Tikva, Israel.

Green Chilli Chicken

Serves 6.

1 large chicken, chopped into desired sizes
1 1/2 kg shallots
1 cup coconut oil
10 green Chillies
5 tomatoes
1 tbsp red chilli powder
1 lemon-sized ball of tamarind
2 pieces of ginger, each 2" long
6 cloves garlic
1 small sprig curry leaves
1/2 tsp turmeric powder
1 or 2 tbsp sugar (optional)
Salt to taste

Slice shallots and tomatoes; finely chop ginger, garlic and 5 green chillies. Slice the remaining chillies length-wise. Soak the tamarind in a little water and squeeze out the juice. It should be of medium consistency.

Heat oil in a deep-bottomed saucepan. Add curry leaves, sliced onions, chopped ginger, garlic and chillies. Fry till the onions turn light brown in colour. Add tomatoes. Cook till the water in the tomatoes dries up and the oil comes out clear.

Add the chilli powder and turmeric. Sizzle for a minute. Add the chicken pieces, mix well and cook for a few minutes.

Add a cup of water and salt and cook covered for 30 minutes on low heat or until the chicken is tender. Remove lid and add sliced green chillies. Cover and cook for 5 more minutes. Add the tamarind extract and cook on a slow fire till oil rises to the top. If needed, add 1 or 2 tablespoons of sugar. This offsets the heat of the chillies and enhances the flavours of ginger and tamarind.

Courtesy: Reema Salem, Synagogue Lane, Kochi, India.

Malli Varutharacha Kozhi (Coriander Fried Chicken)

Serves 6.

This delicious chicken preparation is a favourite across Kerala. The coriander adds a freshness that makes it distinctive from other dishes.

1 kg chicken, cut to desired sizes	*1/2 tsp turmeric powder*
4 tbsp coriander powder	*3/4 cup coconut oil*
3 large onions, sliced	*1 or 2 sprigs of curry leaves*
5 cloves of garlic, chopped	*1/2 cup water*
1" ginger, grated	*Salt to taste*

Grind coriander powder, sliced onion, garlic and ginger to a paste. In a deep bowl, on medium heat, cook the chicken in water until meat is almost done. Stir in the coriander paste, add some more water and cook covered until the liquid is all gone.

In a large frying pan, heat the coconut oil and fry the cooked chicken for about five to ten minutes. Serve with rice or bread.

Courtesy: Queenie Hallegua, Synagogue Lane, Kochi, India.

Marak Oaf
(Cochin Jewish Chicken Soup)

Makes 12-15 servings.

Marak Oaf is a hearty chicken soup with vegetables and meatballs and is a great starter course. The dominant flavour is coriander.

1kg chicken, cut into pieces, bone in	2 large onions - peeled and sliced
3 large potatoes	4 stalks celery
3 medium carrots	1 bunch coriander leaves
3 large tomatoes	Salt and pepper to taste
	1 1/2 tbsp of vinegar

Fill a big pot with 2 litres of water, add all ingredients, except the coriander. Boil on high flame. Add 3/4 tsp of turmeric. When the pot starts bubbling, lower the heat and close the lid. Cook for 30 to 40 minutes.

Check if the chicken is done; then add the coriander leaves. Take pot off fire and let cool for 30 minutes as spices mingle with the broth.

Courtesy: Rachel Roby, Petah Tikva, Israel.

Mutta Kari
(Eggs Cooked In Rich Onion Sauce)

Serves 6-8.

This delicious egg dish is a favourite all over Kerala and also goes by the name of *Mutta Masala*. Hard-boiled eggs buried in a soft pile of fragrant, browned onions, with tiny jolts of chillies, cardamom and cloves at every bite and may be a hint of cinnamon or fennel, is eaten with rice or any type of bread and is a perfect meal any time of the day.

12 eggs, hard-boiled	4 cardamom pods, skinned and crushed
5 large onions, sliced	2 tsp red chilli powder
3 tomatoes, chopped rough	3 tsp coriander powder
6 garlic cloves, chopped fine	5 cloves, crushed
2" ginger, grated	2 tsp fennel seeds
4 green chillies, halved and slit lengthwise	1/2 tsp cumin powder
2 pieces of cinnamon	1/2 tsp turmeric powder

1 tsp ground black pepper	1 sprig curry leaves
1 bunch coriander leaves, chopped	4 tbsp coconut oil
	Salt to taste

"*The curry we usually ate on Saturday night was eggs cooked in sauce... because we had no time to cook meat as we must have hot meal,*"[3] was how Ruby Daniel wrote about this delicious dish.

Shell the hardboiled eggs. Make about seven or eight thin gashes on the sides of each egg. Keep aside. In a heavy, deep-bottomed pan, heat the coconut oil. Add onions, garlic, ginger, green chillies, fennel seeds and the curry leaves. Fry on low heat, stirring often until the onions begin to glaze and brown.

Add the powders - cumin, coriander, red chilli, turmeric and salt. Stir and let mix well with other ingredients. Add the chopped tomatoes. Keep stirring for about three minutes. Add the hardboiled eggs. Add the pepper and cook on medium flame until the fragrant mixture begins to leave the sides of the pan. Sprinkle the chopped coriander leaves. Leave for about an hour to allow the spices to soak through the eggs.

(You can halve the hardboiled eggs before adding to the pan, if you like. The addition of 2 pieces of cinnamon will produce a more aromatic sauce. Leave the fennel seeds out, if you don't like its sweet bite).

Adding a cup of coconut milk and simmering for a few minutes before taking the dish from the stove is an option for another taste experience.

Courtesy: Matilda Davidson, Petah Tikva, Israel.

---

[3] Daniel & Johnson, *Ruby of Cochin*, p. 32.

Chapter 4

Kubbah, You Adorable Dumplings!

The *Kubbah* (or *Kubba*) meaning 'ball' in Arabic, is a dish of bulghur, onions, spices and ground meat that originated in Baghdad. It became an instant hit around the 17th century with the Cochin Jews as the recipe spread among Sephardic and Mizrahim communities. However, instead of bulghur, the Cochinis used rice or all-purpose flour.

It has been reported that "...in the mass *aliyah* of 1950/51, many families took with them their heavy brass mortar and pestle for pounding the *kubbas*, as a priority item of their luggage". [1]

Queenie Hallegua of Mattancherry, Cochin, spells it out as *Koubbah* and describes it as "chicken or fish minced and encased in round balls made of flour and cooked in gravy. The gravy can have vegetables in it, like (okra) lady's fingers and gourd." It is served with the fabled *Resaya Pulav* of the Cochin Jews. *(See recipe on page 97.)*

There have been paeans sung to the *kubbah*. Here are two examples:

The first poem was written by Benjamin Koheleth, who was a Tel Aviv Magistrate Court Judge in Israel in the 1980s. Translated by Meer Basri it was printed in the *The Scribe* (Journal of Babylonian Jewry), London, January 1993, Issue No. 56. The second by Gad Ben Meir of Melbourne, Australia, was printed in *The Scribe*, June 1993, Issue No. 58. Both poems reprinted with permission from *The Scribe*/Dangoor Family.

[1] *The Scribe* (Journal of Babylonian Jewry), London, January 1993. Issue No. 56.

The Kubbah

A Kubbah, which everyone would like to eat,
has been pursuing me day and night.
Tasty, its beautiful shape equals its savour and fragrance.
It went gracefully into the throat
like a gentle wave into the calm sea.
> *Its pure rice covered a ball of excellent meat.*
> *I would forsake every food to satiate my hunger*
> *when it entices me to a ravenous appetite.*
> *When I beheld it, I left my "regime" and decided to forget it.*

And I said to those who questioned me,
"No more hunger, no more fasting".
O, our lady friend, I praise you
for making such nice food in quality and quantity
> *Make more Kubbahs to satisfy a heart crushed by pain.*
> *As if these pies emulated their maker's gracious soul*
> *to be the nourishment of body and spirit.*

•••••

Saga of the Kubba

O my kubba, O my kubba
you are my stomach's love.
With you I comfort my hunger,
your fragrance is my wine.
> *Blessed be the hand*
> *that fashions this wonder.*
> *I chew you with relish,*
> *and prolong my enjoyment.*
> *I have loved you since my youth,*
> *as now in my old age.*

Every fan has his idol;
my idol is my kubba.
Wa K..bati fi kubbati:
my K..ba is my kubba!'

Kubbah Varuthathu (Fried Kofta Balls)

Makes about 16 servings - Meat is optional. (In northern India, a similar dish made with vegetables is called *kofta*).

For the Kubbah covering:
3 large potatoes, peeled
1 1/2 cup matzo meal
2 tbsp oil
Salt to taste
All-purpose flour or plain wheat flour for dusting

For the filling:
1/2 cup oil
1/2 pound boneless chicken or ground beef
3 hard-boiled eggs, chopped
1/2 cup carrots, sliced thin
1/2 cup cabbage, chopped fine
3 onions, chopped
1 potato, sliced thin
1/2 cup mushrooms, chopped
1/4 cup almonds, chopped
1/4 cup cashew, chopped
2 green chilli pepper, chopped
1 tsp turmeric
3 tbsp wine vinegar
1/2 tsp black pepper
Salt to taste

For frying:
6 eggs, lightly whisked,
1 cup oil
Salt and pepper to taste

Boil the peeled potatoes. Mash. Add matzo meal, oil and salt and form dough. Set aside. Heat 1/2 cup oil in a large pan or wok. Fry the chicken until meat turns white. Add the chopped vegetables one by one, stirring constantly. Cook for 20 minutes over medium heat.

Add salt, pepper, turmeric, vinegar and the nuts and cook for another 15 minutes, stirring frequently. Add the chopped eggs and remove from heat. Dust a work plate with the flour. Roll the dough into about 9 or 10 equal-sized balls. Flatten balls with a rolling pin into patties of four or five inches in diameter.

Fill each patty with just enough filling so that the dough can be folded and pinched closed. Add salt and pepper to the beaten eggs. Brush the patties with the egg. In a deep fryer or wok, fry each *kubbah* one at a time, until it turns golden brown.

Courtesy: Shlomo Mordechai, New York, United States.

Kubbah
(Cochin Kofta Dumplings in Gravy)

Makes 25-30 balls.

For *kofta*:
1/2 kg ground meat (beef or chicken)
5 large onions, chopped fine
1/4 kg all purpose flour
1/2 tsp turmeric powder
8 green chillies, seeded, chopped fine
1/4 cup mint leaves or celery, chopped fine
1 tsp ground pepper
Salt to taste

Boil the ground meat in enough water until cooked. Drain and keep aside. Immerse the chopped onions in salted water for about two hours. Squeeze out salt and water from the onions and mix with the chopped chillies, meat, mint, turmeric powder and pepper. Mix a little water and salt with the flour and knead till it forms dough. Make small balls from the dough, flatten them out with a rolling pin. Place a heaped tbsp of *kofta* in centre of flattened dough. Close and seal edges.

For gravy:
3/4 cup cooking oil
3 large onions, sliced
1/2 kg pumpkin or carrot or beetroot or 15 okra, chopped
4 tomatoes, chopped
3 tsp coriander powder
1 tsp red chilli powder
1 tsp ground pepper
1 1/2" piece of ginger, chopped
4 cloves of garlic, chopped
Lemon-sized ball of tamarind pulp (soak pulp in 1/4 cup warm water and extract juice)
1/2 tsp turmeric powder
8 cups water
Salt to taste

Heat oil in a deep saucepan and fry the sliced onions with ginger and garlic until onions soften. Add tomatoes, coriander, turmeric and salt; cook until the mixture becomes mushy and paste-like. Add pepper and 8 glasses of water or stock. Bring to a boil. Add tamarind water when the vegetables are half-cooked. Let simmer, drop in the *kofta* dumplings and cook covered for 10 minutes. Turn over the *kofta* balls and let boil for another 10 minutes, until gravy thickens.

Courtesy: Sarah Cohen, Synagogue Lane, Mattancherry, Kerala, India.

Kubbah Hamidh - Soup
(Baghdadi Jewish Recipe)

This is an original Indo-Baghdadi Jewish recipe which became popular in Cochin in the middle of the 18th century. On festive occasions, it is made with a thick gravy to accompany coconut rice and other main courses. Different Cochini Jewish congregations adapted the recipe to their tastes. It even went vegetarian!

The *kubbah* dumpling is boiled when it is used for making soups (called *Marak Kubbeh*) or fried when used as a snack.

Serves 10.

For the casing:
2 cups rice
1 cup ground meat
(lamb preferred)
For the filling:

2 cups ground meat
1 large onion, chopped fine
1/2 bunch coriander leaves,
chopped fine
Salt and pepper to taste

Soak the rice in water for about an hour. Drain. Grind the rice and mix with the ground meat. Make a small ball with the meat paste and flatten it. Spread a tbsp of the filling and turn the casing back into a ball. Seal the edges with fingers. Repeat process until all the casing and filling are done.

For the soup:
1/2 kg lamb (mutton)
with bones
8 cups water
1 large zucchini/or eggplant,

chopped
1/2 a small squash, cubed
1 large tomato, chopped
4 tbsp lemon juice

In a large bowl, bring the mutton pieces to a roiling boil. Add the eggplant, squash and tomato. Reduce heat and let simmer for about an hour.

Add the *kubbah* balls and let it come to a boil again, uncovered about 20 minutes. Serve *Marak Kubbeh* hot.

Courtesy: Pearly Simon, Haifa, Israel.

Chapter 5

THE LURE OF THE PASTELS

Pastels, known to most Jews as *burekas* or *borekas* has been a traditional food item for the Cochinis for several hundred years. The Cochini pastel was mentioned by Shlomo Reinman in the 1850s in his book *Masa'oth Shlomo b'Kogin*.[1] Reinman was a merchant from Galicia in northwest Spain, who came to Cochin in the 1840s and married the daughter of merchant Samuel Chaim Rahabi of Mattancherry. He stayed in Cochin for about 25 years, before returning to Europe and writing his fascinating travelogue.

In Synagogue Lane, Mattancherry, in the waning years of the 20th century, 'pastel hunting' was a favourite hobby for Jewish bachelors during the Shabbat. In their book *The Last Jews of Cochin*, Nathan Katz and Ellen Goldberg write of how Isaac Ashkenazi and Raymond Salem (both now deceased) "went from house to house in search of the perfect pastel."[2] Every Cochin Jewish family made the pastels in a different way and every variation became a gourmet delight.

Pastel itself is a Portuguese word that denotes a crisp pastry with assorted fillings. In Brazil, the pastel is called *salgado* (salty snack), primarily sold on the street as a thin pastry envelope containing cheese, ground beef, chicken, fish or other fillings and then deep fried. Sweet pastels are

---

[1] Reinman, Shlomo, *Masa'oth Shlomo b'Kogin*. p.39.
[2] Katz & Goldberg, *The Last Jews of Cochin*, p. 221.

also made, containing combinations of fruits or chocolates. In Israel, the pastel's cousin - the *bureka* - is a popular street food made with phyllo dough that is cut to size, filled with your choice of vegetables, meats or cheese, garnished with sesame seeds and baked in an oven. In Cochini homes, *burekas* are always dairy (with cheese), while cheese is never added to pastels.

Kadathala Pastel

Here is the delectable Kadathala Pastel, mentioned by Schlmo Reinman and made today by Cochinis according to the same ancient recipe. I tasted this for the first time at the home of Shalom and Esther Nehemia in Moshav Nevatim, Israel. Delicious! - *Bala Menon*.

Makes about 30 pastels.

For the Batter:	*3 large onions, chopped fine*
1 cup rice flour	*3 potatoes, chopped*
2 cups coconut milk	*1 lime, juiced*
3 eggs	*A few mint leaves*
Salt to taste	*1/4 tsp turmeric*
For the Filling:	*1/4 cup ghee/coconut oil*
2-3 eggs, hard-boiled, chopped	*Salt and pepper to taste*

Heat a little oil/clarified butter in a saucepan and fry the chopped potatoes until they begin to brown and crisp. Keep aside.

Heat oil/clarified butter in a wok and fry the chopped onions until browned. Add the fried potatoes, turmeric, salt, pepper, mint leaves. Stir well and cook for a few minutes. Keep aside.

•••

Break the eggs into a bowl and beat lightly. Add the rice flour, coconut milk and salt to taste. Heat a saucepan and brush the pan, first with some oil and then with some egg yolk. (In Cochin, the brush was made from threads of coconut husk twisted together.) Pour enough batter into the pan and cook for 2 to 3 minutes (till the edges curl). Transfer to a tray lined with paper towels. Continue till the entire batter is used up.

Take each *kadathala*, put a little of the filling and fold over to form a puff. Fry in heated oil in a wok.

The Kadathala Pastel (without the filling) can be eaten for breakfast or tea with scrambled eggs or jam etc. It is sometimes eaten along with a fenugreek dip called *hulba*, said to have originated hundreds of years ago in Yemen. Many Yemeni Jews believe the fenugreek is an auspicious food item mentioned in the Talmud (Talmudic Rubia) and is a mandatory item on the Rosh Hashanah table.

Fenugreek is called *uluva* in Malayalam, *hylbh* in Hebrew and *methi* in Hindi.

The Ancient Hulba Dip

2 1/2 tbsp ground fenugreek *1 bunch coriander*
2 tomatoes *2 green chillies*
2 cloves garlic *1 lemon, juiced*

Soak the ground fenugreek overnight in water. This removes the bitterness. Drain the water. What is left is a paste-like mixture. Chop the tomato, garlic, coriander and chillies. Pour all ingredients into a blender. Add the lemon juice and salt to taste.

Blend until the concoction becomes frothy. Pour out and serve in a dipping bowl. Vinegar or additional lemon juice can be used to thin the sauce, if needed.

Cochin Pastel

This recipe is from Shlomo Mordechai (from Paravur/Chennamangalam and now in New York). Here is what he has to say: "As a result of the expulsion of Jews from Portugal during the Inquisition and immigration to Cochin, India, where a 1500-year-old independent Jewish community already resided, we now have the Cochini Jews' version of pastel with a filling called *hooba*.

"*Hooba* (a mixture of cabbage, vegetables, potatoes, egg, cashews, spices and sometimes chicken) was filled in dough balls (dumplings) that were cooked on low heat overnight for Shabbat mornings. During festivals, Cochini Jews filled the *hooba* in a flat dough that was fried in oil. I made an adaptation using egg roll wraps to make cooking less time-consuming and more convenient. This recipe takes about one hour to prepare and yields about 20 pastels."

2 medium onions, chopped	1/4 tsp turmeric powder
10 oz cabbage, chopped	2 tsp soup mix
5 whole mushrooms, chopped	2 oz cashew nuts, chopped
1 potato, chopped	1 boiled egg, chopped
2 carrots, chopped	1 raw egg
2 tbsp vinegar	1 pkg egg roll wraps
1/2 tsp ground black pepper	Cooking oil

Heat 1/3 cup oil in a large pan and sauté the chopped onions until they turn translucent. Add cabbage. Cook until it softens. Add mushrooms, potatoes and carrots. Add chicken and continue stirring.

Add black pepper, turmeric and soup mix. Stir until all vegetables are cooked (around 20 minutes). Add the cashew nuts and chopped egg. Mix all together and let it sit for 5 minutes. This is the *hooba* mix.

Beat the egg. Fill each egg roll wrap with 1 tbsp *hooba* mix. Brush the edges with the egg. Crimp the sides to seal the dough. Bring the oil to boil and fry the pastels until golden brown (around 2 minutes).

If adding chicken:

Before you begin, take a 1/4 cup of diced chicken breast and sauté in oil until it turns brown. Keep aside. Then follow the instructions above and add the chicken after adding the vegetables.

Sarah Tovachy Elias's Chicken Pastel

Makes 40 servings.

Dough:

3 cups all-purpose flour	1 tbsp vegetable oil
4 tbsp margarine, melted	Salt to taste
1 egg, lightly beaten	

This recipe is from Ora Farchy's cousin Hannah Abraham in Israel.

Whisk 2 cups flour and the salt together in a bowl. In a separate bowl, combine margarine, oil, egg and ¾ cup water. Slowly pour the egg and oil mixture into the bowl with the flour, stirring to prevent clumping. Add flour as needed until it forms a soft dough.

Filling:
3 tbsp vegetable oil, or more
1/4 pound chicken breast
2 cups onions, chopped fine
1 potato, peeled, shredded and squeezed dry
1 carrot, shredded fine
2 green chillies, chopped fine
1 tsp coriander powder
1/4 tsp turmeric
1 bunch coriander, chopped fine
1 tbsp white vinegar
Oil for frying
Salt and pepper to taste

Heat the oil in a large pan. Add the chicken and cook over medium heat until the pink disappears. Add onions, carrot, potato, peppers and spices. Cook for about 30 minutes. Stir in vinegar and chopped coriander in the last few minutes of cooking. Let cool completely.

Divide the dough into thirds. Roll it out thinly one at a time. Cut out circles, each the size of a coffee mug. Place a heaped teaspoon of filling on half of each circle, fold, to make half-moons, and crimp to seal. Heat the oil. Deep-fry the pastels until light brown, flipping once. Drain on paper towels.

Ora Farchy's late grandmother Sarah Tovachy Elias from Chennamangalam was among the Cochin Jews who made aliyah in the early 1950s and lived in Moshav Shahar in the Negev, southern Israel.

Classic Cochin Tuna Pastel

Follow the same procedure as the Kadathala Pastel (*page 76*), substituting the filling with flaked tuna, cooked with the desired spices. Cochinis today add bell peppers and some chopped olives into the mix.

Two cans of tuna, with 1 cup of grated carrots and a bell pepper, should yield about 15 pastels.

Rachel Roby's Baked Cheese Burekas

3 cups all purpose flour
100 gms butter
1 large egg

Crumble cheese in bowl. Break egg into bowl and whisk gently. Knead the flour with butter till dough is formed, using water as needed.

With a rolling pin open out the soft dough on a board dusted with flour. Cut into circles with a cup or mug (size 8 -10 cms)

Alternate method: Roll portions of dough into small balls and then roll them open on the board.

Fill with cheese-egg mixture and close it in the shape of a half-moon by pinching the edges. Preheat oven to 180 degrees. Line a baking tray with parchment paper. Place *burekas* and bake for about 20-30 minutes.

Courtesy: Rachel Roby, Petah Tikva, Israel.

· · · · ·

The Chief Rabbinate of Israel issued directives in June 2013 on the shape of *burekas*, according to their fillings. "These new set of conventions are to ensure maximum compliance with Jewish dietary laws," according to a report in the Jerusalem Post. [3]

Pastries that are *parve* must now be triangular or spiral shaped, while dairy *burekas* must be either loopy or like a thick, broad finger. The Rabbinate has also ruled that sweet croissants and *rogelach* must be crescent-shaped if they are dairy or linear if they are *parve*.

It was explained that the new measures were essential because of the 'creativity' in the field of *bureka*-making and the explosion in their commercial availability throughout Israel. The Rabbinate cited the law which prohibits making dough with milk without indicating that it is dairy to prevent it from being consumed with meat.

---

3 Sharon, Jeremy. Meet your new bureka shapes. *Jerusalem Post*, June 14, 2013. http://www.jpost.com/LandedPages/PrintArticle.aspx?id=316521

Chapter 6
Here's The Beef, Although It's Rare![1]

Shlomo Mordechai, from Paravur/Chennamangalam in Kerala, went to Israel when he was 12 years old. He has only faint memories of Kerala, "but the food remained a part of my life."

He now attends an egalitarian and socially active, conservative synagogue, "Beth El" in Massapequa, New York. He prepares several Cochin dishes, including the popular pastel, as part of the 57-year-old synagogue's cooking program. The synagogue is the only one in Long Island with a *kosher* food pantry.

Shlomo, whose name in Kerala was Solomon Pallivathukkal (meaning Solomon from the house near the synagogue door), prefers traditional Kerala food at home, because: "This food, in general, especially vegetarian items, are in sync with our *kosher* laws." Shlomo has shared four of his favourite recipes with us.

(*Newsday* of New York published versions of his recipes under the title *A Passover from India* along with some Bene Israeli recipes after Shlomo was interviewed by a freelance writer Ramin Ganeshram.[2]

(There are many members of the Pallivathukkal clan settled in the United States and several living in Israel.)

---

[1] See chapter on *How We Kept Kosher in Cochin*, p. 14. Beef was a rare commodity in Cochin.

[2] Ganeshram Ramin, *Newsday*, March 19, 2002. URL: http://www.newsday.com/food-day-wednesday-a-passover-from-india-a-seder-from-the-subcontinent-includes-curry-rice-and-dosas-1.356638

Ispethi
(Cochin Jewish Beef Stewed In Rich Sauce)

Serves 10.

1 1/2 kg stewing beef, cut into 2" cubes
2 1/2 tsp red chilli powder
2 green chillies, chopped fine
2 tsp turmeric
1 tsp black pepper
1 tsp salt (assuming that the beef is already salted)
1/2 cup vinegar, divided
1/4 cup vegetable oil (coconut oil is preferred)

3 large onions, sliced
2-4 cloves garlic, sliced
1 sprig curry leaves
4 tsp powdered coriander
1" ginger, grated
1 tsp salt
3 tbsp tomato paste
1/4 cup water
1 large onion, chopped rough
4 bell peppers, chopped
Salt to taste

Marinate the beef with paprika or chilli powder, turmeric, black pepper, salt and 2 tbsp vinegar. Refrigerate for about 2 hours.

Heat oil in large pot. Add sliced onions, garlic and curry leaves and sauté until onions are translucent. Add beef and fry until browned on all sides. Add the remaining ingredients and water except the chopped onion and bell peppers. Cook on medium-low heat, covered, for about 1 hour 45 minutes, or until beef is tender. Add chopped onion and bell pepper and cook for another 20 minutes. Serve over cooked rice.

Courtesy: Shlomo Mordechai, New York.

Ispethi - Curry Style

Serves 10.
This is another version of the famous dish, with thick gravy.

1 1/2 kg beef, cut into big cubes
6 cloves of garlic
A few curry leaves
2 green chillies, sliced
2 onions, sliced
2" piece of ginger, chopped

1/2 tsp turmeric
3 tbsp coriander powder
1 tsp black pepper
4 tbsp coconut oil
2 tbsp vinegar

Heat oil in a deep pan and sizzle the curry leaves along with garlic for a few minutes. Add beef cubes and continue frying. When the juices from the beef begin to come out, add onions, ginger and green chillies. Stir well. Add coriander powder, turmeric and black pepper. Stir again.

Reduce heat and add vinegar and salt. Cook covered, stirring frequently to prevent burning. If you find the gravy too dry, add 2 tablespoons of water at a time. Continue cooking till the meat is done. The gravy should be thick.

(Optional: Add half a tablespoon of sugar or one tablespoon of tomato puree for a milder taste - although this is not part of the original recipe).

Courtesy: Batzion Bezallel, Moshav Kidroon, Israel.

•••••

Delving Into History For Recipes

In modern-day Kochi, there are two hotels that look to history to prepare authentic Jewish dishes.

One is the Brunton Boatyard, run by CGH Earth (formerly Casino Group Hotels), a company owned by the Dominic family that believes all its properties must be "immersive and respect local ethos." They operate a string of 'eco' hotels, with environment and nature taking precedence over concrete structures.

The Brunton Boatyard itself has been resurrected from the remains of a Victorian ship-building yard and its many restaurants bill themselves as 'melting pot of cultures… (and in ancient Cochin) the Jews found coriander both *kosher* and delicious and into the cook pot it went…"[1]

Ajeeth Janardhanan is Executive Chef at the Brunton Boatyard and he tells us that he visited several Jewish families scattered today around Cochin, Ernakulam and Alwaye to collect some ancient recipes. He has also been experimenting with some of them so that the Brunton Boatyard restaurants can present original Jewish dishes or 'close adaptations.' The hotel has a restaurant named The History Cafe. He has shared some recipes with us.

The other is the Koder House, the landmark red building on Tower Road, Fort Kochi, which was the residence of the renowned Jewish fam-

---

[1] Brunton Boatyard site: http://www.cghearth.com/brunton-boatyard

ily of the Koders and the hub of Cochin Jewish life for over a century. It was built by Samuel Koder in 1808, over an early Portuguese mansion. It is believed to have been structured and gabled in Europe and shipped to Cochin. It passed on down the family and in the second part of the 20th century was occupied by Shabdai Samuel (Sattu) Koder (1907–1994) who lived there with his family.

The Friday open houses at the Koder House during the latter part of the 20th century was a Cochin social event and guests included heads of state, diplomats and celebrities from all vocations. Actor Fredrick Marsh with president Eisenhower's daughter, Princess Margaret (Countess of Snowdon) and Rajiv Gandhi (before he became Indian Prime Minister) were some of the personalities who came to meet with the Koders.

After Sattu and his wife Gladys passed away, their daughter Queenie, sold the 20,000 sq feet house to its present owners, Vicky and Praveena Raj, who run it as a boutique hotel. Queenie also gave the hotel a collection of her family recipes and "so our food is always spiced with history," says Praveena.

"You will not get these recipes in any other homes. My children abroad wait for me to cook the *kubbah* and pastel for them, as these are time consuming. These are exclusive to Kochi Jews," says Queenie Hallegua.[23]

Two of the main dishes on the Jewish menu are the *ellegal* made with chicken and the Cochin red beef curry, both with a strong coriander flavour. "We are recreating authentic Cochin-Jewish recipes," says Vicky Raj. Dishes on the menu include *oaf molagirachi* and *oaf kothiporichathu*, both chicken dishes. There is also the Cochin Jewish cutlet, "like the *schnitzel* that we get abroad. Thin chicken breasts dipped in eggs and mixed in crumbs are deep-fried. We flatten the meat using tenderizer," says Hallegua.[4]

Every year, Koder House[5] organizes an Indo-Jewish food festival during Hanukkah at the Menorah restaurant where a huge seven-branched candelabra spreads its glorious light, as Jewish tourists and guests get a taste of Cochini cuisine.

---

[2] Sharma, Priyadarshini, "Food Spiced with History", *The Hindu*, Kochi. URL: http://www.thehindu.com/thehindu/mp/2006/04/22/stories/2006042202720300.htm

[4] Ibid.

[5] http://www.koderhouse.com/

Elaggal
(Cochin Jewish Red Beef Curry)

Elaggal is an attractive red curry with a strong coriander flavour. It is an original Cochin Jewish creation and today a customer favourite at the Jewish-themed Menorah Restaurant, Koder House, in Fort Kochi.

1 kg beef, cut into strips
2 tbsp of 8/8 sauce (made of boiled dates, raisins and tamarind water)
2 tbsp tamarind extract (Worcestershire sauce can be used as substitute)
Some mint leaves
2 tsp crushed red chillies
2 long red chillies, halved, de-seeded, cut lengthwise
3 cloves garlic, chopped fine
3 tbsp coconut oil
1 tbsp sugar
2 tsp of white pepper powder
1/2 cup iceberg lettuce, shredded
1/2 cup celery, sliced fine
1 cup shredded red cabbage
4 tbsp balsamic vinegar
1/2 cup Madras curry paste (coriander, cumin, red chillies, turmeric, paprika & water)
2 bunches coriander leaves, chopped

Heat the coconut oil in a frying pan and sauté the chopped garlic. Add beef strips, the date sauce, tamarind extract, chillies, curry paste and cook covered on medium heat for about 20 minutes. Add the mint leaves, white pepper and sugar. In a bowl, combine lettuce, celery, red cabbage, coriander leaves and balsamic vinegar. Toss. Pour the red beef curry over the salad. Serve.

Courtesy: Vicky Raj, (Menorah Restaurant), Koder House, Fort Kochi.

• • • • •

There is another version of *Ellagal* made in Cochini homes with only chicken being used in the dish. The ingredients and the directions are the same as the *Ispethi - Curry Style* recipe. (*See page 82;* this version is not red and the chicken pieces rest in thick gravy.)

Beef Olathiyathu (Cochin Beef Fry) or Cochin Chilli Beef Roast

Serves 6.

Fried bits of coconut add an indescribable burst of flavour to this beef dish. Combined with roasted ginger and curry leaves, it is delightful with a variety of breads or rice and has today become a featured item at wedding receptions in Kerala.

1 kg stewing beef, cubed
1/2 cup chopped coconut
10 shallots, chopped fine
2" ginger, grated fine
1 sprig curry leaves
4-5 green chillies, halved and sliced lengthwise
6 garlic cloves, chopped fine
2 tbsp vinegar
Salt to taste
Coconut oil for frying (No other oil will provide the right flavour and aroma needed for this dish)

The spice mix:
3 tsp dried red chilli powder
3 tbsp coriander powder
6 cloves cardamom, husked, crushed
1/2 tsp turmeric powder
1 tsp fennel seeds, crushed
2 tsp of ground pepper
1 tsp cinnamon powder
A sprig of curry leaves, chopped

Heat a small frying pan and add all ingredients listed in the spice mix. On low flame, dry roast the mix for about 6 minutes until it browns. In a heavy pan, add the beef cubes along with the fried spice mixture, vinegar and 1 cup of water. Cook over medium heat for about 60 minutes.

In a large frying pan or wok, heat some coconut oil and fry the coconut pieces. Add onions, ginger, chillies, garlic, salt and sauté on low heat for about 10 minutes or until the mixture gently browns.

Add the cooked beef and let simmer over low heat and stir until all the water has evaporated. Garnish with chopped coriander leaves and chopped tomatoes if you so desire.

Courtesy: Pearly Simon, Haifa, Israel

Kurkirachi (With Beef)

(See main recipe with chicken on page 64.)
Serves 8.
This recipe, in which coconut and coriander is also used, is how the Hindus and Christians make the same Cochini dish. Replace the chicken with beef.

The other ingredients are the same as the *Kurkirachi*.

Cook the beef and the *koorka* in separate skillets, with a little oil and turmeric powder. In a saucepan, fry coconut pieces in hot oil, along with the shallots and keep aside.

Combine the beef and *koorka* and add water slowly until there is some thick gravy. Stir. Add the fried coconut pieces and the spice mixture at the end. Serve hot with rice.

Beef Cutlets

1/2 kg ground beef	*1 tsp garam masala*
2 potatoes	*1 sprig curry leaves*
2 onions, chopped fine	*1 bunch coriander leaves,*
4 green chillies, chopped fine	*chopped fine*
2" piece of ginger, chopped	*2 eggs*
6 cloves garlic, chopped	*100 gms bread crumbs*
1 tsp ground black pepper	*Coconut oil for frying*
1 tsp red chilli powder	*Salt to taste*
1/2 tsp turmeric powder	

In a large saucepan, cook the ground beef, ground pepper, chilli powder, turmeric powder, salt and *garam masala (See recipe on p. 201)* until done. Heat 2 tbsp oil in a frying pan and sauté onion, ginger, garlic, green chillies and curry leaves. Boil potatoes in water, drain and mash.

Combine onion mixture with cooked beef, mashed potatoes, coriander leaves and knead well. Make small balls (size of a lemon), flatten with your hands and keep aside. Beat eggs, dip the meat patties in the beaten egg and dust with bread crumbs. Deep fry in oil until brown and slightly crispy on the outside. Serve hot with coriander chutney. Makes about 15 thick cutlets.

Chapter 7
LAMB / MUTTON

*"What do you mean you don't eat no meat? …..
That's OK, I'll make lamb"* ~ Andrea Martin as the character Aunt Voula telling the groom-to-be in the movie, 'My Big Fat Greek Wedding'[1]

Lamb is delicate meat, compared with beef. Although North American consumption of lamb is low, it is the favoured meat in India (where it is often called mutton [chevon] and comes from young goat), Middle East, Australia and New Zealand (the last two are lamb/mutton exporters). Also, lamb easily absorbs the intriguing tastes of spices/seasonings available in India/Middle East.

MALLI ARACHA ATTIRACHI (LAMB IN CORIANDER SAUCE)

Serves 8.

1 kg lamb, cubed
4 onions, chopped
3 tomatoes, skinned, chopped
3 bunches coriander leaves,
5 green chillies, chopped
5 cloves garlic, chopped
2" ginger, chopped
4 tbsp coriander powder

1 tsp turmeric
1 tsp cardamom powder
1/2 tsp cloves, powdered
2 tsp pepper
2 tsp of Kashmiri chilli powder
1 sprig curry leaves
6 tbsp coconut oil
Salt to taste

---

[1] *My Big Fat Greek Wedding* was a 2002 Canadian-American comedy, written by and starring Nia Vardalos and directed by Joel Zwic. It was a runaway hit.

Heat coconut oil in a deep-bottomed pan. Sauté onions until translucent. Add the coriander leaves, chillies, garlic, ginger, coriander powder, cardamom powder, cloves and chilli powder. Mix well with the onions on medium heat. Add curry leaves and fry two minutes.

Add the chopped tomato. Stir. Add the lamb, salt and pepper, a cup of water and bring to boil. Reduce heat, and simmer for about an hour, adding water if the mixture gets too dry.

Kochi Chuttirachi (Cochin Fried Lamb Dish)

In the late 20th century, lamb/kid became a rare treat for the Jews of Mattancherry because the community had no *shohet*. The Jews in Ernakulam had the *shohets*, who slaughtered only chickens, although there were no congregational gatherings in any of their synagogues.

Today, Babu Josephai, caretaker of the Kadavumbhagam Synagogue in Ernakulam and Sam Abraham, who spent several years in Israel before returning to Cochin to run a flourishing automobile dealership, are the community *shohets*.

This dish of tender chunks of lamb/kid, marinated in spices and cooked with shallots, coconut and fennel is an ancient recipe of the Cochin Jews.

Serves 6-8.

1 kg lamb (mutton - in Kerala, this generally means young goat)
10 shallots, chopped
1 tsp cinnamon powder
1/2 tsp turmeric
1 tsp fennel seeds
6 garlic cloves, crushed
1 tsp ground pepper
3 tbsp coriander powder

1 tsp whole black peppercorns
2" ginger, grated
4 green chillies, chopped
2 sprigs curry leaves
5 cloves
2-3 tsp dried red chilli powder
1/2 cup coconut bits
Coconut oil - 5 tbsp

Grind shallots, cinnamon, coriander, ginger, green chillies, cloves, garlic and some salt into a smooth paste. Marinate the mutton pieces and chill for about 3 hours. In a deep pan, cook the mutton with 2 tbsp of coconut oil and 1/2 cup of water for about 30 minutes. Reduce heat and let simmer uncovered for 8 to 10 mins or until all liquid disappears.

Heat 3 tbsp of coconut oil in a wok and sauté the onions, peppercorns, curry leaves, fennel seeds and coconut bits until they turn dark brown. Transfer the lamb/mutton to the wok and stir fry for about a minute. Garnish with skinned and chunky crushed tomatoes for a tangier taste.

Courtesy: Pearly Simon, Haifa, Israel.

Attirachiyyum Pachhakariyum (Lamb With Vegetables)

Serves 10.

This recipe is said to have been written down sometime in the middle of the 19th century in the little Jewish hamlet of Chennamangalam. Today, there are no Jews there and there is no *kosher* lamb available for the remaining Kerala Jews. The dish is, however, popular in Cochini homes in Israel.

1 kg lamb, cut into cubes
1 large onion, chopped
1 tsp ginger grated
5 garlic cloves, chopped
4 cups of mixed vegetables
(peas, green beans, carrots, sweet potato and okra)
1 lemon, squeezed
3-4 green chillies, chopped fine
1 sprig curry leaves
1 bunch coriander leaves
Salt and pepper to taste
Vegetable/coconut oil

Brown the meat in a large pot in a little heated oil. Add the onions, ginger and garlic. When the onions turn translucent, reduce heat and add pepper and salt.

Cook for an hour on low heat. Add all the vegetables. Add the lemon juice and the green chillies. Cook for another two hours on low heat. Towards the end, add chopped curry leaves and coriander. Stir well. Garnish with more coriander.

Courtesy: Ora Farchy, Houston, Texas
(Handed down by grandmother Sarah Tovachy Elias)

Cochin Lamb Soup

Serves 8.

1 kg lamb, with lots of bones
3 onions, chopped
10 shallots, sliced
1 tsp fennel seeds
1 tsp cumin seeds
4 cloves garlic, smashed
3 cloves, powdered
1/4 tsp turmeric
1 tsp red chilli powder
1 tsp cinnamon powder
1 tsp cardamom powder
5 tsp peppercorns, crushed
2" dry ginger, grated
1 sprig curry leaves
5 tbsp coconut oil
Salt to taste

Heat 2 tbsp oil in a deep saucepan and sauté the chopped onions. Add garlic, ginger, cloves, fennel seeds, turmeric, peppercorns and salt and mix well. Add the lamb pieces along with 10 cups of water and bring to boil over medium heat. Reduce heat, add cinnamon and cardamom powders and grated ginger and simmer until lamb is well done and the liquid is reduced to half. In a frying plan, heat the remaining coconut oil and sauté the sliced shallots till they begin to caramelize. Add shredded curry leaves and cumin seeds and fry for a minute. Add this mixture to the soup, and bring to a boil again. Take off pan from stove and stir well.

(Optional: Half a cup of thick coconut milk can be added to the soup to make it creamier.)

Courtesy: Sippora (Venus) Lane, Tiberias, Israel.

Attirachi Varattiyathu (Cochin Jewish Lamb Chops)

This is a rare, exquisitely flavoured and aromatic dish from the Jewish congregation of Mattancherry in Cochin.

Serves 4.

1/2 kg lamb chops
2 tomatoes, chopped fine
2" ginger grated
4 cloves garlic, crushed
1 tbsp pepper
1/4 tsp turmeric powder
1 tsp cardamom powder
Salt to taste
Oil for frying

Grind tomato, ginger, garlic, pepper, turmeric, cardamom powder and salt to make a mushy paste. Marinate the scored lamb chops with the paste and leave in refrigerator overnight. In a deep-bottomed pan, cook the chops in a little water until almost done. Heat oil in a shallow skillet and fry the chops, turning them over frequently until the chops brown.

Courtesy: Reema Salem, Mattancherry, Kochi, Kerala, India.

•••••

The Jews of Cochin have always been known for their hospitality. It is recorded that in the year 1686, a delegation of Jews from Amsterdam, led by Moses Pereyra de Paiva, arrived in Cochin - granting recognition to the Cochini settlement as one of most far-flung outposts of the Jewish Diaspora. The Dutch were by then the colonial masters of Cochin and the Jewish community was prospering economically and culturally.

Paiva wrote in his *Notisias dos Judeos de Cochin* (published in 1687) "that if the King Messiah had come to them through the door, I do not know if they could have shown greater affection." [2]

De Pavia was full of praise for Cochini cuisine. "On the 24th of November, they entertained us with music consisting of six drums, six trumpets and six brass instruments the harmony of which was pleasant; enjoyable was the splendid lunch which David Raby gave us with such magnanimity... (there is) nothing to match its excellence."[3] There are no details of what was on the banquet table, but Raby's descendents in Binyamina in Israel, believe it was the same rice, chicken and fish dishes of today that so delighted foreign guests in those days.

The Rabys or the Rahabis were the most famous and immensely wealthy of the Cochin Jewish families in the 17th and 18th centuries. They were prominent international traders, shipping magnates and diplomats for the Raja of Cochin. Today, their anglicized name is Roby.

This legendary hospitality continued in the late 20th century. On Friday evenings, the head of the Jewish community, the late Sattu Koder and his wife Gladys held an Open House for friends, acquaintances and Jews passing through from all over the world. Sattu Koder was a teetotaller but he ensured that his guests enjoyed the best of imported liquors and a lavish spread of Cochin Jewish food.

[2] *Noticias de Judeos de Cochin*, reprinted in *Cochin Synagogue Quarter Centenary Souvenir*, Dec. 1968, p. 34.
[3] Cited by Katz & Goldberg, *The Last Jews of Cochin*, p. 90.

Chapter 8
Ris, Riso, Arroz Or *Ari* - Rice Is Nice!

"Rice is a beautiful food. It is beautiful when it grows, precision rows of sparkling green stalks shooting up to reach the hot summer sun. It is beautiful when harvested, autumn gold sheaves piled on diked, patchwork paddies. It is beautiful when, once threshed, it enters granary bins like a (flood) of tiny seed-pearls. It is beautiful when cooked by a practiced hand, pure white and sweetly fragrant."
- Shizuo Tsuji - legendary Japanese chef (1933-1993)[1]

Rice (*ari* in Malayalam) has always been the staple food of Kerala. It also has spiritual and religious connotations, because of its association with weddings, festivals and other life cycle events. During the early part of the 20th century, a substantial amount of rice was imported from Burma, although Kerala is famous for its scenic rice paddies and abundant produce. Burma rice was bold and round and increased to three times in size after cooking and was once quite popular with the Jews from the Ernakulam area. It was also smelly! Today, India's *basmati* variety is the preferred choice. Kerala is also home to one of the oldest rice varieties in the world, the *Pokkali*, said to be in cultivation for about 3000 years.

---

[1] Tsuji Shizuo, *Japanese Cooking, A Simple Art*, Kodansha USA, Inc. (2011), p 271. Excerpted with permission.

Thengha Chor
Cochin Jewish Coconut Rice
(Samuel Sabattai Koder's Coconut Rice)

Many American newspapers have named this famous recipe as Samuel Sabattai Koder's Coconut Rice after the illustrious Cochini Jewish businessman of the 20th century. (S.S. Koder - 1928-1992).[2] However, there is more to it than what has since been copied and disseminated through several Internet sites.

There are two ways to make this distinctive and gratifying main dish, which goes well with meat preparations. One is by adding thinly shredded coconut flesh and spices to the cooked rice and the other is cooking the rice in coconut milk and then adding spices to unleash a delightful aroma and an unforgettable flavour. A third version uses both coconut milk and shredded coconut. All three work!

The Classic Version

Serves 5.

1 1/2 cups Rosematta rice (any parboiled rice or basmati will also do)
2 cups finely grated coconut
1 tsp mustard seeds
6 green chillies
1 pinch asafoetida
1 tsp cumin seeds
1 tsp cinnamon powder
12-15 cashew nuts, split
12-15 raisins

4 tsp urad dhal (skinned & split black lentils)
4 tsp chana dhal (split Bengal gram)
1 1/2" ginger, chopped fine
4 cloves garlic, chopped fine
2 sprigs curry leaves
4 tbsp clarified butter
1 tbsp coconut oil
1/2 cup water
Salt to taste

Cook rice and let cool. In a large saucepan, heat the clarified butter and splutter the mustard seeds. Add the cinnamon powder and cumin seeds and sauté for a minute. Reduce heat. Add the chillies, curry leaves, *urad dhal*, *chana dhal*, ginger and *asafoetida* and fry until the *dhals* begin

---

[2] Sahni, Julie, Passover In India : Why is this night different from all others? *The Los Angeles Times*, March 24, 1991.

to brown. Add the shredded coconut, cashew nuts and raisins and stir fry for about three minutes. Add rice and salt as required and gently fluff the rice, while drizzling the coconut oil over it.

Courtesy: Matilda Davidson, Petah Tikva, Israel.

·····

Kerala Matta rice or Rosematta rice also goes by the name *Palakkadan Matta*. This red variety is a well-kept secret of Kerala and was once available only to royal families. It has a robust flavour that makes it popular for breakfast dishes and the numerous rice-based snacks, the most popular being the crunchy *murukku* (*See recipe on page 162*). The Kerala Matta rice is an ancient grain, mentioned in the Tamil classic *Thirukkural* by Tiruvalluvar, a poet who lived sometime in the 1st century BCE or 6th century CE - long before Jews got official recognition in the Hindu kingdoms of Malabar. (*See page 4* about Cheraman Perumal's grant of the copper plates to Joseph Rabban in Cranganore/Shingly).

·····

Coconut Rice with Shallots, Fennel & Fenugreek

The fenugreek in this rice preparation lends an intriguing bitterness in sharp contrast to the sweet fennel and the coconut.

Serves 5.

1 1/2 cups Rosematta rice (if this is not available, any parboiled rice will do)
2 cups grated coconut
3 pods cardamom, husked
1 1/2 tsp fennel seeds
1 1/2 tsp fenugreek seeds

12 shallots, chopped fine
4 tbsp clarified butter
Salt to taste
A handful of roasted, broken cashew nuts and raisins is optional for sprinkling atop the fluffed rice

Cook the rice and keep aside. In a heavy skillet, heat clarified butter. Add shallots, fenugreek, fennel, cardamom and fry until shallots turn brown. Add coconut and rice. Add salt as needed. Fluff the rice gently.

Courtesy: Reema Salem, Mattancherry, Kochi, Kerala.

COCUNUT RICE WITH COCONUT MILK

Serves 5.

1 1/2 cups Rosematta rice	1 cup grated coconut
3 cups coconut milk	Water

Cook rice in coconut milk and a little water on medium heat in a saucepan. Bring to boil. Reduce heat and cook until most of the liquid is absorbed and rice is cooked. Turn off heat and fold in grated coconut. Fluff with a fork.

Courtesy: Pearly Simon, Haifa, Israel.

COCHINI SPICED RICE

The cardamom, cinnamon, cumin, pepper, garlic and ginger in this rice dish all create tiny explosions of taste with every spoonful. Some fennel seeds can also be added when stir-frying the spices to add another level of flavour.

Serves 6-8.

2 cups long-grain rice	1/2 tsp cinnamon powder
1 large onion, chopped fine	2 tsp coriander powder
1" ginger, chopped fine	1 tsp cumin seeds
3 cloves garlic, chopped fine	5 cloves
4 cardamom pods, husked, crushed	4 tbsp clarified butter or coconut oil (for keeping kosher)
1 tsp ground pepper	Salt to taste

In a heavy-bottomed pan, heat the ghee or coconut oil over medium heat. Sauté the onion, garlic and ginger until the onions become translucent. Add the cumin seeds, cinnamon, cardamom, coriander, cloves, pepper and stir fry for about a minute.

Add rice, 4 cups of water, salt and bring to boil. Cook on reduced heat for about 30 minutes or until the water is absorbed.

(Optional) - Drizzle 2 tbsp of coconut oil over the hot rice or stir in 2 tbsp of clarified butter. Mix well.

Courtesy: Rachel Roby, Petah Tikva, Israel.

Resaya Pulav
(Rice With Turmeric & Coconut Milk)

This attractive yellow rice dish is cooked in coconut milk with turmeric (and chicken stock, if preferred) and is an original Cochin Jewish creation. There is an interesting fusion of warm and spicy flavours here and the *Resaya Pulav* or *Plaf* is accompanied by chicken or beef dishes.

Katz and Goldberg have mentioned a grand banquet in Sassoon Hall (on Synagogue Lane in Mattancherry) during the Simchat Torah celebrations of 1986, "when a lavish meal was laid out - 19 fowls were on the table, not to mention huge trays of steaming yellow rice, *biryanis*, vegetables and other specialties."[3]

The yellow rice is the famous *Resaya Pulav* - as served today on Jewish holidays in Cochini Jewish homes in Kerala and Israel and at the Koder House Hotel in Fort Kochi.

Serves 5.

1 1/2 cups basmati rice	oil (for kosher)
1 cup chicken broth	1/2 tsp turmeric
1 1/2 cups coconut milk	1/2 tsp garam masala (optional)
1 onion, finely chopped	Salt to taste
3 cloves garlic, chopped fine	1/2 cup of raisins
3 tbsp clarified butter or coconut	1/2 cup toasted cashew nuts

Soak the rice for about 30 minutes in a bowl of cold water. Drain. Melt the butter or heat coconut oil in a deep saucepan and stir in the onion and cook on low heat until browned.

Add garlic and *garam masala. (See recipe on p. 201.)*

Add the rice to the pan and stir. Add the coconut milk and chicken broth, season with salt and bring to a boil. Reduce the heat and stir. Add the turmeric and salt. Cover the skillet and simmer until the rice is tender and all the liquid has been absorbed.

Sprinkle the raisins and cashew nuts over the rice.

Courtesy: Matilda Davidson, Petah Tikva, Israel.

---

[3] Katz, & Golberg, *The Last Jews of Cochin* p. 185.

Cochin Jewish Biriyani/Biryani/Buriyani (Rich, Festive Rice With Meat)

The *biryani* is a rich rice dish mixed with chicken, lamb, fish or vegetables and a common household festival item throughout India. However, Cochinis aver that their *biryanis* are more flavourful than those made in other regions of India - because coconut milk replaces the yogurt and the addition of tomato and fennel raises the taste factor exponentially.

In Cochin Jewish homes, throughout the 20th century, it was customary to bring in Muslim cooks to give instructions to make the *biryani* on festive occasions; it was believed that only they knew the secret to create the legendary Malabar *biryani*. The Jewish housewife handled the ingredients and did the actual cooking. In Israel today, Cochin Jews make the *biryani* using the *biryani masala* powder/paste, imported from Kerala.

Note: Although at first glance, the making of the meat *biryani* and the vegetable *plaf* look similar, there is a major difference between these two famous cousins. While the *plaf* is made by cooking all the vegetables, spices and rice together, the *biryani* demands that rice and chicken be cooked separately and mixed together later.

Serves 16.

8 cups basmati or any long-grained rice	12 cloves
2 kg chicken, cubed	6 green chillies, slit lengthwise
6 large onions, sliced thin	1 cup coconut milk
4 cloves garlic, crushed	1/2 tsp turmeric
2" ginger, grated fine	2 tbsp vinegar
6 large tomatoes, chopped	3 pieces of cinnamon
1/2 bunch mint leaves, chopped	1/2 cup oil
2 bunches coriander leaves, chopped fine	1 packet biryani masala powder*
12 cardamoms	Salt to taste
	1 tbsp vinegar

Soak the *biriyani masala* powder in a bowl of water to make a smooth paste. On medium heat, cook the rice for about 15 minutes in a big pot with plenty of water, vinegar, salt, cardamom pods, cloves, fennel seeds and cinnamon and salt to taste. Drain and keep aside.

Heat oil in a deep bottomed non-stick pan and fry the onions and garlic until the onions are caramelized. Add green chillies and ginger and fry for about 2 minutes. Add coconut milk and let simmer for about 5 minutes. Add the *biryani masala* paste and stir well.

Add tomatoes and half the chopped mint leaves and coriander leaves. Stir. Add the chicken cubes along with 1 1/2 cups of water. Add turmeric. When it starts to boil lower heat and cook covered for about an hour, stirring occasionally.

When chicken is cooked, add the remaining coriander and mint leaves. Switch off stove. Divide the cooked rice into three portions. Spread one portion of the rice in the pan and add cooked meat and spread this evenly. Add some coriander leaves and mint leaves. Then make the second layer first with rice and then with meat. Repeat this till rice and meat are done. Garnish with coriander leaves and close the lid. Leave in a heated oven to keep warm until ready to serve.

Optional: Garnish the *biryani* with fried raisins and cashew nuts.

BIRYANI MASALA

4 bay leaves
2 tsp fennel seeds
2 star anise
4 tbsp coriander seeds
6 cardamom pods, husked
2 black cardamom pods, husked (this is popular in northern Indian dishes and has a stronger flavour than the common cardamom)
2 tbsp black cumin seeds/ caraway seeds
8 cloves
2 tsp peppercorn
5 two inch cinnamon sticks
3 mace flowers
1/2 tsp grated nutmeg

In a wok, on medium heat, dry roast all the ingredients. Let cool and grind to a powder. Ideal measure is 1 1/2 tsp of *biryani masala* for each cup of rice.

Courtesy: Rachel Roby, Petah Tikva, Israel.

Majboos

Majboos is an Arabic dish similar to the Malabar chicken *biryani* of the Muslim community. In the Middle East, the Persian Gulf kingdoms and among the Bedouins of Israel, it also goes by the name of *Kabsa*. It is now served regularly in the Menorah Restaurant at Koder House in Fort Kochi as part of its Cochin Jewish fare. The *Majboos* can also be a vegetarian dish, if the chicken is replaced with eggplant and zucchini.

Serves 6.

1/2 kg rice	2 tsp red chilli powder
1 kg boneless chicken, cubed	1" ginger, smashed
2 large onions, chopped	6 cloves garlic, smashed
3 tomatoes, chopped	1/4 cup raisins
4 cloves	1/4 cup split peas, boiled
1 tbsp cardamom powder	1 bunch coriander leaves, chopped
5 whole cardamom pods	
3 cinnamon sticks	Salt to taste
1/2 tsp turmeric	1 1/2 cup vegetable oil

In a bowl, combine chicken with salt, turmeric and chilli powder. Keep aside for an hour. Heat vegetable oil in a pan and fry chicken until it loses its rawness or is half done. Take chicken out with a slotted ladle. Add onions, tomatoes, ginger, garlic, cinnamon powder and sauté for a few minutes. Add raisins and boiled peas. Add rice along with enough water to cover the rice. Stir well. Add chicken, cardamom pods and cloves and let mixture come to a boil. Cook covered on medium heat for 30 minutes. Uncover and stir contents well. Garnish with chopped coriander leaves..

Courtesy: Vicky Raj, Koder House, Fort Kochi, Kerala, India.

•••••

The Venerable Shabbat Dish - Cholent/Hamin

"It was a time [when] we did not have electricity and no oven to keep the food warm for Shabbat.

"One or two rich families had a big oven built, as big as a room, where they kept burning coconut shells on the side and closed the small doors. On Friday *evenings most of the Jews would bring their food, either hamin or rice in a pot, and keep it in one of those ovens."*

- Ruby Daniels about life in Cochin in the early 20th century.[4]

One of the many traditional Jewish foods that survived thousands of years of upheaval, dispersal and settlement has been the *cholent*. It is said that in ancient days, Jewish mothers kept their iron vessels with the meat/vegetables or whatever was then available near embers left burning in their stoves or pottery kilns. All the ingredients cooked on through the night and became a delightful dish for *Shabbat*.

The Ashkenazi Jews called this dish *cholent*, Central and Western Europeans called it *shalet* and in Cochin, it went by the Sephardic name of *hamin* (Arabic for hot), with the distinct flavours of Kerala blending with the ingredients. Like mothers everywhere, Cochini Jewish women also immersed half a dozen eggs in the mixture to be a mystery treat for children the next day when the *hamin* was ladled into the bowls. The main ingredient was chicken that melted from the bones and mixed with the rich gravy.

Cochin Jews in Israel have made one change today in their way of cooking the *hamin*; they use electric crockpots and platas - but the elders aver that the *hamin* does not compare well with the dish cooked with real fire and heat!

There is no fixed recipe, however, for *cholent/hamin*. It is said that anything *kosher* and edible can go into the pot. In 1998, an Israeli-wide *cholent* competition organized in Jerusalem attracted 131 entries. The prize went to a Tripolitanian spinach *cholent* which had stuffed vegetables, chicken and beef, semolina dumplings and a mixture of spices.[5]

I remember we had a big baker's oven, for all of Jew Town, which was used for the Shabbat dish of *hamin*. The oven was called *Porna* - in Malayalam and it was in Puthan Veedu or Sassoon Hall, the house next to Sarah Cohen's home on Synagogue Lane. The name Sassoon Hall still hangs outside the house, which is now the property of the synagogue and has been locked up for years now. 'Porna' came from the Spanish word 'horno' for oven or furnace. This, in turn, came from the Portuguese word for oven or kiln 'forno'. - *Dr. Essie Sassoon.*

[4] Daniel, Ruby, *More Memories of Cochin Jew Town*, Bridges magazine, Volume 7, Number 1, p. 40.
[5] Erdosh G, *Jewish Magazine*, May 2001: http://jewishmag.com/43mag/cholent/cholent.htm

Cochini Hamin
(Made With Chicken And Rice)

Serves 4 to 6.

2 cups rice
1 kg chicken, cut into desired pieces
3 large onions, chopped
5 carrots, grated
3 tomatoes, chopped
1 potato, chopped
2" ginger, grated
5 cardamom pods, husked and crushed
1 tsp turmeric
1 tsp pepper
5 cloves
6-8 eggs
3 tbsp vegetable oil
2 cups water
Salt to taste

Heat the oil in an oven-proof pot (a pot that can be put on the Shabbat plata).[6] Add the onions and sauté until tender. Add salt, turmeric and pepper and fry for a minute. Add the grated carrots, ginger, tomatoes and potato along with the chicken pieces. Mix well.

When the chicken is half done, add the rice that has been thoroughly washed. Add 4 cups of boiling water. Stir well and close pot. Lower heat to minimum and cook for 20 minutes or until rice is cooked. (If a crockpot is being used, allow the rice to cook slowly for 16 to 20 hours)

Hard boil the eggs and place in pot. The eggs will turn a delightful brown color the next day. Transfer the pot to a pre-heated oven or Shabbat plata until lunch the next day. (The oven can be adjusted to Shabat setting.) Remove the eggs and garnish the *hamin* with the shelled and halved eggs.

Courtesy: Rachel Roby, Petah Tikva, Israel.

(Legumes are abundant in India and there are several varieties that can be added when cooking the *hamin*. While the Mattancherry Jews did not use any legumes in their *hamin*, the Ernakulam and Mala Jews added beans or lentils or peas, making the dish more vigorous.)

---

[6] Shabbat plata is a flat, electric warming tray without knobs or dials and which can be left plugged in before Shabbat. This equipment is popular in Israel today.

Meal After 25 Hours Of Fasting

"The ninth day of he month of Ab is a day of 25 hours of fasting and lamenting in memory of the destruction of both the First and Second Temples of worship in Jerusalem and the dispersion of the Jews. For some unknown reason, the Cochin Jews called that day "Seerya" ... No meat is eaten on the first nine days of Ab ... [One] family sent to all Jewish families in the town a sort of porridge made of rice, coconut and a kind of red beans, which would be eaten only during [these nine days]." [7]

Kanji & Payar
(Rice Porridge With Beans)

Serves 6.

Kanji (rice *congee*), is an easily digestible rice porridge and a staple for aged seniors, convalescing patients, those breaking fasts or observing some sort of penance among all communities of Kerala. For the Cochin Jews, this dish was standard during the month of Ab.

The gruel is prepared by boiling 2 cups of rice in water for a long time until the grains soften and begin to disintegrate. The liquid is rich in starch and other nutrients.

(Option 1: Sprinkle 2 tbsp of finely grated coconut over a bowl of *kanji*.)

(Option 2: Mix a tsp of clarified butter into a bowl of *kanji*.)

Payar For Kanji

1 cup red cow peas (vanpayar in Malayalam)
1/2 cup grated coconut
12 shallots, chopped
4 cloves garlic, chopped
5 dry red chillies
1/2 tsp cumin seeds
1/4 tsp turmeric powder

2 tbsp coconut oil
1 tsp mustard seeds
4 cups water
Salt to taste
A few curry leaves

[7] Daniel & Johnson, *Ruby of Cochin*, pp. 161-162.

Soak red cow peas in a bowl of water for about six hours. Drain. Grind the grated coconut and cumin seeds to form a coarse paste. Keep aside. In a deep saucepan, boil the soaked cow peas with turmeric, chilli powder and salt until cooked and the water has evaporated. Add the coconut and cumin paste and mix well. Remove from heat.

Heat the oil in a shallow frying pan and splutter mustard seeds. Add curry leaves and shallots and sauté for about five minutes or until browned. Keep stirring. Pour mixture over the cooked cow peas and mix well. Serve hot with *kanji*.

•••••

For the Cochinis, rice is a vital part of their lives and embedded in their consciousness.

As part of their everyday conversations, when one is asked, 'How are you?' the reply will be the following to denote 'All is just well':

By sifting paddy, I got rice grains, by cooking the rice grains, I got rice, and by eating the boiled rice I had my meal.[8]

•••••

Although rice is *kosher*, it is sometimes not considered to be so during the seven days of Passover (Exodus 13:3).

According to the Torah, a Jew must not eat or have in their possession any of the five grains that come into contact with water for more than 18 minutes. Such grains - wheat, spelt, barley, oats, and rye - are called *chametz* .

Rice is not listed, so several Sephardic Jewish communities from Spain, the Middle East and India find rice acceptable during Passover because it is not a prohibited grain. However, the Jews of Eastern Europe, the Ashkenazim, will not touch rice because it falls into a category of food called *kitniyot*. Lentils, peas and even peanuts and some seeds are considered *kitniyot* (because flour produced from these look like those from the prohibited grains and could cause confusion to the observant).

(Note: See more on kitniyot on page 18.)

---

[8] Gamliel, Ophira, *Jewish Malayalam Women's Songs*, PhD dissertation, p. 374

Chapter 9
Our Bread Basket

*"If thou tastest a crust of bread, thou tastest
all the stars and all the heavens."*
- Robert Browning, English poet and playwright (1812 –1889)

Challah or *Shabbat* bread is eaten at the beginning of the *Shabbat* meal on Friday night and again on Saturday. Before the meal, the blessing *Baruch atah Adonai, eloheinu melech ha'olam, hamotzi lechem min ha'aretz* (Blessed are you, Lord, our God, king of the universe, who brings forth bread from the earth.) In Cochin, instead of *challah*, so familiar to the Western world as the main bread of the Jews, a type of bread/bun called *rotti* was made which was very soft on the inside with soft brown crust. Fresh coconut toddy was used as the raising agent.

Homotzi/Rotti

6 cups flour	*- or active yeast*
1 3/4 cups water	*1 tsp salt*
½ cup coconut toddy (kallu)	*1 tsp sugar*

Mix all ingredients together; cover with a wet cloth and leave it for an hour, allowing the flour to rise. Knead the mixture well to make a large dough ball. Divide this dough into 12 to 14 ping-pong ball-size portions Dust cutting board with flour and roll each ball using a rolling pin. Pre-heat oven to 325 and bake the *homotzi/rotti* until crust turns light brown.

Classic Challah

The classic challah, now being made by the Cochinis in Israel is the spiral variety - the shape of which is said to signify the cycle of life. Also, instead of toddy, yeast is used to make the dough rise.

(Matriarch Sarah Cohen of Mattancherry in Cochin makes these spiral *challahs* even today on special occasions).

6 cups flour	*1 tsp oil*
3-4 eggs	*1 1/2 tsp dry yeast*
1 cup sugar	*2 cups water*
1/2 cup oil	*Salt to taste*

In a large mixing bowl, combine half cup of the oil, salt and about 2 tbsp of sugar and whisk briskly. Add a cup of boiling water; then add a cup of cold water and whisk again. Dissolve the yeast and a tsp of sugar in a cup of warm water.

Break the eggs in another bowl and beat until peaks form. Pour the beaten eggs into the oil/water mixture. Keep a tbsp in reserve. Pour the yeast and sugar solution. Add flour slowly, stirring constantly to prevent clumping until dough is formed.

Dust a bowl with flour and knead the dough into a smooth ball. Daub the bowl with tbsp of oil and roll the ball all around. Keep covered with clean cloth for about one or two hours to let the dough rise. Break up dough into three or four smaller balls. Break these balls again into three pieces and roll into thick strands of about the same length. Braid them with greased hands.

Preheat oven to 375 degrees. Lightly brush all round the loaves with the beaten eggs mixture kept in reserve. Bake until browned - about 40 minutes.

Note: *Sesame seeds or poppy seeds or even spices are sometimes sprinkled on challahs.*

Rachel Roby makes more than 100 *puris/pooris* (fluffed, fried flatbreads) for the *Shabbat* evening meal on most weeks, when relatives and friends gather at their home in Petah Tikva. The *puri* is enjoyed in India across cultures, regions and religions. It is mostly eaten with a spicy gravy of potatoes and/or chickpeas, but also goes well with eggs or chicken. Rachel's family prefers the *puris* with soft *halvas*.

Puris/Pooris (Fried Flatbreads)

3 cups all purpose flour (maida; kemah levan - white flour)
1/4 cup oil for mixing and more for deep frying
Salt to taste
3/4 cup warm water

Mix the flour and salt in a wide-bottomed pot. Add the 1/4 cup oil; mix and then add the water slowly. Knead until you get a soft dough.

The next step depends on the size of the *puris* that you prefer. Rachel Roby makes small *puris*; so she makes small dough balls and then opens them into round shapes of about 6 -7 cms, with a rolling pin dusted with flour.

Deep fry the roll-outs one by one in hot oil in a wok. The *puri* will fluff up quickly; take out with slotted ladle and drain on paper towels.

Matzah Bread

This is the bread made at Passover.

1 cup wheat flour
1 teaspoon all-purpose flour for dusting
1/3 cup water, or more if needed
(In Cochin, it was from purified wells and the water was left outside in earthenware pots to cool)
Salt as needed
Coconut oil (optional)

Mix water and flour till you get the right consistency for the dough. Knead quickly into balls and roll on a flour-dusted flat surface, with a rolling pin. Make about 7 or 8 pieces of bread, about 8" inches in diameter.

Pierce with a skewer all over the rolled dough to prevent it from rising. Place on hot griddle and bake quickly, until the *matzah* becomes brown and crispy. (Optional: Lightly daub coconut oil atop the *matzah* and sprinkle salt.)

Matzah Ball Soup

4 eggs
1 cup matza meal, powdered
matzah bread
4 tbsp oil
Salt as needed
1 cup cold water
1 tsp pepper
1 onion, chopped
2 sticks of celery
2 carrots

Crack the eggs into a bowl and whisk till peaks form. Add cold water, salt and pepper and combine well. Add *matzah* meal. Keep in refrigerator for between 30 minutes to an hour. Form the dough into small balls. Cook the balls in boiling, salted water along with the carrots, onions and celery for about 30 minutes.

Matzah balls can also be fried in oil to become a tasty snack.

Kerala (Malabar) Porotta (Flaky Flatbread)

While the North Indians have their *naans* and their *chappatis* (wheat-based breads), Kerala has its unique flatbread, a delicious flaky one made

2 cups all-purpose flour
1 cup coconut oil
Water as needed
Salt to taste

with all-purpose flour. It is popular with all communities.

Combine flour with water, salt and a little oil in a bowl and knead until it forms dough. Cover with a wet cloth and leave aside for about an hour. Knead it again and make medium sized balls of equal size. Flatten a ball, apply oil liberally on both sides and use a rolling pin to make it as thin as possible. Apply oil again, and fold into pleats, applying a little oil within the folds. Hold one end and make a spiral. Heat a little oil in an iron skillet/griddle and pan fry the porotta till it begins to crisp. Flip over. Take off stove and pat in centre to separate the many flaky layers.

Chappati (Wheat Flatbread)

The *chappati*, so common in Maharashtra (Mumbai) and other parts of north India, is a common flatbread in Cochini kitchens today, although it began as a novelty snack in the middle of the 20th century. Many people from Kerala, including Cochin Jews, went to Bombay in search of employment and were attracted to the *chappati* as a filling food item. It is a simpler version of the Kerala *porotta* and there are no layers. Dough is rolled into thin rounds and pan fried on an iron griddle or skillet.

••••

There is a community of Christians in Kerala called the Knanayas or Cnanites whose many life-cycle practices mirror those of the Cochin Jews. Although there is no historical evidence, it has been disseminated that these 'Jewish Christians' called Nazaranis, led by one Knayi Thomas or Thomas of Cana reached the Malabar coast in 345 CE. Scholars like Dr. Shalva Weil of the Hebrew University of Jerusalem have noted how the Jews and the Cnanites "developed along parallel lines in a similar geographical area both in terms of history and tradition and in terms of group image".[1]

"For Easter, the Cnanites partake of unleavened bread, reminiscent of the Jewish *matzot* and drink wine prepared from coconut milk and plums which is of a faint red colour like the wine drunk by Jews on the Passover Seder night. Biblical songs are sung about the Creation and the Exodus from Egypt and they partake of a Pesach or Passover meal."[2]

The Knanayas also had their base in Cranganore, like the Jews, and fled the area in the early 16th century, after repeated attacks by the Muslims, backed by the Zamorin of Calicut.

The Pesaha (Passover) meal includes local fresh fruits and nuts. A bitter herbal drink mimics the *maror* of the Jews. These Nazaranis, who also call themselves the Jerusalem Community from Edessa, hail Jesus as the Messiah while adhering strictly to Mosaic Law. There are large pockets of Knanaya Christians in various cities in the United States, with the largest congregation in Chicago.

---

[1] Weil, Shalwa Dr., Symmetry between Christians and Jews in India: the Cnanite Christians and the Cochin Jews of Kerala, *Contributions to Indian Sociology*, Vol. 16, No. 2 (1982), Sage Publications. London.

[2] *Ibid.*

Indari Appam & Pesaha Paal
(Unleavened Bread & Passover Drink)

1 cup rice flour
1/4 cup split black lentils
(Uzhunnu in Malayalam)
1 cup grated coconut
5 shallots

2 cloves garlic
1/4 tsp cumin seed
Salt to taste
Water, as needed

This is a recipe from the Knanaya Community. The unleavened bread made by the Knanayas during their Maundy - Thursday (coinciding with the Jewish Passover) is called *Pesaha Appam* or *Indari Appam*. *Paal* is milk in Malayalam and the *Pesaha Pal* is Passover Coconut Milk.

Pesaha Appam

3 cups coconut milk
1/4 kg jaggery
1/4 tsp cardamom powder

1/4 tsp dried ginger powder
1/4 tsp sesame seeds

Soak *urad dhal* for about 3 hours and grind it with a little water to make a fine paste. Add to rice flour. Grind coconut, shallots, garlic and cumin to make a coarse paste and add it to the flour. Add a little water and combine everything well to make a thick batter. Add salt to taste.

Pour the batter into a greased stainless steel plate or line the plate with aluminum foil and spread evenly. Steam in a steam cooker for about 20 minutes. Let cool.

Pesaha Paal

Melt jaggery in about 1/2 cup of hot water. Strain. In a saucepan, heat the coconut milk on low heat until it comes to a boil. Add the melted jaggery and stir for a few minutes. Stir in the powdered ginger, cardamom and toasted sesame seeds.

(Optional: Add some rice flour to thicken the milk. Also optional is adding thin slices of the *poovampazham* variety of small bananas.)

Recipe adapted from website with permission from Jisha Joy.[3]

---

[3] *Kerala Recipes* - http://recipes.malayali.me/menu/indari-appam-and-pesaha-paal

Chapter 10
OUR VEGETABLE GARDEN

Noted cartoonist and writer Abu Abraham (1924–2002) was a welcome visitor at Moshav Nevatim in the Negev in the summer of 1967. Abu's father A.M. Mathew was a lawyer in Cochin and many from the Ernakulam Jewish community knew him and received him with delight. "A young man named Joshua took me around and showed me his poultry farm and all the crops he had cultivated," Abu wrote later.

What struck him most was what the Nevatim settlers did with their *moshav*. "The place, I noticed, was fast becoming a little Kerala. There were, for instance, most of the same fruits and vegetables growing - papayas and mangoes, aubergines (eggplant), okra, drumstick, bitter-gourd and what not." The only complaint from an elder was they could not get Burma rice in Israel and coconuts were very expensive.[1]

•••••

Dr. Barbara Johnson in *Ruby Daniel: A Cochin Woman Remembers* thanks Ruby's sister Rahel Kala (Royal), "for her cheerfulness and for cooking the *sambhar* while we worked" more than 20 years ago in Neot Mordecai, a *kibbutz* in the Upper Galilee in northern Israel. (Rahel still lives on the *kibbutz*).[2] *(While a moshav is an agricultural settlement with individual property rights, the kibbutz is a collective.)*

---

[1] Abraham, Abu. Amid the Alien Corn, *The Sydney Morning Herald*, Thursday, July 13, 1967.
[2] Daniel & Johnson, *Ruby of Cochin*, page ix (Acknowledgments).

The Classic Sambhar

The *sambhar* is a lentil and shallot-based curry that is an everyday dish in Kerala, Karnataka and neighbouring Tamil Nadu state, from where it is believed to have originated. It can be described as a richer cousin to the more well-known *dhal* of northern India. The Kerala *sambhar* is, however, a little different because tamarind pulp/water is used as the souring agent and a pinch of asafoetida adds a mystery aroma and special flavour.

Today, the *sambhar* has travelled far and wide and enjoyed in restaurants and takeouts across India and India-themed eateries abroad, as an accompaniment to *dosas*, *idlis* and *vadas*. It is a staple curry in most Cochini Jewish homes.

Serves 10.

1 cup toor dhal (yellow pigeon peas)
1/4 tsp turmeric powder
3 green chillies, chopped
2 potatoes, chopped
1 carrot, chopped
1 tomato, chopped
8 okra, cut
1 onion, chopped
Salt to taste
Tamarind water (squeezed from 1 lemon sized ball of pulp)
2 tbsp coriander powder
1 tbsp red chilli powder
1/4 tsp asafoetida
1/4 tsp fenugreek seeds
4 tbsp grated coconut
1 tsp mustard seeds
3 tbsp coconut oil
1 sprig curry leaves
1/4 cup coriander leaves chopped

Add two cups of water in a bowl along with the *toor dhal*. Add turmeric powder, green chillies, onion, salt and cook (preferably in a pressure cooker) till *dhal* is done. Add the chopped vegetables and cook until they are tender.

Heat 1 tbsp oil in a frying pan, add grated coconut, fenugreek seeds and fry till golden brown. Add coriander powder, chilli powder and asafoetida. Remove from pan and grind, adding tamarind water. Add this mixture to the cooked *dhal* and vegetables and cook for another 5 minutes. Heat the remaining oil and add mustard seeds. When it splutters add curry leaves. Pour this over the *sambhar* and mix well. Garnish with coriander leaves.

Other vegetables that can be used in a *sambhar* include drumstick, eggplant and/or yam. A *sambhar* made only with shallots and the same spices as the main recipe, simmered in its own juices and tamarind water is considered a specialty dish with a distinctive flavour and aphrodisiacal properties!

Parippu
(Curried Lentils/Plain Dhal Curry)

Lentils (*Lens culinaris*) are one of the most ancient foods in the world. *The Book of Genesis*, 25:34 says: "Then Jacob gave Esau some bread and some lentil stew. He ate and drank, and then got up and left."

Urns containing lentils have been unearthed from Tel Mureybit in Syria, which have been dated to 8000 BCE.

India, which is today the largest producer and consumer of lentils, has found lentils at Neolithic sites in the north-eastern state of Bihar dating to 255 BCE. More than 50 varieties of lentils are grown in India. Canada is another major world producer, with the bulk grown in Saskatchewan and exported to India and the Middle East.

In Kerala, the *dhal* mixed with clarified butter and poured over hot rice is a much-loved dish.

Serves 6.

1 cup red lentils (masoor dhal)
2-3 cups water
1 large tomato, chopped
1/2 tsp red chilli powder
1/4 tsp turmeric powder
1" ginger, chopped
4 cloves of garlic, chopped
4 green chillies, chopped
1 tsp cumin seed
1 tsp mustard seeds
1 onion, chopped
1 sprig curry leaves
3 tbsp clarified butter or coconut oil
Salt to taste
1 /2 bunch coriander leaves, chopped

Wash the lentils; drain. Bring water to a boil in a deep saucepan and add the lentils. Add chilli powder and turmeric. Cook covered for about 10 minutes on medium heat. Add tomato and salt and cook for another five minutes. Heat oil in a wok and splutter the mustard seeds. Add cumin seeds, ginger, garlic, onion and curry leaves. Fry until the onions turn dark brown. Add the onion mixture to the cooked lentils. Stir. Garnish with chopped coriander leaves.

Pineapple Pachhadi
(Pineapple in Creamy Yogurt Sauce)

Some years ago, members of the Brighton and Hove Reform Synagogue in London, England got an opportunity to savour the delights of Cochini Jewish food. As part of a *Discovering Jewish Communities Around The World* project, participants tasted curried salmon fish balls (*meen undas - see recipe on page 46*), curried pineapples and the Cochin Jewish cake (*see recipe on page 181*).

According to Rabbi Meyer of the synagogue: "There is no one normative way of Jewish life, and that the context in which these communities reside has a huge impact on the way they perform their rituals, carry out their customs and, of course, cook and eat their food."[3]

Pineapple (known as *kaitha chakka* in Malayalam) is grown in most districts of Kerala, but industrial farming takes place in the Vazhakkulam area of Ernakulam district, near Cochin. Kerala produces around 140,000 tons of pineapple a year, mainly as an intercrop in rubber plantations and it is in plentiful supply in local markets throughout the state.

Serves 10.

2 cups ripe pineapple, cut into 1" cubes
4 green chillies
1/2 tsp ground pepper
1/4 tsp turmeric powder
1/4 tsp cumin powder
1/2 cup grated coconut
2 tbsp coconut oil

1 tsp mustard seeds
1 sprig curry leaves
1 cup water
Salt to taste
1 litre yogurt (keep at room temperature for some time to make it sour)

Grind grated coconut with green chillies and cumin with 1 cup yogurt. Add rest of the yogurt to the coconut mixture and stir well.

Keep aside. In a deep saucepan, on medium heat, cook the pineap-

---

[3] Jewish Chronicle Online , *Rabbi serves up taste of global communities*, 20/09/2005 - http://website.thejc.com

ple pieces in water with pepper, salt and turmeric powder. Reduce heat and add the coconut yogurt mixture to the pineapple. Stir frequently till bubbles appear on the sides of the pot. (Do not boil after adding coconut-yogurt mixture.) Take off stove.

Heat coconut oil in a frying pan and splutter the mustard seeds. Add curry leaves, fry for about 1 minute and pour it over curry. Stir.

Cochin Pineapple curry

This variant uses ginger, garlic, shallots, red chillies and fenugreek seeds as well. A sprinkling of sugar over the curry is optional.
Serves 8.

1 ripe pineapple
1 cup grated coconut
1 cup yogurt
6 shallots, chopped fine
2" ginger, grated
4 cloves of garlic, chopped fine
4 green chillies, chopped fine
3 dry red chillies, crushed

1/4 tsp turmeric powder
1/2 tsp cumin seeds
1/2 tsp fenugreek seeds
1/2 tsp mustard seeds
1 sprig curry leaves
3 tbsp coconut oil
Salt as needed

Chop the pineapple into small bite-sized chunks. Keep aside. Grind coconut, garlic and green chillies into a rough paste. Keep aside. In a large pan, heat coconut oil on medium flame. Sauté the onion until it is translucent. Splutter the mustard seeds.

Add dry red chillies, green chillies and ginger and fry about three minutes. Add curry leaves, fenugreek seeds, turmeric and salt. Add pineapple along with 1/2 cup of water and bring mixture to boil. Add coconut paste and mix everything well. Switch off stove. Let cool slightly and add yogurt. Mix. Sprinkle a tsp of sugar over the dish.

Maampazha Kaalan
(Ripe Mango in Coconut & Yogurt Sauce)

This attractive and palate-tingling curry is eaten with relish during the summer in Kerala, when the mango is in season.

Serves 10.

2 cups ripe mangoes, skinned and cubed	1 tsp mustard seeds
(Leave some flesh on the seeds; these also go into the pot)	1/4 tsp red chilli powder
	1/4 tsp turmeric powder
	6 green chillies
1 cup winter melon (skinned and cubed)	1/4 tsp fenugreek seeds
	1 sprig curry leaves
Salt to taste	Salt to taste
2 litre yogurt	2 tbsp coconut oil/corn oil
1 cup grated coconut	1 cup water
1 tsp cumin seeds	1 tbsp sugar (optional)

Grind coconut, green chillies and cumin seeds with 1 cup yogurt into a fine paste. Keep aside. Boil one cup water in a deep saucepan and add mango and winter melon cubes. Add turmeric powder, chilli powder and salt. Cover and cook for 6 minutes (till water evaporates). Whisk the remaining yogurt and add this to the saucepan. Reduce heat and stir well. When bubbles begin to appear on the sides of the pan, add coconut and chilli mixture. Simmer for 5 to 6 minutes, stirring occasionally (do not boil). Take pan off from stove.

Heat oil in a frying pan and pop the mustard seeds. Add fenugreek seeds and curry leaves and let sizzle. Remove from heat and pour over the cooked mango curry. Stir well.

A sprinkling of sugar over the curry is optional.

(Note: Keep yogurt at room temperature for a day to let it turn sour before making the *maampazha kaalan*.)

Courtesy: Gila Rosenblatt, Aberdeen, New Jersey.

Spicy Cochin Okra

Okra (known as gumbo or lady's finger, *bhindi* in Hindi, *bam-ya* in Hebrew, *bamay* in Arabic, *vendakkai* in Malayalam), is a green, edible seedpod that can be cooked in several ways. As one of the most popular vegetables in Kerala, it is often the main item in curries or is dry roasted/ stir-fried with spices to make an excellent side dish.

Serves 4.

1/2 kg okra
1" ginger, grated fine
2 onions, chopped fine
4 cloves garlic, chopped fine
3 green chillies chopped fine
1/2 tsp cumin powder
2 tbsp coriander powder
1 tsp red chilli powder or milder cayenne power
1/2 teaspoon turmeric
2 tbsp coconut oil
Salt to taste

Trim ends of the okra and cut into half inch pieces. In a deep frying pan, heat the coconut oil on medium flame. Add the onion, ginger, garlic, chillies and cumin. Cook until the onions begin to glaze. Add the okra. Stir everything well and cook the mixture for about 15 minutes. Reduce heat and add the coriander powder, red chilli powder, turmeric and salt. Stir fry until the okra becomes tender or turns deep brown.

To make a gravy-based okra dish that goes well with rice, follow the directions as above but add 3 tbsp of tomato paste, 1 cup of water and 1 tbsp vegetable soup base, 2 tsp lemon juice or vinegar before the okra turns brown. Cook for half hour on low heat until the okra becomes soft.

For a creamier option, add 3 tbsp of coconut cream. (This pairs well with the *Chuttulli Meen* (*See recipe on p. 44*).

Note: To remove the stickiness of okra, cut each okra into two pieces. Throw away the ends, Heat a little oil in a skillet and stir fry the okra on medium heat. The stickiness goes away. You can also add a tbsp of white vinegar to okra when it is being cooked. This should also take care of the stickiness.

Courtesy: Ora Farchy, Houston, Texas.

Okra In Coconut Milk

This is a variation of the Spicy Okra.

Along with the same ingredients, also include:
2 tsp ground fennel
1 cup thin coconut milk.

Follow the same steps until you add the coriander, red chilli powder, turmeric and salt. Here, add the fennel powder as well. Instead of stir frying, pour coconut milk over the mixture and simmer for a couple of minutes. Do not boil. Take vessel off from stove.

Olathiya Vendakkai
(Devilled Okra)

This is a side dish served with *Chuttulli Meen* (*See recipe on p. 44*).
Cut 12 okras lengthwise into strips. Dip them into a mixture of chickpea flour (gram flour), salt and pepper. Deep fry in coconut oil.

Koorka Varatti
(Stir-Fried Chinese Potatoes)

Serves 4.

20 koorka (Chinese potatoes), peeled, cut into small pieces
10 shallots - crushed
2 red dry chillies, crushed
3 cloves garlic, smashed
1/4 cup grated coconut
1/2 tsp turmeric

1/2 tsp mustard seeds
1/2 tsp cumin seeds
1/2 tsp urad dhal (decorticated or dehusked- split)
2 tbsp coconut oil
10 to 12 curry leaves
Salt and pepper, as needed

Cook the *koorka* in a boiling water along with turmeric and salt. Heat the coconut oil in a wok, splutter mustard seeds; add the cumin, curry leaves and *urad dhal* and sizzle for a few minutes. Combine the crushed shallots, chillies and garlic and add it to the ingredients in the wok. Sauté.

Add cooked *koorkas* and grated coconut. Stir. Cover the wok and cook for ten minutes on a low flame. Drizzle 1 tsp coconut oil over mixture. Serve hot.

The *koorka* can also be stir-fried with a little coconut oil and salt to make a delightful side dish.

Unakki Vevichathu (Stir-Fried Vegetables)

This dish can be made with a combination of vegetables like beans, peas, carrots, zucchini or pumpkin. *Unakki* means dry in Malayalam and *vevichathu* means cooked.

Serves 6.

1 1/2 cup mixed vegetables
2 onions, chopped rough
1 sprig curry leaves
1" ginger chopped
3 cloves garlic, chopped

1/2 tsp turmeric
1 bunch coriander leaves, chopped
3 tbsp coconut oil
Salt and pepper to taste

In a deep skillet, heat the coconut oil. Fry onions, garlic, curry leaves and ginger for about four minutes or until the onions turn brown. Add mixed vegetables of your choice, turmeric powder and cook until all the liquid is absorbed. Sprinkle coriander leaves over dish.

(A non-vegetarian version calls for the addition of cooked meat balls to the dish just before serving.)

Courtesy: Sarah Cohen, Synagogue Lane, Mattancherry, Cochin.

(This recipe has been mentioned in a magazine *Live Encounters*.)[4]

•••••

The *thoran* is a signature side dish in Kerala cuisine and part of every feast along with being a common, everyday dish. Cabbage, beans or raw banana are the main vegetables used in this Cochin Jewish stir-fried, no-fuss dish. Coconut dominates, while onion and ginger are optional. Sometimes, carrots are added for colour and crunch.

---

[4] Ulyseas, Mark. Jews in God's Own Country. Special Report, *Live Encounters*, September, 2011. - http://issuu.com/liveencounters/docs/september2011

The Konkani community that lives in the vicinity of Synagogue Lane and elsewhere in Cochin (and that had centuries of dealings with the Cochin Jews) call this stir-fried dish *Sukke* and add chopped potatoes into the mix. (The Konkanis came to Cochin in the 16th century, mainly from Goa and surrounding areas, fleeing the Inquisition by the Portuguese and were given refuge by the Raja of Cochin.)

Cochin Mottakoose Thoran
(Stir-Fried Shredded Cabbage)

Serves 5-6.

2 cups cabbage, shredded and chopped fine
1/2 cup grated coconut
4-6 shallots
1 sprig curry leaves
4 green chillies, chopped fine

1/4 tsp, chilli powder
1/4 tsp turmeric
1 tsp mustard seeds
2 tbsp coconut oil
Salt to taste

Mix turmeric powder, chilli powder, salt and chopped cabbage and keep aside. Heat oil in a wok and splutter mustard seeds. Add curry leaves. Add chopped cabbage and mix well; cover pan and cook for 5 minutes. Coarsely grind green chillies, shallots and coconut. Add this mixture to the cabbage and stir well. Close pan and cook for another 2 minutes on low flame.

Cochin Payaru Thoran
(Stir-Fried String Beans)

Serves 5-6

2 cups beans, chopped fine
2 cloves garlic, chopped fine
1 tsp cumin powder

Plus all the ingredients used in the cabbage thoran (except cabbage)

The ingredients and directions for this dish are the same as the cabbage *thoran*, except that cumin and garlic have been added to the mix.

Follow the same directions, but add the cumin and cloves when grinding the coconut and chillies mixture.

Cochin Kaaya Thoran (Stir-Fried Raw Banana)

(This tasty preparation can also be made with the skin of the Nendran plantain, in place of the bananas. See more about Nendran plantains in the *In Banana Country* section, *pp. 154-157*).

Serves 6.

4 raw bananas
1 cup grated coconut
5 green chillies, chopped fine
8 shallots, chopped fine
1 tsp cumin seeds
1 tsp mustard seeds

2 cloves garlic, chopped fine
1" ginger, grated
1 sprig curry leaves
Salt to taste
3 tbsp coconut oil

Again, this dish has the same ingredients as the cabbage *thoran* (except the cabbage), with the addition of garlic, ginger and additional shallots. There is more grated coconut added.

Cut the bananas into small cubes and cook in water with turmeric, salt and chilli powder till done. Drain water and keep aside. Coarsely grind coconut with green chillies, shallots, garlic and cumin. Heat coconut oil in a wok and splutter mustard seeds. Add curry leaves and ground coconut mixture. Stir for 2 minutes. Add cooked bananas and stir well. Cook over low flame for a few minutes, stirring constantly.

Cochin Jewish Vegetable Stew

This preparation is similar to a *cholent* (without the meat and is made on weekdays). Serves 6.

2 large onions, chopped
1 kg mixed vegetables of your choice (potatoes, carrots, any variety of beans, green peas, eggplant, zucchini or others cut to bite-sized pieces)
4 cardamoms, husked, crushed
4 cloves, crushed

2 sticks cinnamon
1 cup coconut milk
1" ginger, chopped fine
1 sprig curry leaves
12 whole black peppercorns
2 tbsp all-purpose flour
Salt to taste
(6 hard-boiled eggs - optional)

In a deep-bottomed pan, sauté the onions in 4 tbsp of oil on medium heat until they glaze over. Add ginger and curry leaves and fry for about 3 minutes. Add the flour and continue frying. Add 3 cups of water and bring to a boil. Add salt, cinnamon, cardamom, cloves, peppercorns and all the vegetables.

Cover pan, reduce heat and let simmer until vegetables are done. If you find the mixture is thick, add more water. When the vegetables are cooked, add coconut milk and let simmer for a few minutes. Do not boil. Take off from stove. Cut hard-boiled eggs into halves and add to stew. Do not stir. Just tilt the pan from side to side. Serve hot.

Courtesy: Matilda Davidson, Petah Tikva, Israel.

•••••

Tova Simon, a Cochini Jew in Moshav Machesiya, near the northern Israeli industrial area of Beit Shemesh, cooks with lots of coconut, cardamom and fresh Kerala spices at her popular takeaway.[5] Her full-set home-cooked meals include delectable fish and vegetarian dishes that can be ordered and picked up for Shabbat and special occasions. The Israeli Tourism department has listed Tova's takeaways as 'authentic rural ethnic cooking", and blog writers have described her tapioca dish as "tasting like heaven".[6]

The tapioca plant was introduced into Kerala by the Portuguese in the early 17th century. There was a time when *kappa* or *marachini* (Malayalam for tapioca/yuca/cassava) was found only in the homes of poor agricultural labourers or in toddy shops across Kerala. Over the past three decades or so, the tuber slowly went mainstream and is today served in high-end restaurants in Cochin and elsewhere. It becomes a main dish when combined with coconut and spices or a dessert when steamed with butter, sugar/jaggery and coconut. The most popular version is *Kappa/Meen* (red hot sardine curry poured over mashed tapioca).

In Kerala, tapioca is also thinly sliced and fried like potato chips or ground into flour to make specialty breads.

---

[5] Jewish Agency for Israel - www.jewishagency.org/NR/rdonlyres/.../tourismguidewithlinks.xls
[6] http://www.jewish-art-and-gifts.com/ethnic-cooks-in-mateh-yehuda

Kappa - Cochini Tapioca/Cassava

Serves 8.

1 kg tapioca
5 green chillies, chopped fine
6 cloves garlic, chopped fine
1 cup finely grated coconut
1/2 tsp turmeric powder
1/2 tsp powdered cumin

1 sprig curry leaves
6 shallots, chopped fine
1 tsp mustard seeds
2 tbsp coconut oil
Salt to taste

Grate the skin off the tapioca and cut into pieces. Remove inner stems. In a bowl, boil the tapioca in salted water with the turmeric on high heat until it softens. Drain. Mash the tapioca with a flat spatula (it will be of slightly thicker consistency than creamy, mashed potatoes). Add salt, grated coconut and chillies. Mix well. In a frying pan, heat the coconut oil. Splutter mustard seeds and brown the onions and curry leaves. Pour the mixture onto the tapioca. Stir.

•••••

Kerala's Principal Festival of Onam

The main festival of Kerala is known as *Onam*[7] and celebrated by Keralites with food and cultural programs wherever they settle. However, it took around 60 years for the Cochinis in Israel to begin public Onam celebrations. Many said they marked it in their own homes even through the early years of hardship and difficulty of getting the required ingredients for the various recipes.

It was Sima Molly Muttath Pal of Hadera, a town close to Haifa, who first organized a community Onam feast. In her book, *Being Indian, Being Israeli*, Prof. Maina Singh Chawla, quotes Sima as saying in 2008: "We have been talking nostalgically about Onam as we celebrated it with our childhood friends in Kerala and in 2004 we decided to call in a few friends ... and more people joined in every year."[8]

---

[7] *Onam* is a harvest festival falling in August/September. Legend has it that a demon-king called Mahabali once ruled over a prosperous Kerala. The Gods were envious and connived to push him down into the netherworld, allowing him to visit his people only during *Onam*. Keralites celebrate this homecoming.

[8] Chawla, Singh Maina, *Being Indian, Being Israeli*. p. 185.

Chawla adds that Onam "became an occasion to bond together along ethnic lines and reconnect symbolically with an Indian past."

Over the next few years, the festival grew exponentially and in 2011, the Onam celebrations, with a variety entertainment program and a traditional feast, attracted more than 2,000 people at the Central Bus Terminal hall in Tel Aviv.

Onam feasts are strictly vegetarian with food served on banana leaves. The spread is sumptuous and comprise 14 or more dishes, ending with one or two desserts called *payasams* (*See a payasam recipe on page 177*). Two of the principal dishes of Onam are presented here. One is the rich and delightful medley of vegetables called *Aviyal* and the other is the delicately flavoured *Olan*.

Avial
(Mixed Vegetable Medley)

This is a dense mixture of vegetables in a coconut & yogurt sauce. Serves 10.

200 gms string beans
200 gms yam
200 gms snake gourd/pumpkin/ winter melon
2 raw bananas
2 carrots
3 drumsticks
1/4 tsp turmeric powder
1 tsp chilli powder

6 green chillies
1 cup grated coconut
1 tsp cumin seed
2 cups yogurt
1 sprig curry leaves
2 cups water
4 tbsp coconut oil
Salt to taste

Grind cumin seeds, green chillies and ¼ cup grated coconut with ½ cup yogurt to make a fine paste. Coarsely grind the remaining coconut with yogurt and combine with the fine paste. Thinly slice vegetables into 2" pieces, wash and drain. Boil the vegetables in 2 cups water with salt, turmeric powder and chilli powder till almost cooked. (Don't overcook.)

Add the ground coconut and yogurt mixture to the vegetables and stir well and cook on low flame till bubbles appear on the sides of the pot. Add curry leaves and coconut oil and mix well. Remove from heat.

Sima Molly passed away in December 2012 after battling with cancer. Sima was very helpful with her inputs on Jewish life in Cochin and for tidbits on Kerala cuisine for this book.

Olan
(Melon in Coconut-Milk Sauce)

This delectable dish of delicate winter melon cooked in coconut milk and flavoured with curry leaves and fresh chillies is served on all special occasions. Coconut milk has a tendency to separate when cooked at high temperatures, so be careful not to let it get too hot.

Serves 6.

500 gms winter melon
8 green chillies, slit lengthwise
1 tbsp thinly sliced ginger
1 cup coconut milk
1 sprig curry leaves
3 tbsp coconut oil
1 cup water
Salt to taste

Peel and slice winter melon into thin 1" pieces. Boil melon with green chillies, ginger and salt in one cup of water. When vegetables are cooked and water is almost absorbed, add coconut milk and bring to a boil. Reduce heat immediately. Add curry leaves, drizzle the coconut oil and stir well. Remove from stove.

(In southern Kerala, string beans and pre-cooked cow peas are used along with the winter melon).

Chapter 11

CHUTNEYS & SALADS - THINGS TO RELISH!

Chutney is a word common to all Indian languages. It describes a type of spicy preparation, generally used as a side dish or a spread. It is derived from the Sanskrit word *chatnī* (to lick). In English, chutney today denotes a blend of spices with any combination of mashed vegetables/fruits.

• • • • •

Bezallel Eliayahu is a renowned Israeli horticulturist, who became famous in Israel as the man who made the Negev desert bloom. He was one of the pioneers of modern Israeli agricultural techniques and the man behind the successful export of flowers to Europe. He received the Best Exporter award from then Prime Minister Levi Eshkhol in 1964. The Israeli parliament (*Knesset*) awarded him the Kaplan prize, one of the highest civilian awards of Israel, in 1994 for his contributions to agriculture.

He was honoured with the Pravasi Bharatiya Samman, the highest award given by the Indian government to persons of Indian origin. Several Indian ministers, former Prime Minister Deve Gowda and intellectuals like Jean Paul Sartre and Simone de Beauvoir have all been guests at Bezallel's farm in Moshav Shahar. Bezallel made *aliyah* in the early 1950s from the little Kerala hamlet of Chennamangalam.

One of the items he offered us during a visit to his other farm in

Moshav Kidroon was the *mango chutney*. He makes it on a traditional black rectangular stone called *ammi*, which he brought from Kerala. A pounding stone or rolling stone is used to smash coconut, onions etc. "It is only this pounding that releases the real flavours," says Bezallel.

Maanga Chammanthi (Mango Chutney)

1 large raw mango
1 cup grated coconut
2 tsp mustard seeds
4 dry red chillies
5 or 6 green chillies
3 shallots, chopped
1" ginger, grated
1 small bunch coriander
1 tsp turmeric powder
3 tbsp coconut oil
Pinch of asafoetida
1/2 a lemon, juiced
Salt, as needed

Cut mango into small pieces. Leave skin on. Smash the mango pieces along with coconut to a pulp. Heat the oil in a pan. Add mustard seeds, turmeric, asafoetida, green chillies and red-chillies. Remove from heat after mustard seeds finish crackling. Mix with mango, lime juice and salt.

Courtesy: Bezallel Eliyahu, Moshav Kidroon, Israel.

Queenie's Coconut & Coriander Chutney

Queenie Hallegua of Mattancherry, Cochin, has given this recipe to several chefs in Kochi, who now use it as part of their special Cochin Jewish fare.

1 cup grated coconut
2" piece ginger
8 shallots
4 green chillies
1 bunch coriander, chopped
2 tsp vinegar
Salt, as needed
1 tsp sugar (optional)

Use a blender to grind all the ingredients into a smooth paste. In traditional Kerala, this is done on a flat stone or mashed in a mortar and pestle. This chutney is delightful when spread over fried fish. It also goes well with crêpes, fried chicken or a hot bowl of rice.

Variant Of Coriander Chutney

This is another fresh-tasting variant of the coconut and coriander chutney on the previous page.

1 tbsp coriander seeds	3/4 cup coconut milk/or
2 cups fresh coriander leaves	1 tbsp lime juice
1 1/2 " ginger, chopped coarse	1 tsp white pepper, ground
2 green chillies, seeded & chopped fine	3/4 tsp sugar
2 cloves garlic	Salt to taste

In a non-stick pan, toast the coriander seeds for 3 to 4 minutes. Crush in a mortar or coffee grinder. Process the garlic, chillies, ground coriander, pepper and coriander leaves. Add coconut milk or lime juice, sugar and salt and process again until it becomes a paste. Spoon the chutney into a bowl. Serve fresh with rice, bread etc., as a side dish/relish or as a dip.

•••••

Two types of coconut chutneys are made in most Kerala homes. The liquid version is served as a dip with *idli* and *dosa,* while the solid one - called *chammanthi* - is an excellent side dish with rice. Ingredients used are coconut, dried red chillies, shallots and ginger, all smashed together. In other variants, tamarind, curry leaves, garlic and coriander powder are also added in different proportions. The red chillies are dry roasted in a shallow pan before being crushed. The white version of the *chammanthi* is made with green chillies.

Thenga Chammanthi (Ground Coconut Chutney)

This dip has a unique Kerala flavour derived from dry-roasted coconut.

1/2 cup chopped coconut	Small ball of tamarind pulp
5 shallots, chopped	A few curry leaves
6 dry red chillies	1 tsp coconut oil
1" piece ginger	Salt to taste

In a heated wok, stir fry the coconut pieces and the red chillies, until the coconut begins to brown. Let cool. In another pan, heat coconut oil and fry the shallots, ginger, and curry leaves. In a processor, blend the coconut and onion mixtures along with tamarind and salt to a coarse powder. Add a tbsp of water if you prefer it moist.

Ulli Chammanthi (Shallots Chutney)

2 cups shallots, peeled
6 dried red chillies
A few curry leaves
A small ball of tamarind pulp
1 tbsp coconut oil
Salt to taste

Heat coconut oil in a wok and sauté shallots and red chillies, until the shallots brown. Add tamarind, curry leaves and salt and cook for another minute. Let cool and grind to a coarse paste. Drizzle a tsp of coconut oil over paste and mix well.

Cochin Cucumber Salad

Serves 4.

4 medium cucumbers
2 large tomatoes
2 green chillies, chopped fine
1 green bell pepper, diced
(optional - there were no
bell peppers in Cochin of
yesteryears.)
1 tsp ground pepper
1 small bunch coriander, chopped fine
1/2 lemon, juiced/or 1 tbsp white vinegar
Kosher or coarse salt, as needed
Pinch of sugar

Use a grater to remove the skin of cucumbers and cut into small pieces (quarters of a ring). Cut tomatoes the same way. Mix the tomatoes and cucumber in a bowl with the lemon juice/vinegar, salt, pepper. Garnish with coriander. Add a pinch of sugar to enhance the tang of lemon and tomatoes.

Almost every home in Kerala has a couple of mango trees in the compound. Many varieties of the fruit are available during the months of March to June, ranging from the legendary *Mulgova* and the delicious *Alphonso* to the fleshy *Moovandan* and the juicy *Priyoor*. During these months, the Jews of Cochin added mango to everything - from fish dishes to simple curries and the fruit also went into the making of delicious salads and pickles. These continue to be made in Israel.

Toasted Mango Salad

Serves 6.

4 large mangoes, sliced into small cubes
10 small cucumbers, sliced fine
4 cups coriander, coarsely chopped
2 cups fresh mint, chopped
2 lemons - juice squeezed
2 limes - juice squeezed

1 tsp ground cumin
2 tsp pepper
4 green chillies - sliced fine (optional)
1 tbsp coriander powder
6 tbsp coconut oil
1/4 vinegar
Salt to taste

Mix all ingredients, except the mango, in a large salad bowl. Toss. Toast the mango slices over a hot grill after brushing them with a little oil until they turn brown. Add to salad. Stir, adding three or four cubes of ice.

Spicy Pineapple Salad

A fresh and tangy salad, ideal as a starter for lunch. Serves 6.

1 pineapple, cut into small chunks
Juice of 2 limes
1 large onion, chopped fine
2 tsp red chilli powder

2 green chillies, chopped fine
2 tbsp brown sugar
1 tsp ground white pepper
1 bunch coriander, chopped fine
Salt to taste

In a salad bowl, briskly whisk the lime juice, red chilli powder, salt, pepper and brown sugar. Add the pineapple, green chillies, chopped onions and coriander and mix well.

Cochin Jewish Pineapple Salad

Serves 6.

1 pineapple, chopped
1/2 cabbage, shredded
6 carrots, grated fine

3 cloves garlic, chopped fine
2 tbsp vinegar
2 tsp olive oil

Combine pineapple, cabbage, carrots, garlic. Add vinegar and stir well. Drizzle the olive oil over the salad. Serve chilled.
Courtesy: Vicky Raj, Menorah, Koder House, Fort Cochin

Ulli Sarlas
(Kerala Onion Salad With Vinegar or Yogurt)

This rustic salad, made with red onions and green chillies, is a popular accompaniment to biryanis, *plafs* and fried rice.

Serves 4.

2 large red onions, sliced thin
4 green chillies, chopped fine
1 lemon, juiced

2 tbsp vinegar
(or 1 cup of yogurt)
Salt and pepper to taste

Combine all ingredients in a bowl. Squeeze the onions/chillies firmly until they begin to go soft and the onions take on a deep pink colour. Add a couple of crushed ice cubes or chill before serving.

Plain Pulip (Salad)

Serves 4.

3 small potatoes, boiled
1 large onion
4 green chillies, chopped fine
1 tsp toasted cumin powder

2 tbsp Cochin Jewish vinaigrette dressing (See p. 135)
1 bunch coriander
1/4 cup grated coconut

Chop up potatoes and onion. Mix with green chillies, coconut, coriander cumin and vinaigrette dressing. Serve chilled.

Pulip - A Variant

Mix boiled and chopped potatoes with chopped coriander leaves, toasted cumin, salt, pepper, mint leaves and pour coconut milk over it instead of the vinaigrette.

Koorka Sambola (Native Potato Salad)

This dish was one of the favourites of the Jews while most were in Cochin. Because the *koorka* was not available in Israel, the community began making it with ordinary potatoes, although the taste doesn't compare with the original. Recently, horticulturist Bezallel Eliyahu has started growing the *koorka* in his Moshav Kidroon farm.

Serves 6.

1 kg koorka (Chinese potato) *12 shallots, chopped*
1 large bunch coriander, chopped *1 cup coconut milk*

Peel and chop the *koorka*. Boil *koorka* and shallots together in a large bowl of water until *koorka* is cooked and soft. Reduce heat, add coconut milk and simmer for a few minutes. Sprinkle chopped coriander.

Cochini Cabbage Salad

Serves 4.

1 kg cabbage *4 tsp sugar*
Some curry leaves or mint leaves *2 tbsp vegetable oil*
1 bunch coriander *3 or 4 tsp vinegar*

Cut the cabbage into strips. In a bowl, combine the chopped cabbage with vegetable oil, coriander/mint, sugar, and vinegar. Stir well, chill for 30 minutes and serve.

Courtesy: Goulie Sheer, Ora Farchy's cousin, Houston, Texas

The pomegranate - known as *maatalanaranga* in Malayalam, *rimon* in Hebrew and *anaar* in Hindi - is said to be the fruit that Moses received from scouts who ventured into the 'Promised Land'.

Exodus 28:33-34 describes embroidered pomegranates on the *me'il* ("Robe of Ephod"), worn by the Hebrew High Priest. The Book of Kings 7:13-22, says the fruit was carved on the pillars in front of King Solomon's temple in Jerusalem. The pomegranate has been found emblazoned on ancient Judean coins. The fruit is also named among the special produce of the Land of Israel (Hebrew Bible - Deuteronomy 8:8).

Pomegranates are said to have originated in ancient Persia, but is now grown across the world. It is a popular fruit in India where it has been used in Indian traditional medicine, called Ayurveda, especially in Kerala, for thousands of years. For the Cochin Jews, like Jews elsewhere, the exquisitely coloured and flavourful *arils* of the pomegranate symbolized prosperity and abundance and it became traditional to consume the fruit during Rosh Hashanah.[1] Pomegranate juice has long been a favourite health drink throughout India. In Israel, a dessert wine made with pomegranate has been developed by a winery in the Upper Galilee.[2]

Pomegranate Salad

Serves 4.

1/2 cup pomegranate arils
1 tbsp lemon juice
1/2 tsp vinegar
3 tbsp coconut/olive oil
Pepper and salt to taste
1 bunch spinach, shredded
1 bunch lettuce, shredded
3 oranges, peeled, slices separated
1/4 cup cashew nuts, chopped
1/4 cup blanched almonds, chopped

Mix lemon juice and vinegar together in a small bowl. Pour the oil into bowl and gently whisk the mixture. Add salt and pepper to taste. Combine spinach and lettuce in a large bowl. Pour lime and vinegar mixture and toss salad. Decorate with orange slices and garnish with pomegranate seeds, cashews and almonds.

---

[1] The pomegranate is said to have 613 seeds, corresponding with the 613 *mitzvot* or commandments of the Torah.
[2] http://www.lasplash.com/publish/Beer_Wine_%26_Spirits/Rimon_Winery_Dessert_Wine_Review.php

Tarator
(Cucumber Salad)

Serves 3.

1 long cucumber, grated	1 cup water
1 large dill, finely chopped	6 cashew nuts, crushed
3 cloves garlic, smashed	3 tsp olive oil
4 cups yogurt	Salt to taste

The Tarator is a newcomer to Cochini Jewish cuisine. Similar to the cucumber salad made in Mattancherry homes, this starter dish comprises pieces of cucumber served with yogurt and coriander/mint. The *tarator* is a traditional Balkan dish, and popular in Israel and in all Mediterranean countries. The cucumbers can be substituted with lettuce or carrots.

Chef Ajeeth Janardhanan serves the *tarator* as part of his Jewish repertoire in the restaurants at Brunton Boatyard, Cochin. Combine all ingredients together and mix well. Garnish with cashew nuts, olive oil (or any other favourite oil). Serve chilled or with crushed ice mixed in.

Queenie Aunty's Fruit Salad

This light and fresh summer dessert was a big hit with the Jewish children of Mattancherry during the 1970s. All the children of Synagogue Lane are, however, long gone - and so are Queenie Hallegua's own children, a son who is a doctor in California and a daughter who lives in New York. Queenie Aunty's Fruit Salad, which soaks up earthy, local flavours, however, lives on and is now served in the Menorah Restaurant, Koder House. (The apple is a late 20th century add-on, when the fruit started coming to Kerala from north Indian orchards.)

Serves 8.

1 ripe banana (Nendran variety preferred)	1/4 papaya
	1/2 cup green grapes
1 apple	1/2 cup red grapes
1 orange	1/4 cup cherries
1/4 water melon	1/4 cup sugar
1/4 pineapple	

Cut the larger fruits into small cubes. Mix with fresh/whipped cream. Chill. Sprinkle sugar over the fruits and serve in a bowl.

Courtesy: Vicky Raj, Koder House, Fort Cochin.

Cochin Jewish Salad Dressing

Serves 4.

This vinaigrette or salad dressing can be made with assorted fruits and vegetables. Although many consider it similar to the north Indian *raita* (a yogurt-based dressing), in Cochin it was/is made with coconut milk, so that it can accompany meat dishes in keeping with *kosher* food laws. Flavours can be enhanced with coriander or mint and your choice of spices.

1 cup, fresh coconut milk ,	*2 green chillies*
thinned with water	*1 large bunch coriander*
1/2 large, unripe mango	*1/2 teaspoon cumin powder*
1 medium tomato	*1/2 tsp curry powder**
1 large onion	*Salt to taste*

Cut the mango into small bits and add it to the coconut milk. Chop tomato, onion and coriander and green chillies finely. Reserve a little of the coriander for garnish, add the rest to the coconut milk. Stir in the cumin and the curry powder. Garnish with the coriander held in reserve. You can use ripe mango instead of raw ones, if you want the dressing sweet and tangy. In this case, add two rings of chopped pineapple as well.

CURRY POWDER *is an aromatic medley of some of Kerala's fine spices. Coriander seeds, cumin seeds, cardamom seeds (3 tbsp each), 1/2 tsp turmeric powder and $1^{1/2}$ tsp red chilli powder are ground together and bottled. Use as needed.*

Yogurt & Cucumber Sauce

1 cup plain yogurt	*1 lemon, squeezed*
1/2 cup cucumber, grated fine	*1/4 tsp red chilli powder*

Mix all ingredients together. Add salt to taste. Finely chopped coriander provides a delightful garnish. (Finely chopped green chillies - without the seeds - makes the sauce more appealing).

Date Sauce

20 dates, seeded, boiled, mashed into paste
1 large onion, chopped fine
1 bunch coriander
1 tsp cumi n powder
3 tsp dried red chilli powder
4 tbsp vinegar or juice of one lemon
Salt to taste

Combine all ingredients and whisk briskly until you get the desired consistency.

Inji Thairu
(Ginger & Yogurt Dip)

In Kerala folklore, this simple recipe is considered equivalent to 108 dishes. With just three ingredients, it is an important component of all feasts and a tiny quantity is placed symbolically on the main dining plate or banana leaf.

1" piece of ginger, grated fine
1/2 cup yogurt
3 green chillies, chopped fine
Salt to taste

Mix all ingredients well. Serve.

Parippu Chammanthi
(Ground Lentils Chutney)

50 gms urad dhal
50 gms yellow split dhal
50 gms coconut powder
1 tsp red chilli powder
1 sprig curry leaves
1 tsp tamarind paste
1 onion chopped fine
2 tbsp coconut oil
1/2 cup water
Salt to taste

Dry roast *urad dhal*, yellow split *dhal* and coconut powder. Coarsely grind and keep aside. Heat oil and sauté onion until golden brown. Add curry leaves, chilli powder, tamarind paste and salt. Add water and bring to boil. Remove from heat and add coarsely ground *dhal* and coconut mixture. Mix well. Serve with rice or bread.

Chapter 12

PICKLES & PRESERVES - THINGS IN JARS!

Meen Achaar or Fish Pickle was a 'must' accompaniment at all meals in most homes of the Cochin Jews. Fish was abundant at all times and I remember my mother and our neighbours all making these pickles. My mother (Reema Salem of Synagogue Lane, Mattancherry) still makes this delightful pickle and I bring over some bottles to Toronto every fall when I visit my parents in Kerala. Fishes such as seer fish, sardine, mackerel, butter fish, pomfret and anchovies are some of the popular species for pickling. Fillets of tuna and *veluri* (white sardine) are also used. For sardines and anchovies, the bones are left in - because they are crisply fried before they go into the jars - *Kenny Salem.*

MEEN ACHAAR (FISH PICKLE)

1 kg fish, cut into small pieces
1 tbsp red chilly powder
(Kashmiri chilli powder gives a brighter red colour)
1/2 tsp - fenugreek powder
1/2 cup - garlic, chopped fine
1" ginger, chopped very fine
1 1/2 tbsp pepper, ground
1 tsp cumin, crushed
1/2 tsp turmeric powder
2 tsp mustard seeds
6 green chillies, chopped fine
3 sprigs curry leaves
Salt as required
1/2 cup vinegar
2 cups sesame seed oil (called nallenna in Malayalam)
Coconut oil for frying

Marinate the fish pieces with 1 tbsp chilli powder, 1/2 tsp pepper, 1/2 tsp turmeric, 2 tbsp vinegar and salt for about three to four hours. Fry the marinated fish pieces in coconut oil in a deep pan on low heat, until crisp and dark brown. Keep aside. Heat the sesame oil in a heavy wok and splutter the mustard seeds. Fry the curry leaves in the same oil. Add the ginger, fenugreek powder, cumin, garlic, green chillies and the remaining vinegar. Reduce heat. Add the fried fish, salt to taste and stir gently. Let the mixture heat through. Cool. Transfer to glass jars, drizzle some sesame oil over it and seal. It will keep for months when refrigerated.

Courtesy: Reema Salem, Mattancherry, Kerala, India.

•••••

A simpler *Meen Achar* is made without the cumin, pepper, fenugreek, green chillies and ginger. Use the other ingredients as the recipe above.

Marinate the fish in a paste made of a little sesame oil, garlic, turmeric, red chilli powder and salt. Deep fry the fish in coconut oil. Drop the fried fish in a jar with enough vinegar to cover the fish. Pop mustard seeds in sesame oil, add the curry leaves and add them to the jar. Seal.

Puli Inji or Inji Puli (Tamarind & Ginger Pickle)

A special type of pickle - which is tart and sweet and spicy - and made only on festive occasions or feasts in Kerala is the *Puli Inji* or *Inji Puli*. It is excellent with rice and yogurt. Serving size is 1 - 2 teaspoons.

3 pieces of ginger (about 2" each), grated fine	1/2 tsp mustard seeds
	1/4 tsp fenugreek seeds
2 ping-pong sized balls of tamarind pulp	1/4 cup jaggery, crumbled
	1 sprig curry leaves
4 green chillies, chopped fine	2 tbsp coconut oil
3 dry red chillies, crushed	A pinch of asafoetida
1/4 tsp turmeric powder	Salt to taste

Soak the tamarind in 1 cup of hot water for a 10-15 minutes. Squeeze pulp to extract juice. Strain it through a cheesecloth. Heat coconut oil in a heavy-bottomed pan and fry ginger until brown. Remove, let cool. In a blender, grind the fried ginger into a powder. Pour tamarind juice into the pan. Add salt, chilli powder, turmeric powder; stir and bring mixture to a boil. Reduce heat and simmer until gravy thickens. Melt the jaggery in a cup of boiling water. Heat coconut oil in a shallow pan and splutter mustard seeds. Add fenugreek seeds, asafoetida, green chillies, curry leaves and sauté until the mixture turns dark brown. Pour spice mixture into tamarind mix. Stir. Add crushed ginger and melted jaggery. Reduce heat to medium and let mixture thicken to the consistency of heavy sauce.

KANNIMANGA ACHAAR (TENDER MANGO PICKLE)

Made with small green mangoes, this pickle sits at the top of the pyramid among all Cochin pickles. The flavour of sesame seed oil, the jolt of chillies and the delight of biting into the wrinkled fruit has made this a favourite, spanning generations and centuries. The pickle is left to mature in a beige/brown ceramic jar called the *bharani*, the design of which is said to have originated in 13th century China during the reign of Kublai Khan. (These jars are still called *cheena bharani* - Chinese jars - in Kerala.)

1 kg baby green mangoes
2 tsp mustard seeds
1 tsp fenugreek seeds
4 tbsp red chilli powder
1/4 tsp asafoetida
3 tbsp sesame seed oil/
(gingelly oil)

Immerse the mango in heavily salted water in a jar for about 3 weeks. (Alternately, in a jar layer mangoes over crystalline salt, repeating process until many layers are formed. Seal jar and keep aside for three weeks.) Dry roast mustard seeds in a deep frying pan, along with fenugreek seeds and asafoetida. When mustard splutters, remove pan from stove. Let cool. Grind mustard and fenugreek to a powder. Dry roast the red chilli powder, stirring constantly. Add ground mustard/fenugreek powder and mix well. Drain the salt water. In a saucepan, boil 3 cups water and add the spice mixture. Let cool. Put the shrivelled mangoes into a clean jar and pour gravy on top. Mix well. In a pan, on low flame, heat the sesame oil/gingelly oil. Let cool and pour into jar. Seal jar with clean white cloth, soaked in oil and close it tight with lid. Store in a dark, cool place for about 2 months.

Cheru Naranga Achaar (Lime Pickle)

Lime is call *cheru naranga* or little orange in Malayalam. (*Naranga* is a generic word for all citrus fruits. Limes, not lemons, are used in Kerala to make this 'finger-licker.')

6 limes	Pinch of asafoetida
2" ginger, grated	Salt as required
3 tbsp sesame seed oil	2 tbsp vinegar
1 tbsp red chilli powder	

Boil the limes in a bowl of water. Let cool and drain. Cut limes into quarters or smaller pieces. Heat half the oil in a shallow pan and sauté the lime pieces for 3 minutes. Set aside and let cool. Heat the remaining oil in another pan and sauté the ginger. Add chilli powder and asafoetida. Add the limes, salt and mix well. Add vinegar. Stir and store for three days. Add salt or chilli powder, as needed. Transfer pickle to ceramic jar and keep in a cool, dark place for about 3 weeks.

•••••

"And you shall take on the first day the fruit of the beautiful (hadar) tree, branches of palm trees and boughs of leafy trees and willows of the brook, and you shall rejoice before the Lord your God for seven days!" - Leviticus 23:40.

The fruit mentioned in the Bible is *etrog*, a citron used in the waving rituals of the festival of Sukkot - the Feast of the Tabernacles (usually between late September and late October). The fruit is believed to predate other citrus species and has been found engraved on several antiques in Israel and archaeological findings. In Cochin and Ernakulam (until the mid-1950's) Jewish families erected *pandals* (temporary shelters) with coconut palm fronds and open to the elements outside their homes. They spent some time and ate some meals in these shelters. Sukkot commemorates the 40-year travails of the Israelites in the Sinai desert. (Today, a communal shelter is symbolically erected at the synagogue in Mattancherry where all the remaining 40 or so Jews of Kerala gather.)

The *etrog*, called *narthanga* in Malayalam/Tamil has a valued place in south Indian kitchens, where it is used for making pickles and preserves.

Narthanga Achaar
(Etrog Pickle)

(Some call this *vadukapuli achar* - although *vadukapuli* is not etrog, it is 'wild lemon'). This pickle is easy to make.

2 etrogs	2 green chillies - sliced
1 tsp mustard seeds	1" ginger - chopped fine
1 tsp fenugreek	3 tbsp coconut oil
2 tsp red chilli powder	Salt to taste

Combine salt, green chillies and ginger. Fry the mustard seeds, fenugreek and red chilli powder together in a little coconut oil. Mix the etrog pieces well with the spices and the pickle is ready to serve.

(In Tel Aviv, there is a brewery that uses the rinds of the etrog to make a brand of beer during the Holiday of Sukkot.)[1]

Etrog Jam

A jam or jelly made of citron (*etrog*) is distinctive because of its strong and tangy flavour; it can be a favourite with children. In Cochin, sweet oranges were mixed into the jam, while in Israel, apples are also added into the mix.

1 etrog	5 cups of water
1 orange	1 or 2 cups sugar

Cut the etrog into thin slices. This helps for easy removal of the numerous seeds. Do likewise for the orange. Soak the slices overnight in water. Drain the next day. Put fruit slices in a pot of water and bring to boil. Change the water and bring to boil again. Drain water again. (This removes the bitter aftertaste.) Pour sugar over the fruit and simmer on low heat until it starts congealing. Keep stirring to prevent burning. The process should take between 30 to 45 minutes. If it is a little runny, add some orange marmalade. For observant Jews, the fruit spread invokes the spirit of Sukkot for weeks together.

---

[1] http://articles.philly.com/2011-09-29/entertainment/30217084_1_etrog-beer-styles-belgian-style-witbier. The brewer calls it "Sukkot in a glass!"

Guava Jam

Many Cochinis remember the guava jam they enjoyed during the summers in Kerala. The guava comes from the Spanish word *guayaba* and is abundant in Kerala. Called *pera* or *perrakka* in Malayalam, it is similar to the pear, and the inexpensive fruit is a favourite with Kerala's squirrels and birds (especially parrots), as well. The Kerala guava is round, has a slight citrus aroma and the rind, pulp and seeds are all eaten with relish.

1 kg ripe guava
1/2 kg brown sugar
2 tbsp lime juice
Water

Cut guavas into halves. Remove seeds with a teaspoon. Cut the remaining fruit into small pieces. Boil the guavas in water in a saucepan filled up to level of the fruit on medium heat. Remove from heat when mixture turns mushy. Strain using a cheese cloth. Add the lime juice and sugar to the guava mush. Bring to boil. Reduce heat and let the jam change colour and thicken. When it starts bubbling, take off stove. Let cool.

Chakka Varattiyathu (Jack Fruit Jam)

The fleshy jack fruit can be made into a wonderful jelly-like jam; and this rich brown confection is exclusive to Kerala.

1 kg pieces of jack fruit flesh
1/2 kg brown sugar/jaggery
1 tsp cardamom powder
1 tsp dry ginger powder
8 tbsp ghee

In a large saucepan, boil the jack fruit pieces in 3 cups of water. Dissolve jaggery in a little warm water to make a thick syrup. In a heavy-bottomed pan (in Kerala, a copper vessel called *uruli* is used), mash the boiled jackfruit with the jaggery syrup. Cook on moderate heat, stirring constantly to prevent clumping. Drizzle ghee slowly; keep stirring until the mixture turns into a dark brown jam. Fold in the ginger and cinnamon powders. Let cool. The jam has a long shelf life when refrigerated.

Chapter 13

WINE & OTHER FINE DRINKS

Kiddush literally means "sanctification." It is one of the main segments of the *Remember the Sabbath Day* commandment (Za'chor et Yom Ha'Shabbat- Exodus 20:8). *Kiddush* is recited over a glass of wine: "Remember the Shabbat day and sanctify it. Remember the day over wine."

All meals on Shabbat and on Jewish holidays begin with this combination of ritual and wine. Many Cochini families have special silver goblets which are heirlooms and used as the *Kiddush* cup.

Ruby Daniels talks about wine in Cochin:

"The Jews of Cochin made wine for their weddings. They usually used dry grapes boiled with water, maybe because they could not get kosher wine at that time. They made this raisin wine called *mai* for their ceremonies such as circumcisions, Shabbat and specially for the Passover Seder. There were also some Jews who made real wine at home for such occasions".[1]

During the 18th century, a Yemenite Rabbi Yahya ben Yosef Salih (Mahris) was reported to have sent coffee and raisins to the Cochini jews 'in return for spices and fragrant oils'.[2] Kerala does not grow much grapes and in earlier days it had to be imported from elsewhere in the country,

---

[1] Daniel & Johnson, *Ruby of Cochin*, p. 179.

[2] *The Yahya ben Yosef Salih story was from a letter sent to Salih from Cochin, quoted in a book *Come Thou South - Bo'i Teman; Studies and Documents concerning the culture of the Yemenite Jews*, ed Jehuda Ratzaby (Tel Aviv, 1967 Heb, 250, in which he cites a Sassoon manuscript. (Salih, Yahya ben Joseph (known as Mahariz; c. 1715), Yemenite scholar; Av beit din and Rabbi of San'a.

sometimes at great expense. Shlomo Reinman talks about wine in his book: "In any festival, they [the Cochin Jews] drink alcohol, the juice of the liquid from the palm tree of the coconuts [arrack[3], made from distilled toddy]. As they do not have wine and India is not a land of wine, they sanctify the Shabbat and festival with wine made from raisins that are imported from Persia and Arabian countries."[4]

The Cochinis called this raisin juice *mai* or *yeynin*.

Katz and Goldberg have also mentioned the vast quantities of imported alcohol - rum which was called 'petrol', brandy was 'high octane petrol' and whiskey 'aviation fuel'- that was drunk during Simchat Torah and other celebrations in Cochin up to the 1980s.[5]

One of the cocktails today on the wine list of restaurants during many food festivals in Fort Kochi is called *Jew Town*, made with rum and orange juice, blended with bananas and cinnamon. There is another drink evocatively called *Spice Route*.[6]

•••••

Note: Apparently, one of the reasons why Jewish men do not become alcoholics can be traced to their infancy. The story is that boys lose their taste for alcohol during their circumcision on the eighth day after birth. A piece of cloth dipped in wine is tapped many times on the child's lips to comfort him or try to get him to sleep. This leads to the baby associating the pain with the wine and this is enough to put him off alcohol for life.[7]

•••••

Kosher Mai (Kiddush Wine)

2 cups raisins   *4 cups water*

Pour the water into a clean bottle and drop all raisins into it. Leave it at room temperature for about 24 hours. Shake the bottle several times during this time. Strain the liquid and you have your basic *Kiddush* wine.

---

[3] *Arrack*, made from the fermented sap of coconut flowers is extremely intoxicating and is usually consumed with spicy, boiled eggs and potatoes. The Cochin Jews, especially those of Mattanchery, owned vast estates of coconut which yielded plentiful toddy and arrack, before the land reforms of the communist governments in Kerala came into effect

[4] Reinman, *Masa'oth Shlomo b'Kogin*, pg 39.

[5] Katz & Goldberg, *The Last Jews of Cochin*, pp 185-186.

[6] http://www.hindu.com/thehindu/mp/2002/08/08/stories/2002080800390300.htm

[7] Gila Berkowitz, *The New Jewish Cuisine*, p.178.

Sarah Cohen's Kosher Mai

For several decades now, Sarah Cohen of Mattancherry has been making *Kosher Mai*, following this recipe:

> 4 kg red grapes, the darker the better
>
> 2 kg sugar

Wash the grapes thoroughly. Pour a layer of grapes into a large container. Add a layer of sugar. Repeat the process, making as many layers as possible. Seal the container. Every 24 hours, open the container, stir the contents and seal again. On the 12th day, drain the liquid using a colander. Keep as reserve. Squeeze the grapes in a piece of muslin or cheesecloth. Combine this liquid with the one in reserve. You now have *Kiddush* wine. One kilogram of grapes will yield about a bottle of wine.

Chorka/Vinaagri (Raisin Vinegar)

Many older residents in Kodungalloor (Cranganore), some 30 km north of Cochin, still remember the vinegar they purchased from Chennamangalam and Paravur Jews. The vinegar was brought to town in bottles, ferried over by boat across the Periyar River around the middle of the 20th century. Obviously, it must have been a centuries-old tradition. Described as 'fresh' and 'tangy', this *chorka* or *vinaagri* as it was called in Malayalam, was made from raisins left over after making *Kiddush* wine. The entire Chennamangalam and Paravur congregations left in the big 'aliyah' of the 1950s to become farmers or raise poultry in the New Land.

> 2 cup raisins left over after the making of wine
>
> 4 cups water

Mix the raisins that have been used for making wine with water and store in a pot. Allow it to stand for about two months at room temperature. (In Kerala, this meant at around 30-35 degrees C.) This natural vinegar has a wonderful, fruity quality.

Ginger Wine

Chopped ginger and some spices are boiled together for several hours, yielding a refreshing drink. Add some brandy or rum to it and it becomes a high-quality, delicious 'ginger wine'. Serve as a welcome aperitif.

1/4 kg ginger *Juice of 2 limes*
1/2 kg sugar *Water - 2 1/4 litres*

Chop ginger into small pieces. In a large saucepan, bring water to a boil; add ginger pieces. Add sugar; reduce heat and let simmer for about 30 minutes. Let cool. Add lime juice, stir well and refrigerate.

Spicier/Sweeter Ginger Wine

1/4 kg ginger, chopped *6 cloves*
1/2 kg sugar *5 cardamom pods*
8 tbsp honey *Juice of 3 limes*
8 cups water *8 tbsp brandy*
3 pieces cinnamon

In a food processor, coarsely blend ginger, cloves, cardamom and cinnamon. In a large saucepan, bring water to a full boil; add the ginger and spices and Bring the water to a boil in a pot and add the crushed ingredients. Reduce heat and simmer for about 30 minutes. In another pan, melt sugar in a little water on low heat and let brown. Add the caramelized sugar to the simmering ginger brew. Let cool; add honey and lime juice. Stir well. Add brandy. Refrigerate.

•••••

A Cochini Jew named Irit and her Italian-born husband Sandro run the organic La Terra Promessa winery, along with a restaurant, in Moshav Shahar, on the road to Kiryat Gat and Asheklon. Terra Promessa means "The Promised Land" in Italian. Irit's family comes from the Chennamangalam hamlet in Kerala. The winery is reputed for its series of wines and liqueurs and visitors can also enjoy meals which include Italian and Cochin Jewish dishes.

Ruby Daniel writes: "During the two days of Simchat Torah in Cochin ... my father entertained people with *sherbet* as they came by." [8]

•••

Ruby mentions *sherbet* again: "... the Shabbat before the wedding is called *Nadakana Shabbat*. After a festive lunch at the bridegroom's house, all the women go to the bride's house where they are treated with cakes and a cool drink called *sherbet*." [9]

Ruby Daniels has not mentioned the type of *sherbet* that was served. Most Cochini elders in Israel and in Mattancherry believe that the drink Ruby mentioned is the ginger lime *sherbet*. However, other kinds of cool drinks were also popular among the different congregations in the early 20th century in the then Kingdom of Cochin. Most are listed here.

Ginger Lime Sherbet

3 pieces fresh ginger (1" each)
1 cup lime juice
1 cup water
2 tbsp water
2 cups sugar

Wash, peel and grind ginger to a fine paste. Add 2 tbsp water, wring with a clean piece of muslin or cheesecloth to extract juice. Dissolve sugar in one cup water on low heat. Add ginger and lime juice. Bring to a boil. Remove from heat and let cool. Pour into glass bottles and chill. Use as concentrate.

For Immediate Serving:

2 green limes
2 cups water
2 tbsp sugar
1/2 tsp ginger juice
(grated/smashed ginger stirred in a little hot water and filtered)
Pinch of salt

Cut limes in halves and squeeze out juice into a bowl. Add ginger extract, sugar and salt and whisk. Pour chilled water, stir well and serve.

---

[8] Daniels & Johnson, *Ruby of Cochin*, p. 173
[9] *Ibid*, p. 178

• • • • •

In Kerala, in the days before refrigeration, water was cooled in earthenware pots kept in a dark corner of a room, and used for such *sherbets*. Ginger *sherbets* are still popular in Mattancherry town. At Cherlai Junction, one of the busiest trading areas, business is brisk at several small shops selling this drink with the same ingredients; but the glass tumblers are today topped up with carbonated water.

• • • • •

Ambrosia

Ambrosia is the food and drink of the Gods in Greek mythology and was believed to bestow immortality on those who drank it. Semantically, the word *ambrosia* is related to the Malayalam/Sanskrit word *amrita* (which also means nectar of the Gods). In Cochin today, ambrosia is a fruit cocktail of orange and the fruit of the all-giving tree *kalpakavrisha* - the coconut.

Fill a tall glass with alternate layers of sliced orange and grated coconut. Sprinkle cinnamon powder and granulated sugar between layers. (Pineapple rings can also be added to the layers). Eat with a spoon.

An Ambrosia recipe was published in The International Jewish Cook Book of 1919.[10]

• • • • •

Tha Nanari or Naruneendi drink, also called the Indian Sarasaparilla, was very popular across Kerala in the early and middle years of the 20th century.[11] At a time when there was no soda pop or artificial ingredients available, the *nanari* root allowed households to make a refreshing drink during the summer months. Senior members of the Cochini Jewish community still remember this drink, although it is difficult to come by in Israel and urban Kerala seems to have forgotten its health benefits.

---

[10] Greenbaum, Kreisler Florence, *The International Jewish Cook Book*, p. 10

[11] In Kerala, the root (*Hemidesmus Indicus* or *Anantamuli* in Hindi) is considered effective in treating arthritis, bowel problems, rheumatism, insect bites and skin infections. It is interesting to note that the Sarasaparilla root was once available in drugstores across the United States to make tonic and was a principal component of root beer.

Nanari Soda Sherbet
(Limeade Sarsaparilla)

10 tbsp naruneendi syrup
(The syrup is made by boiling
the roots with jaggery or sugar)
4 tbsp lime juice
Cold water or club soda

To make the syrup:
3 pieces 2" naruneendi root
1/2 kg sugar
8 cups water
1 egg

Immerse the *naruneendi* pieces in a small bowl of water for about 12 hours. Drain. Smash the soaked roots and add to a large saucepan with about 8 cups of water. Add sugar and bring the solution to boil over medium heat, stirring constantly. When the syrup becomes thicker, add egg and mix well. Let it come to a boil again. Remove the brown froth. Take off stove and pour the syrup into tall tumblers with crushed ice and carbonated water. Garnish with lemon slices.

Pineapple & Banana Cocktail

Serves 6.

3 ripe bananas
1/2 a fresh pineapple
4 tbsp sugar

6 tbsp lime/lemon juice
3 cups of pineapple juice
1/2 tsp salt

Cut banana and pineapple into small cubes. Place in bowl. Pour lemon juice and pineapple juice over the fruit. Sprinkle sugar and salt. Ladle the cocktail into tumblers along with crushed ice.

Kokum Sherbet

Kokum is the fruit of an evergreen tree (*Garcinia indica*) that grows only in India. It resembles a small, purple plum. When dried, the flattened rind has a sharp, tangy sweetness and a good aroma.

Serves 12.

1 cup dried kokum
3 cups sugar
1 tbsp lemon juice

2 tsp cumin powder
6 cups water

Soak the *kokum* in a large bowl of hot water. Leave it overnight. Use a cheesecloth and extract the juice from the *kokum* pieces into another bowl. Add 6 cups of water and bring the solution to a boil. Add sugar, cumin and lemon juice. Stir and let simmer on low heat until syrup thickens. Let cool. The concentrated syrup can be taken out in spoonfuls and mixed with cold water to make the refreshing *kokum sherbet*.

•••••

The *kokum,* like the tamarind, is also used as a souring agent mainly in northern India. The fruit came to the Cochin Jews through the Bene Israelis who use it in their cooking. (For the Bene Israelis, a raisin *sherbet* is a popular drink to end fasting on the days leading to Yom Kippur. This *sherbet* is made by boiling a handful of black raisins in water and then mashing them. The water is then strained and cooled.)

•••••

Kurumulaku Rasam (Cochin Pepper Water)

The *Cassell's Dictionary of Cookery*, published in London in the 1870s, tells of a recipe from Kerala (but calls it Anglo-Indian). This pepper water, known as *rasam* to the Jews of Cochin and others in Kerala, provides quick relief if you have a cold. Drink it hot! Also, in Kerala, tamarind is used instead of lemon juice. It is equally delicious.

1 or 2 fresh lemons /or a small ball of tamarind	*3 dried red chillies*
	4 cloves of garlic
1 large onion	*1 1/2 tbsp of curry powder*
10 shallots	*Pinch of asafoetida*
15 peppercorns	*1 tbsp of butter*

Squeeze the lemon into a 3 cups of cold water. Slice the onion and mash it along with the pepper, garlic, curry powder and salt. Bring the liquid to a boil in a a saucepan. Cover and let simmer for about 20 minutes. Strain. Chop the shallots and fry them in butter, until golden brown. Add to liquid and let boil again. The 'pepper water' is ready. The British version says: "Bottle the pepper water when cooled, cork closely, and store in a cool, dry place."[12]

[12] *Cassell's Dictionary of Cookery,* p. 534.

Jeeraka Vellam
(Cumin Water)

The cumin is an ancient seed and has been referred to as *ketzah* in the Old Testament in the Book of Isaiah 28:25, 27:

"*"When he has levelled its surface,*
does he not sow the black cumin and
scatter the cumin ...

"... for the black cumin is not threshed with a threshing sledge,
nor is a cart wheel rolled over the cumin,
but the black cumin is beaten out with a stick,
and the cumin with a rod".

Cumin water is served as a warm, golden coloured water, even in small tea shops across Kerala, instead of plain tap or well water. It is considered a powerful digestive aid and mouth freshener. The cumin seed (*nigella sativa*), is a principal ingredient for creating the toasty flavour and fragrance in Kerala recipes. To make *cumin water*, add a heaped teaspoon of cumin seeds to boiling water. Simmer for a few minutes and let cool.

Paanakam
(Spiced Jaggery Water)

The *paanakam* was a popular thirst-quencher in old-time Cochin.

4 tbsp grated jaggery
4 tumblers of water
4 cardamom pods, skinned, and crushed

10 peppercorns, crushed
3 tsp lemon juice
1/4 tsp dry ginger powder

Dissolve the jaggery in a bowl of water. Add all the ingredients and stir well. Chill and it becomes a refreshing drink to beat the humid Kerala heat. Sometimes, a pinch of edible camphor is added to create an enticing aroma to the drink. Using sparkling water can give you a zesty and bolder drink.

Sambhaaram
(Spiced Buttermilk)

This is another refreshing/hydrating drink for the Kerala summers.

6 leaves of the lime tree, crushed	3 green chillies, crushed
2" ginger, grated and smashed	Salt to taste

In a bowl of thin buttermilk, add the lime leaves, ginger, salt and chillies and stir briskly. Serve chilled. (In old Cochin, the buttermilk was kept in earthenware pots which helped cool the drink).

Mooli
(Coriander & Fennel Drink)

This is a drink served on special occasions in Cochin Jewish households; at community gatherings for making *matzah* for Passover, after noon prayers in the synagogue or when prayers are conducted in houses observing a period of mourning. Ruby Daniel wrote about this drink: ""If there is a house where someone had died that year, they invited people and read the Psalms there and they are served a hot drink and cakes.

"For this day, we usually made a special drink instead of coffee and tea. Coriander seeds and cumin seeds are boiled together in water and a little cardamom, cloves and cinnamon are added; then it is served hot with sugar. Good for health and it is also tasty."[13]

1 or 2 cups coriander seeds - fried in a dry pot without any oil	3 litres water
	2 pieces cinnamon
	6 cloves
2 tbsp fennel seeds or anise seeds (not cumin, as Ruby wrote...)	6 pods cardamom

In a wok, stir fry coriander seeds. Let cool and gather it in a gauze bag. In a separate bag, tie the fennel seeds, along with the cardamom powder, cinnamon and cloves. Drop the bags in a bowl of boiling water. Let boil/simmer for about an hour until the water turns brown. Taste. If too strong, dilute with warm water. The *mooli* can be served with or without sugar.

---

[13] Daniel & Johnson, *Ruby of Cochin*, p. 165.

•••••

Tea is drunk everywhere in Kerala, as in most of India. The advantage for Kerala is that much of the tea is locally grown in the high ranges. Scores of beautiful tea plantations dot the hills of Munnar, Devikulam, Anayirankal, Chithirapuram, Grampi, Pathanamthitta, Vilangakunnu, and Ponmudi with several thousand workers employed in each gardens.

From homes to small tea shops in every Kerala village, tea is a brew taken with milk and sugar. However, the Cochini Jews - like their Hindu, Muslim and Christian neighbours, sometimes spiced up their tea, adding cloves, cardamom and ginger or cinnamon for an extra punch. Ginger is a favourite additive, especially after a heavy meal or when you get that uncomfortable, bloated feeling. No tea bags, however; loose tea needs to be boiled the old-fashioned way to get that original, refreshing taste.

SPICED CHAAYA (SPICED TEA)

(Use either ginger or cardamom.)
Serves 4.

1" ginger, grated;
6 cardamom pods, husked and crushed
6 cloves, crushed
1 cup milk

6 tsp. sugar
4 tsp loose tea (Earl Grey, Darjeeling etc.)
3 1/2 cups water

In a saucepan, bring water to a boil. Add the crushed cloves, cinnamon and cardamom/or ginger. Reduce heat and let simmer for about 10 minutes. Add the tea leaves, milk and sugar and bring it to a full boil for about 2 minutes and simmer for another 3 minutes. Strain. Pour into another vessel and back again to aerate the tea. Repeat. Pour into cups.

Chapter 14

IN PLANTAIN/BANANA COUNTRY

Kerala is indeed a true *banana country*. The fruit is said to have been cultivated in the hot and humid Malabar lowlands since 500 BCE and there is mention of the Kerala banana (*kadhali pazham*) in Indian epics like the *Ramayana*. There are 27 varieties of bananas that grow in Kerala's rich, red soil - large ones like the *Nendrakka*, small ones like the *Njalipoovan*, *Chundillakannan* and *Palayankodan*, the *Kadhali* (small golden *Kadhali* and the large red-skinned *Chenkadhali*) and about a dozen varieties of cooking and table plantains, that are grouped under the name of *Robusta* in Kerala. Bunches of several varieties hang in wayside tea shops across the state.

The King of Bananas, however, is the *Nenthrapazham* or *Nendran*, a horn plantain cultivar known in scientific circles as *Kochchi Kesel*. This is a **BIG** banana, much larger than the commercially popular *Cavendish* (*Chiquita*) variety. The *Robusta* is part of the *Cavendish* family.

The *Nendran* has firm flesh, is not very juicy and is sometimes treated as a delicious meal in itself, when fully ripe. In Kerala, this banana is steamed and is a popular breakfast item, mashed into *puttu* (*see recipe on page 35*). Also popular with the *puttu* is the *Njalipoovan* which is a plump, sweet and fragrant fruit. The *pazham pori* or banana fritters is a delicacy that spans all cultural, religious and income segments of the Kerala population. Inexpensive, nutritious and delicious, the *pazham pori* is a staple snack enjoyed at any time of the day. For the Cochin Jews in Israel, it still remains a great treat at tea time, as it was in Kerala for hundreds of years.

Pazham Pori
(Banana Fritters)

4 fully ripe plantains/ Nenthrapazham/Ethapazham
3/4 cup rice flour
1/4 cup all purpose flour/
3 tbsp sugar (if you wish to sweeten the bananas further)
2 cardamom pods, crushed
1/2 tsp turmeric powder
1 1/4 cup water
Coconut oil for frying

Mix the rice flour, all purpose flour, turmeric, cardamom and sugar with water and make into smooth batter. Slice the bananas diagonally into pieces that are about 2" long and about 1/2" thick. Coat the banana slices well in the batter. Heat coconut oil in a wok. Slide the slices into the hot oil and deep fry on medium heat till the edges start to brown. Turn frequently so that they are evenly cooked. Remove the slices with a slotted ladle and place on paper towels to drain.

Serve with hot tea or coffee. (As they say in Kerala, it is now 4:00 in the evening, it is *Pazhampori Samayam - Time for Banana Fritters*).

Spicy, Gingered Plantain
In Cashew/Coconut Sauce

In Kerala, there are scores of ways to make use of the many varieties of bananas. This recipe is suited for the *Nendran* or other varieties with a firm flesh. Do not use very ripe ones.

2 large Nendran plantains/ ethakkya
1/2 cup dry coconut (copra), chopped
3 tbsp cashew nuts, roasted
3 tbsp ginger, chopped fine
1/2 tsp red chilli powder (or more if desired)
1/4 tsp turmeric
Pinch of cumin powder
1 coriander, small bunch
2 tsp jaggery
1 cup sour cream
1/2 tsp cumin seeds, crushed
Clarified butter/ghee for frying
Salt to taste

Peel and slice the plantains into 2" or 3" pieces. Set aside. Blend the cashew nuts, coconut pieces, chilli powder, jaggery, turmeric and ginger, along with the sour cream in a processor. Coat the plantain slices with the paste. In a skillet, heat the clarified butter and gently slide the spiced slices in. Cook on medium heat for about 3 minutes for every three slices, turning once. Let it brown slightly. Add a little water to thin the sauce if needed. Remove from heat, sprinkle a little salt (this brings out the sweetness) and the cumin. Garnish with chopped coriander.

(Optional: You can use thick yogurt instead of sour cream and sugar instead of jaggery.)

Variant of Spicy Gingered Plantain

2 large Nendrans
1/2 cup lemon juice
3 tbsp smashed ginger

2 tsp red chilli powder
1/2 tsp cinnamon powder
Coconut oil for frying

Pour the lemon juice over the skinned and sliced plantains. Coat well. Mix the ginger, red chilli powder and cinnamon powder in a separate dish. Coat the 'lemony' plantains with the spices and fry in coconut oil oil until brown.

Steamed Plantain

Take a ripe *nendran* plantain, make some slits in the skin. Put it in a steamer/pressure cooker for about 20 minutes. Let cool, cut into three pieces, remove skin and serve. The steamed bananas are much sweeter and juicier - ideal to mash into the breakfast *puttu*.

Bananas Sautéed in Butter/Ghee

This is an instant dish to satisfy a sugar craving or as a rich evening snack with tea/coffee. Children will love it.

6 medium sized bananas
6 tsp sugar

4 tsp clarified butter/ghee

Cut bananas into two; slice the two halves vertically - so now you have a dozen slices. In a skillet, melt the butter and slip in the banana slices. Fry three to four minutes on each side or until it starts browning. Lower the heat and sprinkle sugar over the bananas. The sugar will start melting and crust atop the banana slices. Remove from heat and let cool. Eat is as is or topped up with ice-cream of your choice.

Upperi or Kaaya Varuthathu (Fried Nendran Plantain Chips)

3 raw Nendran bananas *2 tsp salt*
1/4 tsp turmeric powder *1 cup coconut oil*

Peel the bananas and slice each into thin rounds. (The thinner the rounds, the crunchier they fry.) Dissolve the salt in a bowl of water along with the turmeric. Immerse the sliced bananas in the liquid for about an hour. Drain. Heat oil in a deep frying pan. Fry the banana rounds in batches until the water in the slices evaporates. When they start turning crisp and golden, take out with a slotted ladle. Drain on paper towels.

Sharkkara Upperi (Jaggery-Coated, Fried Plantain Chips)

Deep fried in coconut oil and flavoured with a hint of ginger, cardamom and cumin, this is an item served on all festive occasions.

3 raw Nendran plantains *1/4 tsp cumin powder*
1/2 tsp ginger powder *1 cup jaggery*
1/4 tsp cardamom powder *1 cup coconut oil*

Peel the bananas and slice them into chunky rounds. Cut them into halves again. Heat the coconut oil in a big wok over medium heat, almost to boiling and slide the chunky pieces. Flip them over with a slotted ladle when half done. Keep frying until the pieces are golden red in colour. Drain on paper towels. In a saucepan, melt the jaggery in some water on low heat. Keep simmering until it takes on the consistency of a thick syrup. Remove from fire and add the fried banana bits, ginger powder, cardamom power and cumin powder and mix well. A sprinkling of icing sugar over the dish makes the *upperi* more appealing.

Chapter 15

SAVOURIES - THE COCHIN SURPRISES!

Ora Farchy of Houston, Texas, remembers her mother Rebecca making this savoury snack in Moshav Shahar in southern Israel. Her mother learnt to make it in the Jewish settlements of Paravur/Chennamangalam and most Cochini Jews consider this a traditional, centuries-old snack.

The Syrian Christians of Kerala claim it is their main snack for festive events and Sojo Joshua (who has a popular food blog remembers "my mom making this in large quantities during New year, Christmas and every month in between[1] ... I think it is a Syrian Christian snack as it is more popular in Christian-dominated areas like Kottayam. And I have heard from my grandmom that *achappam, kuzhalappam, avalose unda* etc also have Syrian Christian roots."

KUZHALLAPPAM /COIL APPAM (CIGAR SHAPED SNACK)

5 cups flour
1/3 cup grits
1 1/2 tsp salt
2 eggs
2 tsp sugar

5 tsp vegetable oil
1 1/4 cups sesame seed, roasted and ground.
1/3 cup coconut, grated
1 onion, chopped/mashed

---

[1] Personal communication. Joshua's blog is at http://sojosmasala.blogspot.ca Note: *All these savouries are everyday snacks in Cochin Jewish homes and Cochinis say they were the earlier settlers.*

1/3 tsp turmeric
1 tsp mustard seeds, ground
1 tsp caraway seeds

1/2 tsp cumin
2 1/4 cups of Water
3 tsp sesame seeds, whole

Makes about 20 *kuzhallappams*.

In a wok, roast the grated coconut until golden brown. Set aside. Add a little water and knead the flour into dough. Mix all ingredients into the dough. With a rolling pin flatten the dough to a thin paper-like layer and with a cup or can cut out circles. Roll the circles into cigar shape and close edges tight. Fry in a deep pan until the coil appam turns brown.

Courtesy: Ora Farchy, Houston, Texas.

Aloo Bonda / Potato Vada (Cochini Potato Fritters)

Makes about 30 croquettes.

Filling:
1.5 kg potatoes
Salt / kosher salt to taste
10 ml fresh lime juice
50 gms fresh coriander/cilantro
5 gms turmeric powder
5 gms fresh ginger
4 green chillies

Coating:
150 gms chickpea flour (besan)

/ lentil flour (gram dhal)
50 gms rice flour
20 gms cornstarch
Salt / kosher salt to taste
4 gms baking soda
3 gms turmeric powder
5 gms garam masala
2 gms asafoetida
5 gms cayenne pepper
Water as needed.
Vegetable/peanut oil for frying

Peel potatoes, wash and clean in running water and place in pan with water add salt and boil till fork tender. Mash the potatoes while still warm. Combine the warm, mashed potatoes with salt, lime juice, turmeric powder, chopped chillies, cilantro and ginger.

In a large bowl, combine the flours and add the spices and baking powder. Add enough water to make a thick batter without lumps. Make the mashed potato mixture into small lemon sized balls. Allow the batter to rest for 30 minutes and keep aside. Heat oil till medium hot. Dip the balls into the batter and fry till golden brown. Remove with a slotted spoon and drain on paper towels. Serve hot or at room temperature with tamarind, coconut or mint chutney.

Courtesy: Ajeeth Janardhanan, Executive Chef, Brunton Boatyard, Fort Kochi.

Cheeppappam/Chipappam (Semolina-Coconut-Sesame Snack)

Serves 8.

1 kg rice flour
1 cup semolina
1 egg
1 large onion, chopped
1 cup coconut flakes
1 cup sesame seeds
2 tbsp sugar (optional)
Salt to taste
Coconut oil for frying

Grind onion, coconut, salt, sugar and a little water to make a coarse paste. Whisk an egg into the paste. In a bowl, combine paste with rice flour and semolina. Mix well. Add a tbsp of oil and knead to make smooth dough. Roll the dough into large circular shape of 1/4 inch thickness. With a cookie cutter, cut dough into strips. Score on surface with a serrated knife. Roll strips into shape of rings and deep fry until browned on all sides.

(Optional - Melt a cup of sugar in a saucepan with about 1/12 cups of water. Let thicken. Mix the fried rings well in the syrup and take out. Let cool.)

Kallu Appam or Stone Appam (Rice & Semolina Crisp)

(*Kallu* is stone in Malayalam), Makes 3 appams.

This crispy and savoury item was made by the Cochin Jews on Friday afternoons for Shabbat. The tradition continues in Israel.

2 cups flour (rice flour preferred)
1 cup semolina
1 cup grated coconut
1 egg
1 onion, chopped fine
5 green chillies, chopped fine
1 sprig curry leaves
3 tbsp oil
Salt to taste

Mix all ingredients except oil to make a batter. Grease a frying pan with 1 tbsp of oil. When the pan is hot, pour 1/3 of the batter and tilt the pan from side to side so that batter evenly covers bottom of pan. Cover and cook for a couple of minutes. Turn it over and cook the other side till appam becomes hard and crispy.

Nula Mala / Sev
(Spicy, Fried Flour Strings)

8 cups ground chickpea flour
4 tbsp toasted sesame seeds
2 tbsp red chilli powder
1 tsp pepper
1/2 tsp asafoetida

4 tbsp coconut oil
Oil for frying
2 - 3 cups water
Salt to taste

In a large bowl, combine chickpea flour, sesame seeds, chilli powder, pepper, asafoetida and salt with 4 tbsp of oil. Slowly add water and knead to make a soft dough. Heat oil in a heavy bottomed pan. Using an *idiyappam* press or *seva nazhi* (a kind of noodle maker), squeeze balls of dough directly into the oil. Fry the strings until golden brown.

Rachel Sopher's Cheeda
(Crispy, Fried Spiced Rice Dough)

Rachel Sopher of Moshav Taoz, a Cochini settlement near Beit Shamesh, presented this snack as part of her repertoire at the Israeli Ethnic Aroma Food Festival in Washington DC in May, 2010.[2] The *cheeda* is also a popular snack of the Knanaya community of Kerala.

Serves 8.

1 kg fine rice flour
1/2 cup black gram flour
1 cup semolina
1 large onion
10 green chillies, chopped
1 cup grated coconut

1 cup sesame seeds
1 1/4 cups water
2 tbsp sugar
A pinch of asafoetida
Salt to taste
Coconut oil for frying

---

[2] Ethnic Cooking Workshop, organized by the Jewish Agency for Israel and the Jewish Federation of Greater Washington: http://www.jewishagency.org/JewishAgency/English/Israel/Partnerships/Regions/Beitshemesh/Cookbook/Washington - Accessed: Dec. 12, 2010.

In a blender, grind onion, coconut, chillies, salt with a little water to make a smooth paste. In a bowl, combine rice, gram flour and semolina with the paste, some water and a little coconut oil. Knead until it forms dough. Make small balls with the dough and flatten them with a rolling pin into thin circles. Heat coconut oil in a wok and deep fry the dough circles until golden brown.

Murukku
(Crunchy Rice Spirals)

1 cup urad dahl powder
2 tbsp sesame seeds
2 tbsp cumin seeds
1 tbsp chilli powder
1 tsp asafoetida
3 tbsp clarified butter/ghee
Salt to taste
Water as needed

Mix rice flour and *urad dhal* powder with butter until crumbly. Add sesame seeds, cumin seeds, salt and asafoetida and mix again. Slowly add water and knead to make dough. Heat oil in a heavy-bottomed pan. Fill *murukku* mould with dough and squeeze batter through the star disc in a circular motion into heated oil. Fry until golden brown and crispy. Take out with slotted spoon and drain on paper towels. (The *murukku* mould, also called *chakli press*, is available in Indian grocery stores.)

Chapter 16
Eating Brick & Mortar - The Charoset

Charoset is one of the symbolic Jewish foods for Passover (Pesach) Seder, the ritual feast that marks the beginning of this major Jewish holiday. It is conducted in the evening of the 14th day of Nisan (Jewish calender) and also on the 15th by traditionally observant Jews living outside Israel.

The colour and texture of the *charoset* is intended to remind the Jews of the bricks and mortar the Israelites were forced to make for 40 years, during their enslavement in ancient Egypt. The word *charoset* itself comes from the Hebrew word *cheres* or "clay."

The Seder tells the story of the liberation of Israelites from slavery (*You shall tell your child on that day it is because what the Lord did for me when I came out of Egypt.*) It is needless to say that this brown lump is delicious and vanishes quickly off the plate! - *Dr. Essie Sassoon.*

•••••

There are as many recipes for *charoset* as there are Jewish communities in the Diaspora. While the Jews of Eastern Europe made *charoset* with apples, walnuts and honey, spiced with cinnamon and sweet wine, in the Middle East it was made with dry dates, raisins and figs. In Greece and Turkey, they added almonds and the Italians used chestnuts.

The Cochini Jews followed the Sephardi/Mizrahi traditions and dates became the main ingredient in their *charoset*. Some congregations also used coconuts, bananas and pomegranates. After reciting the blessings, a sandwich with the *charoset* and some *maror* (bitter herbs)* was eaten, with the rest of the *charoset* enjoyed plain.

Maror, refers to the bitter herbs eaten at the Passover Seder in keeping with the Biblical commandment *"with bitter herbs they shall eat it."* (Exodus 12:8). In Cochin, lettuce was used as *maror*.

Duwoo
(Cochin Charoset)

2.5 kg dates, seeded   *Water*

Put the seeded dates in a big stainless steel pot. Pour water till it is 4 fingers above the level of dates. Cook till the dates become soft/mushy; Cool. Strain the paste through cheese cloth three times. Use water to help in extraction. Put the pot back on the fire with the strained date paste. Cook on low fire for about 4 hours till it is thick and syrupy. (Stir frequently so that the paste does not burn at the bottom of the pot.) Preserve in dry, clean bottles. It will keep for a long time.

•••••

Bernadette Baum is an editor of financial market and general news at a global news agency in New York. Having spent her childhood in Malaysia, she traces her roots to the Cochin Jews. In her words: *"Many years ago, in a tropical paradise far away, a little girl grew up in a jasmine-fringed house with orchids, mango trees, papaya trees, banana and coconut palms, jackfruit, soursop, tomato vines and curry plants. She watched as her Grandmother cooked and baked in a fragrant kitchen. That was me, and I have been cooking since I was ten."* [1]

Bernadette Baum's
Charoset for Passover

"*Charoset*, the fruit and nut jam-like confection which, at Passover, recalls the mortar which the enslaved Jews of ancient Egypt bonded bricks together with, is relatively simple to put together. This version is similar to the charoset made in Egypt, which includes dates, nuts and cinnamon.

[1] Bernadette, who converted to Judaism from Catholicism some 15 years ago, speaks French, Indonesian, Malay, Malayalam, some Hebrew and writes a popular blog *http://divaindoors.com*

I have substituted orange juice for the more traditional red wine, and thrown in coconut as a nod to my Jewish predecessors in Cochin, Kerala."
- Bernadette Baum.

1 Fuji apple, grated
1 cup dates
1/2 -3/4 cup apricot
2 tbsp preserved orange peel
3/4 cup walnuts
1 orange, zest and juice

1 tbsp brown sugar,
1/2 cup coconut shavings
1/2 lemon, juiced
1/4 cup red wine (optional)
1-2 tsp cinnamon

Put all the ingredients together in a food processor and blend, but not too finely. Serve at the Passover Seder and on toasted *matzah* for breakfast.

Reprinted with permission from Bernadette Baum, New York.

CHAROSET (MALA VERSION)

The Cochini Jewish congregation of Mala[2] was among the earliest in India to make *aliyah*. By 1950, they had made all arrangements to go to the Holy Land and as gratitude to the community which hosted them for several centuries, they bequeathed their magnificent synagogue and its estate to the town council. (The only stipulation was that it not be converted into another place of worship or a slaughter house.)

Mala has grown over the past 60 years and today the Mala Jewish cemetery finds itself located in the heart of the town, walled and surrounded by attractive homes... and there is not a single Jewish family anywhere near! There have been demands to convert this valuable piece of real estate into a playground or park - but a court edict, in response to a petition filed by the Ernakulam Jews, has ordered *status quo* on the property.

The synagogue structure still stands and is being used as a community hall for social/cultural functions and meetings. The yard is used as a communal area by local traders for drying red chillies and pepper.

This *charoset* is from the Jews of Mala, part of the erstwhile Kingdom of Cochin.

---

[2] Mala is a small, picturesque town near Kodungalloor (Cranganore), some 40 km north of Kochi. Mala has several inlands waterways and the area boasts acres of rich coconut, ginger and pepper plantations.

1/2 kg dates, seeded
2 cups sugar
4 tbsp sesame seeds
1/2 kg raisins
1 cup cashew nuts

1 cup almonds
1 cup wine vinegar
1 tsp salt
3 cups water

Process all ingredients in a blender until it becomes a paste. Add more water if it is too thick. (In the old days in Cochin, Jewish homes used a large stone mortar and iron pestle to grind the fruits into a pulp.) In a saucepan, let the mixture simmer over low heat for half an hour. Cool and cut into pieces.

Rachael Roby's Charoset

Rachel Roby of Petah Tikva, Israel, starts making the *charoset* immediately after Purim, with the process taking her about two days. The mixture is then bottled and kept in special room for about a month. When it is taken out, it just tastes right!

This recipe is similar to the *Duwoo* of Sarah Cohen of Mattancherry in Cochin, but Rachel squeezes the juice out of each date individually and leaves it to cool overnight.

Place 1 kg of pitted dates in a pot with sufficient water. Cover and boil the dates until pulpy. Let the pot cool overnight. Squeeze out the juice out from each date into another pot. On a high flame, bring the juice to boil. Continue boiling uncovered until all the water evaporates. Cool the remaining syrup mixture. Bottle. When the *Seder* night arrives, mix the syrup with chopped walnuts/other nuts of choice and serve.

(In Cochin, where walnuts were not available, the Jews used cashew nuts which were abundant or peanuts).

•••••

Typically, the *charoset* should include fruits and spices mentioned in the *Song of Songs*: apples, figs, pomegranates, grapes, walnuts and dates with the addition of wine, saffron and cinnamon.[3] However, as mentioned earlier, Jewish communities from different regions had their own recipes,

---

[3] *Song of Songs*: 3 2-3, 2-13, 4-3, 2-15, 6-11, 7-7, 1-2, 4-14 and 4-14.

refined over the centuries. At a *charoset* tasting event at the Houston Jewish Community Centre in Texas some years ago, Hebrew school teacher Ora Farchy's offering was judged as the *'farthest from traditional.'* Amidst the numerous Ashkenazi-style *charoset*, what Ora presented and stood out was one of the Cochin versions, her late mother Rebecca's nut paste held together by pureed dates. Taster Rabbi Yakov Polastek took one bite and declared it *"the most way-out of the evening."*[4]

Rebecca's Charoset

1 cup roasted sesame seeds
1 cup roasted almonds
1 cup roasted peanuts
1 cup roasted cashews
2 cups dates syrup or date puree

½ cup of sweet wine
1 cup honey
A good pinch of ground cardamom
1-2 drops of rosewater

Crush the nuts into rough small pieces. Mix with other ingredients in a pot and heat atop stove. Sir continuously until everything blends together. Turn off the heat and let cool. Store in glass jars. (There is no need to refrigerate... it will vanish in no time.)

Courtesy: Ora Farchy, Houston, Texas.

Spiced Ernakulam Charoset

This *charoset* popular with some members of the Ernakulam congregations includes ginger, red chilli powder and coriander seeds as well - and is a little similar to the charoset made by Yemeni Jews.

1 cup dates, chopped
1/2 cup sesame seeds, roasted
1/2 cup raisins
3 tsp coriander powder

1" piece ginger, smashed
1/2 tsp red chilli powder
1/2 cup sweet wine

Combine all ingredients in a food processor and blend thoroughly. In a saucepan, heat the mixture. Add a little water if too thick. Let cool. Cut into pieces.

[4] Schindler, Janice, Seder foods play a meaningful part in Passover tradition, *Houston Chronicle*, March 31, 2004.

Chapter 17

OUR SWEETS ARE SUBLIME!

A balanced diet is a cookie in each hand. ~Anon

Rachel Roby (née Sassoon) of Petah Tikva is an expert when it comes to Cochini cuisine and often takes the lead in making authentic Cochin-Jewish food for community celebrations in Israel today. Most of the Jews from Mattancherry gather during their many festivals in Binyamina, at the home of Simmi and Sammy Koder.

There is a synagogue nearby, which is the centre for all celebrations for the Cochinis and Rachel and other women cook the food at the Koder residence.

Rachael has also been featured in a popular children's book, *Passover Around The World*,[1] in which the writer tells how Rachel's grandson Ovadya helps his grandmother during *Seder*; arranging the silver *kiddush* cups on individual silver plates and how the 12 pieces of *matzah* are placed around the *seder* tray. (Rachel Roby is Dr. Essie Sassoon's younger sister.) The book also features a recipe "*Grandma Rachel Roby's Charoset*". (*See recipe on page 166.*)

---

[1] Lehman-Wilzig, Tami, *Passover Around The World*, Lerner Publishing (Kar-Ben), Minneapolis. US. 2007. pp. 26-28.

Motta Salada
(Sweet Egg Yolk Strings)

The Motta Salada is a delicacy served during Cochini Jewish weddings and *bar mitzvahs* (Jewish coming of age rituals - 13 for boys and 12 for girls). In November 2011, at the wedding of Gilad Salem and Noagah, in Haifa, it was Rachel Roby, who took charge of making the *Motta Salada*. More than 100 eggs were used, with several Cochin Jewish women working late into the night to make the egg strings.

These ultra-sweet bites were consumed at a party after the bride and bridegroom prayed at their synagogue in Haifa on Saturday after the Thursday wedding. (The *Motta Salada* has also been mentioned as a sweet made of the yolk of the egg, along with bananas given to the bridegroom on the wedding day, by Prof. P.M. Jussay in his book *The Jews of Kerala*.)[2]

Many of the Cochinis in Haifa, Binyamina and Petah Tikva remember Rachel Roby's wedding in Mattancherry some 53 years ago when more than 1,000 eggs were used to make the sweet egg strands. (However, some say they cannot bear the taste of egg yolk and sugar syrup!) The Muslims of northern Kerala make a similar dish - called *Mutta Mala* - Egg Garland- for their festive occasions). - *Kenny Salem.*

30 eggs
1/2 kg sugar: (You can add more sugar if desired)
3 cups water

Directions for the yolk:
Crack the eggs and transfer the yolks and whites to different bowls.

Boil water and sugar in a large pan over low fire and bring to a boil, stirring occasionally. Remove scum that rises to surface.

Strain the syrup using a fresh cheesecloth. Take a glass bottle with a thin nozzle and fill it with the egg yolk. Or improvise with a hole at the bottom of a small plastic bottle. Heat the syrup again on low fire, until it begins to thicken.

Add some water if it gets too thin. Squeeze out the yolk into the hot syrup in a circular motion. It should be coming out like noodle strings. Continue until all the yolk are done.

Sprinkle some cold water into the syrup. This halts the cooking pro-

[2] Jussay, P.M. Prof., *The Jews of Kerala*, p. 100.

cess. Remove the yolk strings using a strainer spoon, after draining the syrup into another vessel. (In Cochin, a small hole was made in a coconut shell to make the strings; and the strings were lifted with thin coconut leaf sticks. In Israel, they now use Chinese chopsticks!). Ensure that the strings do not clump together and place them in a flat dish.

Keep aside the syrup for use with the egg whites.

Ingredients for the egg whites dish:

4 pods cardamom, husked and crushed	1/4 cup raisins or other dried fruits/nuts of your choice.
1/4 cup cashew	

Whisk all the egg whites in a bowl. Add the leftover syrup to the bowl and whisk again. Add the raisins, cashew nuts and cardamom. Steam the mixture in pressure cooker; it cooks to the consistency of cake. Let cool and cut into required shapes. This is called the *Kinnathappam* and can be eaten with the *Motta Salada* or as an individual dessert.

Sheera
(Semolina Sweet)

This delicious, textured sweet is made across Kerala. In northern India, it is called *Kesari* and is part of Hindu temple offerings. The Jews of Cochin make this as part of their many soft *halwa* preparations.

Serves 6.

1 cup semolina/sooji	8 almonds/chopped
2 cups water	8 cashew nuts roasted/chopped
3/4 cup sugar	12 raisins
1/2 cup clarified butter/ghee	5 strands saffron
1/4 tsp cardamom powder	

Heat *ghee* in a heavy bottomed pan and add chopped almonds, cashew nuts and raisins. Fry until golden brown, drain and keep aside. Add semolina to the same pan and sauté for a couple of minutes till the semolina turns a light brown. Boil 2 cups of water with sugar, cardamom powder and saffron strands. Slowly pour this sugar solution over the semolina, stirring constantly. Reduce heat and let simmer for 2 -3 minutes. Remove from heat and cover the pan with a lid. After a few minutes, take off lid and add roasted almonds, cashew nuts and raisins. Mix well.

Unniyappam or Neyyappam (Cochin Jewish Hanukkah Fritters)

Makes about 40 *appams*.

These delicious, golden-brown rice dumplings, deep-fried in clarified butter, were much-anticipated treats at Hanukkah time and the day before Yom Kippur in Cochin. The Hindus also make them as offerings to temples during their many festivals and consider it an ancient specialty.

The *unniyappams* are made in a special cast-iron pan with round indentations, called *appakkara*, similar to the Danish pans called *aebleskiver* used to make apple pancakes. The Greek Jews also have a look-alike pan with seven wells for making their *bimuelo*, the fried dough for Hanukkah celebrations. - *Bala Menon*.

2 cups basmati rice or idli rice
2 cups brown sugar
2 over-ripe bananas - (the Robusta variety called Chiquita)
2 tbsp black sesame seeds

1 tsp cardamom powder
4 tbsp dry coconut (copra), chopped into fine pieces
1 cup clarified butter
Oil for frying

Wash and soak rice for about 5 hours. Grind soaked rice with water, brown sugar and mashed bananas. Transfer to a bowl and add cardamom powder, sesame seeds, and coconut pieces and mix well. The batter should have the consistency of *idli* (or pancake) batter. Keep this batter in fridge for 4-5 hours, allowing the ingredients to blend well. Heat *appakkara* and fill 3/4th of each depression with equal amounts of oil and clarified butter. Pour batter gently into the oil to fill half the well and cook for 2 minutes. Turn the *appams* and cook for another 2 minutes. Use a skewer to check whether the appams are done (skewer will come out clean). Remove *appams* from the *appakkara* and drain on paper towels.

(The bananas help create the soft and spongy interior in delightful contrast to the crusty exterior).

Cochin Jewish Holiday Cookies

This is a favourite recipe of three families of Cochin Jewish cousins - the Farchys, the Gadots and the Abrahams (they now live in different parts of the world). Makes about 35 cookies.

> 2 cups all-purpose flour
> 1 cup clarified butter/oil
> 2 cups sugar
> 1 cup almonds, chopped fine
> 1 cup grated coconut
> 1 tsp cardamom powder
>
> 5 drops food coloring
> Few drops rose water
> Icing sugar
> Salt to taste

Preheat oven to 350 degrees. Line a baking pan with butter paper/parchment paper. Grease lightly. Mix all ingredients in a large bowl and knead until dough is formed. (Red food colouring will make the cookies attractive). Shape chunks of dough into size of ping-pong balls. Place evenly on parchment paper and bake for about 25 minutes. Let cool and sprinkle icing sugar atop the cookies.

Courtesy: Ora Farchy, Houston, Texas.

Coconut Rice Pudding

Serves 6.

> 2 cups thin coconut milk
> 1/3 cup rice
> 4 pods of cardamoms
> 1 cinnamon stick, broken/smashed
> 1/4 cup raisins
>
> 1/4 cup chopped almonds
> 1/4 cup chopped cashew nuts
> 3/4 cup brown sugar
> 1/2 tsp grated nutmeg
> 1/2 tsp vanilla (optional)
> 1 tsp rosewater (optional)

Pour the coconut milk into a medium-sized saucepan. Add rice and bring to a simmer over medium heat. In another saucepan, toast the almonds and cashew in a tablespoon of clarified butter. Add raisins. Add the crushed cardamoms and cinnamon and continue cooking for about 20 minutes. Stir frequently, until the mixture thickens. Add the sugar, chopped almonds, cashew and raisins. Stir. Cook for another 10 minutes. Add the vanilla extract/rosewater and nutmeg.

Cochin Jewish Coconut Cake

Serves 8. This is another dish that also goes by the name of *Appam.*

1 cup semolina	1/4 cup almonds, chopped
1 cup grated coconut	1/4 cup raisins
1 cup coconut milk	1/2 cup cashew nuts, chopped
2 eggs	1/4 tsp cardamom powder
1 cup brown sugar	1 cup coconut oil/clarified butter

In a frying pan, heat coconut oil/*ghee*. Add the semolina and fry until lightly browned. Stir frequently. Let cool. In a bowl, combine eggs and sugar and whisk briskly. Add grated coconut, chopped nuts, raisins, cardamom powder and coconut milk. Add the fried semolina and mix well. Pour batter into a greased dish and bake in a pre-heated oven for about 30 minutes at 325 degrees. Test with a skewer if cake has firmed. These cakes can also be baked in small moulds to make separate cakes.

Courtesy: Reema Salem, Mattancherry, Cochin, Kerala.

Neyyappam
(Cochin Hanukkah Cakes)

These cakes or fritters were popular treats during Hanukkah and just before Yom Kippur in old Cochin. Makes 25-30 cakes.

1 cup flour	10 cashew nuts, chopped
1 cup semolina	1/4 cup raisins, chopped
1/2 cup brown sugar	1/2 tsp cardamom powder
1 tbsp sesame seeds	1/2 cup coconut oil
10 almonds, blanched/chopped	2 cups water
2 cups water	Salt to taste

Dry roast the semolina. Combine with flour, almonds, cashew, raisins and sesame seeds. Add sugar and salt to water and bring to boil in a saucepan over medium heat. Stir in cardamom powder. Remove from heat. Pour over the semolina/flour mixture. Cover and let stand overnight. Add baking powder to the batter. In a wok, heat the oil on medium heat. Pour a small ladle of batter into the oil and fry. Remove when the *neyyappam* browns on all sides. Repeat in batches. Drain on paper towels.

In the 15th century, when Spanish and Portuguese Jews were being expelled from their homes, they took with them the art of chocolate-making. In their new homes, they continued their chocolate making traditions and towns like Bayonne, in southwestern France, became centres of Jewish chocolates. (Many of the expelled Jews, like the Castiels and the Halleguas came to Cochin). In Cochin, however, cacao beans were not available and it was only in the 20th century that wealthy Cochin Jews started using chocolate. The Koders had by then become major importers of fine chocolates, liquors and luxury goods from Europe. For most Cochinis, however, chocolate was an unheard of item until well into the 1960s or so.

Today, chocolate is one of the favourite foods in Israel and is affordable fare for all Cochinis.

The Menorah Restaurant in Koder House, Fort Cochin serves this Cochin Jewish Chocolate Pudding, a mousse made of cacao, coffee and chocolate, a recipe from Queenie Hallegua of the Koder family.

Chocolate Mousse

Serves 8.

3 cups semi sweet choco chips *4 tbsp dark rum*
1/2 cup coffee, brewed strong *8 egg yolks*
4 tbsp sugar *8 egg whites, whisked*

Use a blender to process chocolate chips until ground very fine. Pour hot coffee and add sugar to bowl. Process mixture until the chocolate is melted. Pour the rum and the egg yolks gently into the bowl. Pulse. Pour into another bowl, gently fold in the whisked egg whites. Chill.

Courtesy: Vicki Raj, Koder House, Fort Kochi.

•••••

During Yom Kippur (Day of Atonement), the holiest day in the Jewish calendar, the Cochinis usually fasted for around 27 hours, spending most of the time in intensive prayer in their synagogues. After returning home at around 8:00 pm, the fast was broken with a wheat pudding called *Ural*. This dish is akin to the *halwa*.

Ural Halwa

Serves 10.

400 gms whole wheat
500 gms sugar
2 cups ghee
Optional:
Some blanched almonds

Some broken cashews
Cardamom powder
Saffron strands

Wash the wheat thoroughly and leave it to soak overnight. Drain the water, grind the wheat and add more water. Keep it again overnight. Drain this water too; the paste left behind must not feel glutinous. Add about four cups of water to the smooth, milk-like paste. Cook the paste that is left behind with a little water over low heat. Boil sugar with some water in a pan, until it becomes a thick syrup. Add the wheat paste and the nuts, cardamom powder and saffron.

Keep stirring until the paste becomes translucent, with the chewy consistency of *halwa* or jelly. Add the *ghee* a little at a time, mixing it well with the paste. The whole process takes about an hour. Let cool in a flat, greased tray until the mixture jells. Cut into squares.

(Rose water or vanilla flavouring can be added in place of the cardamom powder. Use rosewater sparingly as an excess will turn the *halwa* bitter.)

A plain variety of *Ural* is also made, using only wheat and sugar.

Wash and soak the wheat overnight. Drain water and grind the wheat well. Mix with a small amount of water to form a smooth paste. Strain through a cheesecloth and remove the milky substance from the husk of the wheat until the water runs clear. Allow to settle. Discard excess water. Add sugar and boil over low heat until it becomes thick, stirring constantly. Pour into flat dishes. Allow to cool and jell.

Sarah Cohen's Kodithiyal Kashuandi Mittai/ Chikki (Cashew Nut Brittle)

The nut brittle is a universal snack. In Kerala, where cashew nut is relatively abundant, this is a delightful, easy-to-make, anytime snack, especially for children.

In India, the legendary *Lonavala chikki* (named after a hill station near Mumbai) of Maharashtra, is made with peanuts and available in packaged form all over the country.

Makes 12-15 pieces.

1 cup broken cashew nuts
1/2 tsp ground cardamom
1/3 cup dry coconut
4 tsp clarified butter
1 cup jaggery, grated
(or two cups sugar, caramelized)
A pinch of salt

Pan roast the nuts in *ghee* on low heat. Add dry coconut and roast for another three minutes. Spread out the nuts/coconut in a baking dish, brushed lightly with 2 tsp of clarified butter. In a heavy iron skillet, pour a quarter cup water, add the grated jaggery and bring to boil on medium heat until the syrup thickens. Reduce heat. Add 2 tsp of *ghee* to syrup and the cardamom and stir.

Pour mixture over nuts in the baking dish. Even the top lightly with a rolling pin. The mixture will cool quickly. Turn it onto a large platter and cut or break into desired shape/pieces. The *Kodithiyal* (brittle) has a long shelf life, when stored in air tight box.

(Roasted, skinned peanuts, almonds and pistachios can all be used instead of cashew nuts to make crunchy, fast-vanishing brittles. Use the same method. If sugar is preferred, heat the sugar in a skillet until it melts and caramelizes to a golden brown colour. You can add a pinch of baking soda into the sugar syrup and shut the heat down when it begins bubbling. The peanut brittle, called *kappalandi mittai* is inexpensive and available in roadside shops across Kerala).

Payasam
(Rice or Vermicelli Pudding)

Serves 6 - 8.

The Kerala rice pudding called the *payasam* is a beloved treat, a soupy dish served as dessert at every feast. The *payasam* is also made with vermicelli (known as *lockshen* in Israel and *semiya* in Malayalam), instead of rice. Adding condensed milk will add richness to the *payasam*. Other varieties of *payasams* are also made throughout Kerala: with bananas, jackfruit, *moong dhal* and jaggery (the last is a temple offering of the Hindus). There are also some types made with coconut milk.

For Cochin Jews, it was a wedding custom for women in the community to gather at the bride's home early in the morning. They sang songs and they prepared 'a sweet rice dish in a huge pot called *chembu* and the rituals were called *chembidiale*....'[3] This dish was, of course, the *payasam*.

1/2 cup basmati rice	1/2 tsp cardamom powder
4 cups milk	12 raisins
1 1/2 cups water	6 cashew nuts, crushed
1 cup sugar	2 tbsp ghee

Wash and soak rice for 2 hours. Drain and squeeze the soaked rice with your hands. Boil water, add rice and cook for 5 minutes. Boil milk in another pan and add to the rice and cook on low heat stirring occasionally until the milk thickens. Add sugar and cardamom and cook for another 5 minutes. Heat *ghee* in a frying pan and fry crushed cashew and raisins till golden brown. Add this to the *payasam* and mix well.

Modakam or Kozhukottai
(Sweet Rice & Sesame Dumplings)

In Jewish Cochin, this was just a sweet dish. However, in Hindu households it was specially made on festival days and offered to the deities as temple offerings. The Bene Israeli Jews of Mumbai call this item *Modak* and is even today an important item at their weddings and served when the bridegroom brings the bride home for the first time.

---

[3] Katz & Goldberg, *The Last Jews of Cochin*. p. 229.

1 cup rice flour
2 coconuts, grated
3/4 cup jaggery
1/2 tsp cardamom powder
1 tbsp clarified butter/ghee
1 tsp sesame oil
Pinch of salt

Serves 6.

Mix the grated coconut well with the jaggery. Heat the *ghee* in a deep pan and stir in the coconut/jaggery. Cook until mixture thickens. Add cardamom powder. Stir. In another pan, bring 2 glasses of water to boil. Add the rice flour and sesame oil. Add salt. Stir to prevent clumping. Let cool. Roll the dough into small balls. Hollow out the centre and put the coconut/jaggery mix into each. Pinch the edges to close the dough balls. In a steamer or vessel with a sieve, grease the base and arrange the dough balls. Steam for about 15 minutes. The *modakam* is ready when the stickiness of the dough goes away. Let cool.

Halwa - The Oldest Confection In The World

The *halwa* (also known as *halwa, halva, halava, helva*, etc.) is one of the oldest known confections in the world and one of the favourite sweets in Israel today. The basic *halwa* recipe is said to date back some 3,000 years and to have originated in India or Turkey, but it is claimed as their own by every country in the Middle East, Central and South Asia and even the Balkans. In modern Israel, the *halwa* is a flaky, *tahini*-based candy, but this is only one of hundreds of varieties consumed in the Middle East and South Asia. *Halwah* comes from the Arabic word *alw* for "sweet".

In Cochin, the Jews made the *halwa* during Rosh Hashanah mainly with semolina, similar to the sweet made in Iran, Turkey and Afghanistan. In Israel, they now use *tahini* (sesame seed butter) and honey, along with nuts. This *halwa* is distributed among neighbours and friends and reminds you of *mishloah manot*, the exchange of treats on Purim.

Whatever its origins or vegetable/nut-based ingredients, including pumpkins and squashes, the *halwa* is the best *kosher* dessert available - because it is *parve* (containing no meat or dairy).

If you visit Jerusalem's Machane Yehuda market you can see streetside tables laden with slabs of *halwa* in a rainbow of colours and a plethora of ingredients. In the United States, the *halwa* was popularized by a company called Joyva, that introduced this ancient sweet to the continent in 1907. The company produced its first batch of *halwa* on the Lower East Side of Manhattan and more than a century later, the product remains a consumer favourite. - *Bala Menon.*

Modern Israeli Honey-Sesame Halwa
(As Made By Cochinis In Israel)

3 cups honey
2 cups sesame butter (tahini)
1 cup toasted cashew nuts
1 cup almonds, blanched and toasted
1/2 cup grated coconut

Heat the honey in a bowl on low heat until it can be made into a soft and sticky ball. Heat the sesame seed butter in another bowl until hot. (Don't let it bubble). Add the sesame seed butter to the honey and stir for several minutes until they combine to become a paste. Add nuts. Stir for about 5 minutes until the batter stiffens. Preheat oven to 350 degrees. Pour batter into a greased baking pan and bake 20 minutes. Let cool in refrigerator for up to 2 days for the *halwa* to acquire its individual texture. Invert onto serving dish and cut into pieces. Makes about 20 pieces.

Kashuandi-Thenga Halwa
(Cashew Nut & Coconut Halwa)

1 medium coconut, flesh cut into tiny pieces
1/2 kg cashew nuts
1/4 cup raisins
1 kg sugar
3 tsp cardamom powder
8 tbsp clarified butter/ghee
1/4 tsp vanilla essence

Heat a tbsp of *ghee* in a pan and fry coconut pieces until brown. Keep stirring to prevent burning. Remove from pan. Heat the remaining *ghee* and fry the cashew nuts until they all turn a golden brown. In a deep saucepan, combine sugar with about 1/12 cups of water. Bring to a boil over medium heat and let simmer until the liquid turns into syrup. Add the fried coconut and cashew nuts along with the *ghee* and cook until mixture solidifies. Add cardamom powder and vanilla essence and stir well. Daub the bottom of a tray with cheesecloth dipped in *ghee*. Transfer the mixture to tray and let cool. Cut into desired sizes and shapes. Makes 8 pieces.

Rice Halwa With Coconut Milk

Serves 12.

1 kg rice flour
2 litres coconut milk
2 kg sugar
6 tbsp clarified butter/ghee
1 tbsp cardamom powder

1/2 cup cashew nuts, chopped
1/4 cup raisins, chopped
1/2 tsp vanilla essence or
rose water (optional)

In a deep-bottomed pan, combine rice flour with coconut milk and sugar. Cook on medium heat, stirring well to prevent burning. When the mixture gets to a thin porridge-like consistency, add the cashew nuts, raisins, cardamom powder and *ghee*.

Reduce heat and simmer uncovered until it thickens like heavy batter. If desired, add vanilla essence/rose water, stir and remove pan from stove. Grease a flat tray with *ghee* and transfer the mixture, which will set as it cools. Cut into desired sizes and shapes.

Thenga Halwa
(Coconut Milk Halwa)

Serves 8.

2 cups coconut milk
1 cup 3.25% milk
1/2 cup grated coconut
6 tbsp clarified butter/ghee

1 cup sugar
A pinch of cardamom powder
A pinch of salt

Combine coconut milk and 3.25% milk in a bowl and bring to a boil on medium heat. Add grated coconut and sugar. Reduce heat and cook uncovered, stirring often till the mixture gets thicker. Add the clarified butter, cardamom powder and salt and stir well. Remove from stove, transfer to a tray greased with *ghee* and let it set. Cut to desired sizes.

Cochin Jewish Cake
(Also Known As Wedding Cake or Rosh Hashanah Cake or Cochin Jewish Spice Cake)

These cakes are special items made for the Jewish New Year and community weddings. Spices like cardamom and cloves give it a deliciously warm flavour. The addition of cinnamon and nuts like almonds are optional. Some families make this cake also for the Festival of Shavuot which comes 40 days after Passover. - *Dr. Essie Sassoon.*

•••••

The Cochin Jewish Cake is considered a jewel in the community's culinary repertoire. Mathew Anthony, son of Dr. Mary Anthony (née Malkah Salem) of Mattancherry, who had a flourishing medical practice in Ernakulam in the latter half of the 20th century, speaks wistfully of this beloved 'Jew Town food'.

"There was this very rich Jewish Cake which my mother used to make and distribute to friends. I used to take this cake to school and it was a big hit with my school principal's wife. She tried to make it several times using my mother's recipe but it always turned out to be a dud, apparently. The real taste of the cake is now only a memory for me…"[4]

Katz and Goldberg have written: "All during the week preceding Rosh Hashanah, every house is filled with the sweet aromas of cakes and cookies in the oven. A Rosh Hashanah specialty is the delicious "wedding cake." …(A) rich batter of semolina, eggs, sugar, ghee, nuts and raisins… (are mixed)…in a large bowl called *kangalam*. The individual sized cakes …are distributed among neighbours, especially non-Jewish friends."[5]

Serves 10-12.

1/2 kg semolina	12 cardamom pods, husked and crushed
1/2 kg sugar	
1/2 kg cashew nuts	12 cloves, powdered
1/2 kg raisins	2 or 3 nutmegs, powdered
12 large eggs	1 1/2 ounce brandy or rum

Roughly chop cashew nuts and raisins together or rough grind them.

[4] Personal communication.
[5] Katz & Goldberg. *The Last Jews of Cochin*, pp. 173-174.

Crack the eggs into a large bowl, add sugar and whisk at speed until it becomes a creamy yellow. Slowly add the powdered spices - cardamom, cloves and nutmeg to the egg and sugar mixture, stirring well with each ingredient. Add the crushed cashew nuts and raisins. Mix well. Add the semolina gently, stirring well to prevent clumping. Add the *ghee.*

Add brandy or rum. Let mixture stand for about two hours.

Preheat oven to 180 degrees and grease baking trays with parchment/baking paper. Pour mixture into tray, level off and bake for between 30 to 45 minutes or until the top starts browning. Test with a toothpick or skewer. If it comes out clean, the cake is done. In not, bake for another few minutes. Don't use a knife for testing; it can cause the batter to collapse.

(For small, individual sized cakes, grease and line small baking tins with butter paper and pour batter into them.)

Courtesy: Matilda Davidson, Petah Tikva, Israel.

Burdoor/Bolkasria (Cochin Jewish Sponge Cake)

Flour, eggs and sugar are combined to create this light, fluffy cake. It is similar to the pound cake of the U.S. or the Madeira cake in Britain. Only a little butter is used and a variety of fillings can be used between the cake layers. This cake with sweet fillings is popular in Israel where it is called *tort*. The Cochin Jews also cut up the cake into pieces which are then dried in the oven to create the crisp and dry *bolkasria*, similar to a hard biscuit. Serves 10.

3 cups all-purpose/self raising flour	2 tsp lemon rind, chopped fine
12 eggs	2 tsp clarified butter
2 1/2 cups sugar	2 tsp baking powder
Juice of 2 lemons, juiced	1/2 tsp salt

Break the eggs into a large bowl. Separate the yolks and place in another bowl. Add the sugar to the yolks and whisk briskly until it is pale yellow in colour and has the consistency of cream. Mix in the lemon juice and rind and whisk again. Beat the egg whites with the salt and baking powder until peaks form. Spread this mixture atop the egg yolk mixture.

Fold in the flour gently with a spatula, mixing well. Pour the batter into a large baking pan, brushed with the clarified butter. Preheat oven to 325 C. Bake for about 45 minutes until the edges begin to come off the pan and the cake is spongy to the touch.

•••••

In old Cochin, the Jewish community abjured meat for all nine days of Ab. On the last day, they fasted for 24 hours. Ruby Daniels described the end of the fasting period thus: "For breaking the fast, we made something special. Rice flour dough is spread on a kind of leaf. They put coconut cooked in jaggery on the dough and fold the leaves and then it is steamed. Jaggery is unrefined sugar, brown in colour, whereas for happy occasions we used white sugar only."[6]

This special and ancient dish that Ruby described is the famous *Sharkkara Ada,* a perennial favourite with every community throughout Kerala. The leaves used are banana leaves. Makes about 10 *adas*.

Sharkkara Ada
(Steamed Rice & Jaggery)

2 cups roasted rice flour
1 cup grated coconut
1 cup jaggery
1/4 tsp cardamom powder
2 tbsp clarified butter/ghee

Salt as needed
4 cups water
Banana leaves, cut into squares of about 9"

In a large bowl, combine roasted rice flour with salt and *ghee*. Pour 4 cups of boiling water over the flour slowly, stirring constantly. Let cool a little and knead well to form a soft dough. Divide the dough into about 10 small balls. Boil 1/2 a cup of water in a saucepan and add the jaggery. Stir until it turns into a thick syrup. Remove from heat and add grated coconut and cardamom powder. Mix well. Flatten a dough ball on one of the banana leaf squares. Use a ladle to spread the coconut jaggery mix over the dough. Repeat process until all dough is done. Fold leaves and steam for about 10 minutes. Thin foil can be used instead of banana leaves.

---

[6] Daniel & Johnson, *Ruby of Cochin*, p. 163.

Meruba
(Chewy Fruit Confection)

Meruba is a special sweet, a jewel-like confection made by Cochin Jews during the blessings of new fruits (*Brakot*) on the night of Rosh Hashanah - Jewish New Year. In Cochin, it used to be made with a fruit called *sabarjilli*, that is similar in taste to the pear. In Israel, of course, we use pears or green apples and pray during the blesssing: *"May it by thy will to renew unto us a good and sweet year"* - Dr. Essie Sassoon.

• • • • •

Fruit has always been a major item for Cochini Jews during the Rosh Hashanah holidays. Katz and Goldberg recounts how the Rosh Hashanah tables in many homes were laden with 'more than a dozen dishes of cut fruit'. These included pineapples, bananas, oranges, green and red grapes, pomegranates, *bablimas* [grapefruit], guavas, melons and sapotas [chikoos], followed by dried fruits like dates, figs and raisins. Also mentioned are plenty of legumes, leeks and green pumpkins.[7]

1 kg pears/green apples
1 kg sugar
Lemon juice to taste
Cardamom powder to taste
Vanilla essence to taste

Remove the skin and cut the fruit into small chunks. In a bowl, mix sugar into the fruit and leave it overnight. Next morning, fill the bowl with enough water to cover the fruit level and boil for two hours. Repeat process every day for five days, until the syrup is thick and reddish in colour. Add lemon juice, cardamom powder and vanilla. Stir, let cool and preserve in clean dry bottle or jar.

Meruba (Made With Red Apples)

1 kg golden or red apples
1 kg sugar
3 tsp lemon juice
Rose water or vanilla essence

Cut apples into small pieces after peeling and coring it. In a bowl, cover the fruit with sugar and leave it overnight to chill in the refrigerator. The next day, using a slotted ladle, remove the fruit pieces from the sugar

---

[7] Katz & Goldberg, *The Last Jews of Cochin*, p. 173.

syrup (the result of the sugar pulling out all water from the fruit). Keep it aside. In a deep pan, bring the sugar syrup to a boil on high heat. Add the fruit pieces along with the lemon juice. Stir. Reduce heat and let the mixture simmer for about 20 minutes. Let cool. Remove the fruit from the syrup and bring it back to boil. Add the fruit bits again and simmer for about 15 minutes. Let cool.

Repeat procedure. You will find the fruit turning brown and becoming translucent after the fourth or fifth time on the stove. Remove the fruit from the syrup and boil it for the last time until syrup thickens and begins to have the look and consistency of honey. Add the fruit bits again and simmer for about 10 minutes. Let cool and add a few drops of rosewater/ or vanilla. Return the apples to the pot and simmer over low heat for another 5 minutes. Store in jars.

Courtesy: Farchy & Gadot families, Houston, Texas.

CHURULLAPPAM/MUTTA KUZHALAPPAM (CREPE WITH COCONUT & JAGGERY)

This is a delightful coconut and sugar-filled crepe-like snack popular with the Cochin Jews. Similar to the *Padhar* of the Bene Israelis of Mumbai, this is also a favourite in Hindu and Christian households in Kerala. The Hindus call this *Motta Paapa* (Egg Delight). In Bengal, a similar sweet is made the same way with thickened milk and without the egg and is called *Patishapta*. Makes 10 crepes.

For the crepes:
250 ml coconut milk
1 large egg
20 ml ghee/clarified butter / coconut oil
30 gms jaggery
Few drops of vanilla extract
A pinch salt/kosher salt

60 gms all-purpose flour or rice flour
For the filling:
100 gms jaggery
Water, as required
300 gms grated coconut (fresh / frozen)
A pinch of cardamom powder

For the Filling:
Melt jaggery, strain and add to the coconut. Add the cardamom powder. Mix well and allow to cool.

For the crepes: Add all ingredients except the flour and whisk till smooth. Add the flour slowly and whisk to make a smooth batter with the consistency of heavy cream. Strain for lumps and set aside for 2 to 3 hours prior to use. Heat a non-stick pan or a cast-iron skillet to medium heat. Use a small ladle to pour about 20 ml batter on the heated pan and rotate the pan to coat the bottom. Once the edges begin to brown, flip and cook till golden brown. Stack between butter papers. Spread 2 to 3 tsp of mixture over each crepe. Roll up or fold, pinching the ends together.

Courtesy: Ajeeth Janardhanan, Executive Chef, The Brunton Boatyard. Fort Kochi, Kerala.

Achappam
(Mildly Sweet, Crispy Rice Rosettes)

Crispy, lightly sweetened, delicate petals of flowers, made of flour and deep fried. This describes the venerable *achappam*, a favourite snack of the Cochin Jews, although it is claimed to be part of their Christmas fare by the Syrian Christian community. It is similar to the Swedish rosettes called *Struva* (which are also made in Norway, with designs ranging from flowers to stars and Santa Clauses). The Kerala *achappams* have only one shape - made with an intricate, flower-shaped, iron mould called *achu*. It is made in large quantities and distributed to friends and neighbours.

1/2 kg rice flour, finely ground
3 eggs
1 cup coconut milk
4 tbsp sugar

1/2 tsp vanilla essence
2 tsp sesame seeds
1 pinch salt
Coconut oil to fry

Makes 20. In a large bowl, combine flour and coconut milk. Beat the eggs in a large bowl until peaks form. Add flour and coconut milk and combine well. Add sugar, vanilla, sesame seeds and salt. Mix well. Heat coconut oil in a deep frying pan or wok on high heat. Immerse the mould in the hot oil. Dip the mould into the batter to cover 3/4 of the ring. Immerse mould again in the oil. Let fry until the batter browns. Push it with a fork or knock the mould gently with a heavy spoon and the *achappam* will slip out into the oil. Fry the other side. With a slotted ladle, remove *achappam* from oil. Drain on paper towel. Repeat until batter is done.

Avalos Unda
(Fried Rice & Coconut Balls)

Popular throughout Kerala among all communities, this is a common evening accompaniment with tea. Made with rice, coconut and sugar - and flavoured with cumin and cardamom, the *avalos unda* or *podi* (the powdered version), can stay fresh for an extended period. It remains popular in Cochini homes in Israel, with brown sugar replacing the jaggery.

Makes 10-12 tennis ball-sized *undas* or 30 golf ball-sized ones.

2 cups coarse rice flour
1 cup grated or desiccated coconut
1/4 tsp cumin seeds
1/4 tsp cardamom powder
2 tbsp water
A pinch of salt
2 tsp ghee
3/4 cup sugar

Mix the coconut and the rice flour well in a bowl. Add salt and cumin seed. Heat a skillet (in Cochin, an earthenware vessel called *chatti* or a bronze vessel called *uruli* was used) and dry roast the mixture. Keep stirring until it takes on a mellow brown colour. Heat jaggery/brown sugar in a pan over medium flame until it liquefies and thickens into a syrup. Add the fried mixture, *ghee* and cardamom powder and mix well. Shape the batter into ping-pong sized balls, while it is still hot. Let cool and store in jars. It stays fresh for a long time.

The powdered version (*avalos podi*) is ready after step two; leaving out the jaggery/sugar and the *ghee*. Sugar or thinly sliced banana is sometimes added when the powder is eaten alone. This is delicious too, with the flavour of roasted coconut and cumin bursting on the taste buds.)

Courtesy: Pearly Simon, Haifa, Israel.

Arikarakal
(Rice & Coconut Crisps)

This is a favourite tea time snack. Makes about 30 crisps.

3 cups rice flour
3 small eggs or 2 large eggs
1 cup sugar
3/4 cup grated coconut
1 tsp baking powder
1 tsp vanilla
100 gms butter/margarine/ ½ cup oil

Mix flour and baking powder with butter/margarine/oil. Add sugar and mix well. Slowly add eggs and knead well. Add vanilla and grated coconut and knead again. Roll dough on flat surface sprinkled with flour with a 1/2" thick rolling pin. Cut into shapes of "8" using a cookie cutter. Pre-heat oven to 150 degree C (300 F) and bake *arikarakal* for 15 minutes. Watch oven to ensure that *arikarakal* does not burn.

Chukunda
(Tiny, Sugared Rice/Coconut Balls)

Shavuot (Pentecost) is the day on which G_d gave the Torah to the Jewish people on Mount Sinai over 3,300 years ago. The Cochinis consider this a very spiritual day, with specific prayers in synagogues, lighting of lamps and special meals. Dairy foods are customary.

Children get special attention on Shavuot. "Before G-d gave the Torah to the Jewish people, He demanded guarantors. The Jews made a number of suggestions, all rejected by G-d, until they declared, "Our children will be our guarantors that we will cherish and observe the Torah." G-d immediately accepted them and agreed to give the Torah."[8]

In Kerala, children were given sweets individually and they also clustered together in the synagogue to enjoy a shower of tiny baked/fried rice balls called *chukunda*.[9] The congregations of Mala, Paravur, Chennamangalam and Ernakulam followed this practice - it has not been recorded as an event in the Paradesi synagogue in Mattancherry.

Makes 80-100 balls.

2 cups grated coconut   *1 1/4 cup sugar*
1 1/2 cups rice   *Coconut oil for frying (optional)*

Soak rice in cold water for about an hour. Drain. Grind the rice to a coarse flour. Dry roast the flour in a deep saucepan. Transfer to bowl. Stir fry the grated coconut. In another pan, on low heat, melt the sugar with a little water. (Don't let it caramelize). Let cool. Add coconut and rice flour to the syrup and mix well. Roll tiny pellet-size balls from the mixture. Fry the pellets in coconut oil in a wok or steam them in a suitable pot.

[8] http://www.chabad.org/library/article_cdo/aid/2151/jewish/The-Role-of-Children.htm
[9] This distribution of sweets in Cochin has also been mentioned by Prof. Sushil Mittal and Prof. Gene Thursby in their book *Religions of South Asia*, Routledge, New York, 2006, p 174

Part III

An Ancient Treasure Chest

Chapter 1

THE SPICE STORY

"He who controls the spice, controls the universe," was the declaration by Baron Vladimir Harkonnen, a villainous character in the 1984 movie *Dune*. The film was based on a novel written by Frank Herbert in 1965. In the story, a special spice is shown as vital for the survival of a great empire and it was essential *"the spice must keep flowing at all times."*[1]

• • • • •

Through the centuries, it was the search for new routes to the spice-rich coasts of Malabar and the East Indies that opened up new worlds to explorers in Europe. The lure of pepper (considered the King of Spices), along with cinnamon and cloves, helped the Portuguese, Spanish, the Dutch and the English establish vast empires from the 15th century onwards, the legacies of which continue even today.

The ancient world talked about Malabar's pepper as one of the most valuable commodities in the world, coveted for its medicinal and culinary qualities and for use in religious practices in the Greco-Roman world. It was also used in the production of perfumes, as incense and to flavour wine.[2] The pharaohs of ancient Egypt were mummified with peppercorns in their nostrils. The Romans exchanged it for gold and writers wove fantasies about the plant. As late as the 14th century, a Franciscan monk named Oderic from Italy visited Malabar and wrote: "(The pepper plant)

---

[1] Herbert, Frank, *Dune*, Chilton Publishing Co., 1965. The novel won the Hugo Award and the Nebula Award for Best Science Fiction in 1966.

[2] Parker Grant, Reviewed work, 'Ex Oriente Luxuria: Indian Commodities and Roman Experience', *Journal of the Economic and Social History of the Orient*, Vol. 45, No. 1 (2002), pp. 40-95. Published by: BRILL Stable URL: http://www.jstor.org/stable/3632707. Accessed: 10/04/2012, p. 45.

grows with numerous bright-looking green leaves and climbs up the trees; the pepper pods hanging down in clusters like grapes."

He wrote an incredible story of a pepper forest: "...crocodiles and huge serpents infest this forest; and in the season of getting the pepper, the people are obliged to make large fires of straw and other dry fuel to drive away these noxious animals."[3]

Riding The Monsoon Winds

An ancient document *Periplus Maris Erythraie* (70 CE), has details about the spice trade and the legendary port of Muziris (known in Malayalam as Muchiri), just off the modern Kerala town of Kodungalloor, at the mouth of the mighty Periyar river.

Periplus credited the discovery of the trade route to the Malabar coast to a Greek navigator named Hippalus (probably 1st century CE), who charted the monsoon winds in the Indian Ocean and mapped the north-south lay of the land on India's west coast. (The Hippalus discovery of the south-west and north-east monsoon winds made the journey from Arabian ports to Malabar possible in 40 days.)[4]

By the time of Pliny the Elder (23-79 CE), pepper had become part of legend. It is said that Alexander the Great introduced the Sanskrit name for pepper - *pippali* - to the Greeek language as *piperi* which then turned into the Arabic *filfil* and Hebrew *pilpel* and later became *pepper* in Europe from the Latin *piper*, coming from ports on the Malabar coast.[5]

Most of the pepper went into the making of food. Marcus Gavius Apicius, who lived in Rome during the reign of Augustus and Tiberius, (30 BCE–37 CE) is credited with writing several gourmet recipes. All the 478 recipes in his book, sometimes attributed to a Caelius Apicius, required spices in various proportions. Nine spices from India are mentioned: pepper, ginger, putchuk (costum - a type of spiral ginger, grown in the Himalayas), folium (nard-leaf), malabathrum (cinnamon leaves or their oil), spikenard (also called muskroot and grown in the Himalayas), asafoetida, sesame seed and turmeric.[6] A document detailing the Apicius recipes, dated 900 CE, was unearthed in the German monastery of Fulda

---

[3] Whitehouse, Rev. Thomas, *Lingerings of Light in a Dark Land: Researches into the Syrian Church of Malabar*, William Brown & Co., London, 1873, p. 5.

4 Vasisth, M.C, "Influence of Monsoon Winds", *Kerala Calling*, Vol. 23, Aug, 2003. A crater on the moon has been named after Hippalus.

[5] Prange, Sebastin R. *Where the Pepper Grows*, SaudiAramcoWorld, Jan-Feb, 2008, pp.10-17.

[6] *Ex Oriente Luxuria: Indian Commodities and Roman Experience*, p. 43.

in the early 20th century and deposited with the New York Academy of Medicine in 1929. It is now part of the academy's Rare Books Collection.[7]

The centre of the world pepper trade was the town of Muziris, described in Pliny's time as *Primum Emporium Indiae*. It was also known in antiquity as Muchiripattanam, Mahodayapuram, Mahadevarpattanam, Makotai, Vanchi, Tiruvanchikulam and later as Cranganore, the first major settlement of the Cochin Jews. The Jews, who belonged to a trade group called Anjuvannam, called the town Shingly (derived perhaps from Changala Azhi, a stream which empties into the Periyar). Today, the town is known as Kodungalloor and remains the mythic capital and historical centre of Kerala.

An ancient Tamil poem refers to Muziris as a "thriving town, where the large and majestic ships of the *Yavanas* [foreigners/Greeks] come bringing gold, splashing the white foam in the waters of the Periyar belonging to the *Cheras* [rulers of Kerala] and return laden with pepper."[8]

Merchants and importers in the Middle East and North Africa dominated the Indian Ocean pepper trade for centuries. In 9th century CE, an Arab traveller Abu'l Qassim Ubaidullah wrote about a Jewish merchant sect called the Radanites that operated on four main trade routes 'partly on land and partly by sea, from the land of the Franks to Sind, Hind ... and China.' In 1948, Rabbi Louis Rabinovitz wrote about these merchants, saying that the Radanites were the only people "who could pass with impunity through the otherwise impenetrable barrier which separated Christianity from Islam. They plied the world by land and sea from Spain to India...".[9]

After a disastrous flood in the late 14th century destroyed the town of Muziris and silted up the Periyar harbour mouth with massive mudbanks, most of the Jews moved southwards to the new harbour town of Cochin and other nearby villages, taking the trade in pepper and other commodities with them. By this time, the prices of spices had become exorbitant and unaffordable even for European elites. By the middle of the 1400s, European royalty felt it was time to act and financed many expeditions

---

[7] *Rebinding of one of the World's Oldest Cookbooks is Completed*: http://www.nyam.org/news/press-releases/2006/2690.html

[8] *Agananuru* is a collection of works by 145 poets, written between 600 BCE and 300 BCE.

[9] Cited by Katz & Goldberg, *The Last Jews of Cochin*, p. 35. (Rabbi Rabinovitz was deputy editor-in-chief of *Encyclopaedia Judaica* and deputy mayor of Jerusalem in the late 1970's.)

to 'discover' India that changed the face of world trade and tilted political and economic power to the Western hemisphere. The Portuguese, led by Vasco Da Gama, landed in Calicut in 1498, followed by the Dutch and the English who set up pepper and other spice factories in various places in Malabar. The French landed on the eastern coast of India.

The Dutch era in Cochin was a 'golden age' for Jewish merchants. One of the wealthiest families at the time was the Rahabis, headed by Ezekiel II, who was a shipping magnate and had "sloops by such names as *Rachel, Daniel, Ashkalon* and *Jerusalem*, emblazoned with the Star of David, [that] plied the pirate-infested seas along the Indian coast, from Sumatra to Muscat and from Colombo to Mocha."[10] The Ezekiel family also owned scores of country boats in the Periyar river and along the coastline carrying cargoes of rice, coconut and other products.

The Spice Route Project

The Kerala Government has launched an ambitious Spice Route Project, centred around Kodungalloor. In February 2011, Kerala approached the UNESCO to get the 'Heritage' tag for the project, arguing that the Spice Route was as important a link in intercontinental trade as the Trans-Asian Silk Route.[11] The 'Spice Route' Project links the Muziris Heritage Project of the government to nearby areas of the erstwhile Kingdom of Cochin, which was the hub of India's spice trade; and remains so even today. The World Pepper Exchange and the Indian Spice Board are headquartered in Cochin, in the heart of the old Jewish settlement.[12] The Mattancherry area is always thick with the fragrance of spices and visitors can see warehouses packed with jute bags of dried ginger, cardamom, cloves, cinnamon, pepper, dried red chillies, nutmeg and turmeric.

Although pepper is grown elsewhere in the world today, the two most desirable varieties remain the ones from Kerala: the Malabar Black and the Tellicherry.

As part of the Muziris project, the synagogues at Chennamangalam and Paravur have been refurbished and converted into museums to reflect the Jewish heritage of the settlements. As one of the characters in Salman Rushdie's novel *The Moor's Last Sigh*, says: "...the pepper if your

---

[10] Parasuram, T.V. *India's Jewish Heritage*, p 42. Cited by Katz & Goldberg, *The Last Jews of Cochin*, p. 95.

[11] *Heritage Tag for Spice Route: Kerala Approaches Unesco* - http://news.outlookindia.com/items.aspx?artid=711456

[12] The Jewish family of the Rahabis were the main pepper agents during the colonial era.

please; From the beginning, what the world wanted from bloody mother India was daylight-clear,' she'd say. 'They came for the hot stuff, just like any man calling on a tart."[13]

Cardamom, the other 'golden spice' was traded from Malabar ports to the Arabian kingdoms 2000 years ago, although Guatemala has now emerged as the top producer. However, the Malabar cardamom - the original one - remains the choice of the world's chefs.

Spice Trade In United States

In the United States, Salem in Massachusetts was the major pepper city, with one of its sons, Elihu Yale[14] making his fortune from his personal trade in pepper in the 1650s while he was the East India Company Governor in Madras (now Chennai) in India. (The Malabar region was at that time part of the Madras Presidency of the British Indian Empire.) The Salem pepper trade continued until 1806.[15]

Most of the pepper imported into Salem from India and Sumatra were re-exported to European ports like Stockholm, Gothenburg, Hamburg, Copenhagen and Antwerp or to Philadelphia, Boston, and Baltimore for local American distribution. In 1806, one single consignment of five hundred tons of pepper was valued at over one million pounds sterling - brought from Sumatra to Salem by the sailing ship Eliza.[16] The Salem pepper trade also produced some of America's first millionaires.

In New Haven, Connecticut, a college was re-named in Elihu Yale's honour, in gratitude for his financial support in the early 18th century. (The college was originally chartered as the Collegiate School with the intention of training political and religious leaders.). That college is today's Yale University. (Note: Elihu Yale was not Jewish, contrary to what many people believe.) - *Bala Menon*.

---

[13] Salman Rushdie, *The Moor's Last Sigh*, Jonathan Cape, London, 1995), pp. 4-5.

[14] *The Old Foodie blog* - http://www.theoldfoodie.com/2006/11/salem-pepper.html

[15] *Encyclopædia Britannica*. Retrieved from http://www.britannica.com/EBchecked/topic/651366/Elihu-Yale

[16] F. Rosengarten, Jr. 1969. *The Book Of Spices,* Jove Publ., Inc., New York. pp 23-96

Chapter 2

Game-Changers In The Cochini Kitchen

"Fire burn, and cauldron bubble."[1]

Kerala's unique plant wealth and their properties were first compiled and printed by Hendrik Adriaan van Rheede, the Dutch Governor of Cochin from 1678 to 1693. *Hortus Malabaricus* (The Garden of Malabar) is a treatise which took Van Rheede more than 30 years to complete with the assistance of physicians practising the local systems of medicine. Originally written in Latin, it was published in 12 volumes of 200 pages each in Amsterdam during his lifetime and contain about 800 copper plate engravings of Malabar flora.[2] The habit, foliage, fruits, colour, smell, taste and practical value of all the great spices are also described in detail.

The books were translated into English only in 2003, after 35 years of painstaking work by distinguished Kerala scholar K. S. Manilal and published by the University of Kerala, in Trivandrum.[3]

---

[1] Shakespeare, William, *Macbeth*, Act 4, Scene 1.

[2] Tot Draakenstein, Van Rheede Adriaan Hendrik, *Hortus Malabaricus, continens Regni Malabarici apud Indos celeberrimi omnis generis Plantas rariores or Horti Malabarici pars prima, de varii generis Arboribus et Fruticibus Siliquosis.* Amsterdam, 1678-1693.

[3] Mohan Ram H.Y., *On the English edition of Van Rheede's Hortus Malabaricus by K. S. Manilal (2003)*, Current Science, Vol. 89, No. 10, November 2005, pp. 1672-1680. The Malayalam translation was released by the University in 2008.

Anise seeds

Anise is sweet and aromatic and the seeds are used powdered or whole in Indian regional cuisine. It is similar to the fennel in taste and goes well in meat dishes and baked goods.

Asafoetida

Known as *kaayam* in Malayalam and *hing* in Hindi, this is a gum tapped from a plant called *Ferula foetida*. As the name indicates, it is the smell of the spice that causes it also to be called Devil's dung. However, when heated with lentils or toasted in ghee or oil, it gives off an enticing aroma. It is available in powdered form or as small, firm jellies.

Bay Leaves

Bay leaves (*Laurus nobilis, Lauraceae*) are used either fresh or dried in cooking for their mild flavor and fragrance. The leaves are ideal in soups, stews and festive rice dishes and tastes a little similar to oregano. In Kerala, it is conspicuous in *biryanis* and is a primary ingredient in the *garam masala* spice mix.

Cardamom

Guatemala is today the major producer of cardamom, but it was not always so. The spice arrived in that country only in the 20th century and the cardamom that grows there is the *Elettaria cardamomum*, a native plant from Kerala's Malabar coast. If pepper is King, cardamom is considered the Queen of spices. The pungent and aromatic seeds were first taken to the west by Alexander the Great and later in the Middle Ages after the Crusades. Cardamom is a revered spice in the Arab world, with Saudi Arabia the world's biggest consumer. Generous quantities of powdered cardamom is mixed with coffee (*Al-Qahwa*) and is a popular drink in all the Persian Gulf kingdoms. The Alleppey Green variety of cardamom from Kerala is rated the best grade of the spice.

Cashew Nuts

Cashew is the edible kernel of *ancacardium occidentale*, an evergreen discovered by Spanish explorers in the Tupi-Indian region of Northern Brazil. The natives called it *acaju*. The Portuguese brought the fruit to the west coast of India, where it is today grown in commercial quantities in Kerala and Goa. The nut is a favoured ingredient in Kerala cuisine, while the fruit is made into a heady liquor called *feni* in Goa.

Chillies

India is the largest producer and consumer of red and green chillies. The attractive red chillies are dried and the powder used as a heat-producer and colouring agent in all regional cuisines of India.

Cinammon/Cassia

Cinnamon is a spice dating to more than two millennia. Obtained from the bark of *Cinnamomum* family of trees, the spice has been mentioned several times in the Hebrew Bible: Moses is ordered to use sweet cinnamon and cassia in the anointing oil; Proverbs talk of cinnamon used to perfume a lover's bed; a song in Song of Solomon describes cinnamon being used to make his lover's dresses smell good. Cassia is also obtained from the bark of a tree and is sometimes substituted for cinnamon. The best cinnamon comes from Sri Lanka. In Kerala, it is used as an accent spice in cakes, sweets, rice, meat dishes and stews.

Cloves

Cloves are the strong-flavoured dried buds of a tree native to Indonesia. It is today grown mainly in Indonesia, India, Madagascar, Zanzibar (*Island of Cloves*), Pakistan and Sri Lanka. The name come from the Latin *clavus* 'nail', because the spice resembles a nail. In Kerala, it is a part of all meat and some rice dishes, and valued for its aroma.

Coconut Milk

Coconut milk, contrary to what is generally believed, is not the liquid found inside the coconut. That is sweet coconut water (a refreshing drink on its own!). Coconut milk is made from the freshly grated flesh of coconuts. The thick, creamy version of coconut milk is obtained by mixing one full grated coconut to some 250 ml of boiled and cooled water and squeezing out the liquid in a hand press or wringing it through a piece of sterile muslin/

cheesecloth. This milk has a high fat content and is rich-tasting. Second and third squeezings - after being soaked in warm water - will provide thinner, less creamier and less sweeter versions. All three are used in the Cochini Jewish kitchen. Coconut cream is what floats to the surface, when the coconut milk is refrigerated. (Note: It has been argued that Kerala gets its name from the word *kera*, meaning coconut in Sanskrit and *alam*, meaning land in Tamil. Hence Kerala, *Land of Coconuts.*)

CORIANDER

Coriander or cilantro is a fragrant leaf used for flavouring sauces and gravies and as a garnish in salads and meat dishes. The dried seeds of the plant have a mild citrus taste when crushed and is used generously in Keralan cuisine to add a distinct flavour to sauces. *See also page 39.*

CUMIN

Cumin has been mentioned in the Bible (Isaiah 28:25-27).[4] This is a warm spice, with a strong flavour, somewhat similar to caraway. The spice is essential for curries, curry powder and savoury dishes and is roasted whole or powdered before use. Cumin is the seed of a plant belonging to the parsley family and is native to the Mediterranean countries and across India. In Kerala, cumin is called *jeera* and is a treasured item in the kitchen.

CURRY LEAVES

The heady aroma and the distinct taste of Keralan dishes come from the leaves of the *Murraya Koenigi* plant, known to us as 'curry leaves'. These leaves floating in our gravies interact with other spices like mustard and chillies, to create a unique fragrance.

The leaf is known by many names - *kariapak, katneem* or *meethi neem* in north India and by other names across South East Asia. In Kerala, it is called *kari veppilla*. (*Vepu* means *neem* in Malayalam. The Neem tree is hailed in India for its medicinal properties.) The plant belongs to the *Rutaceae* family, and the leaves must be used fresh and sizzled in *ghee*/coconut oil for ideal results.

[4] See page 151, *Cumin Water*.

FENNEL

Fennel seeds are crunchy and its licorice-like sweetness is valued in some Cochini meat dishes and *biryanis*. When roasted, it turns aromatic and is considered a potent digestive and breath freshener. The seed is mentioned in Greek mythology in relation to Dionysius, the Greed god of food and wine. The popular liqueur *absinthe* uses fennel seeds and anise as major ingredients.

FENUGREEK

India is the world's largest producer of fenugreek. Like many other spices, fenugreek is an ancient spice and has been mentioned by Hippocrates and Pliny for its medical benefits. Fenugreek seeds have been found by archaeologists in the tomb of Egyptian Pharaoh Tutankhamun.

In northern India the, fresh and dried leaves of the fenugreek plant is used as a vegetable and herb, while in the south, the cuboid seeds are used as a spice. The seeds lose their bitterness when roasted and provide a refreshing crunchiness in certain dishes. Fenugreek sauce is a favourite of Yemeni Jews. It the West, it is used as an agent to simulate maple syrup and butterscotch flavours.

GARLIC

Garlic - *Allium sativum* - belongs to the onion family and has been used in cooking for thousands of years. It is a staple seasoning throughout the world, because of its exuberance and its ability to transfer its succulent flavour to dishes it is cooked in. Garlic loses its pungency when cooked, adding a little sweetness to gravies. In Kerala, it is grown in the high ranges of the Western Ghats.

GHEE/CLARIFIED BUTTER

Ghee (clarified or rendered butter, *hemma meomasath* in Hebrew, *neyyu* in Malayalam, *samnah* in Arabic) is deeply embedded in the Indian psyche, related as it is to the Hindu religion through its extensive use in temples and every regional cuisine in the country. In Kerala, along with coconut oil, it is the favoured medium for cooking. International chefs are now opting for *ghee* for frying and sautéing food because of the rich, buttery flavour it imparts to all items. *Ghee* is pure butter fat, with no milk solids and can be heated to higher temperatures than other oils without burning. *Ghee* has another big advantage over butter: it can be stored for long periods without refrigeration and will not easily oxidize.

Many Cochin Jewish dishes use *ghee* - as a base or as a drizzle over prepared dishes.

Ghee is also very easy to make! Simmer unsalted butter in a saucepan over low heat. When all the water boils off you will find the protein solids settling at the bottom. Pour out the golden liquid at the top without disturbing the milk solids. You have your *ghee*!

If you want the ghee to have a wonderful, nutty flavour, let the liquid boil for some more time until the solids at the bottom turn brown.

Half a kg (500 gms) of unsalted supermarket butter yields about 1 1/2 cups of *ghee*. Ghee from cow's milk, which is yellow in colour, is considered the best for cooking.

In the Indian Ayurvedic system of medicine, *ghee* is aged to become potent health tonics. The *Kumbhiighrta ghee* is aged between 10 and 90 years while the *Mahaghrta ghee* is aged more than 100 years, with traditional physicians preserving it through generations.

Ginger

Ginger or ginger root comes from *Zingiber officinale* plant. Known as *Inji* or *inji ver* in Malayalam, it is used in every kind of vegetable and meat preparations in Kerala, and is among the first ingredient to be fried in oil before the actual cooking begins. India is the world's largest producer of ginger, with Kerala the main exporter of the dried variety called *chukku*.

(*Chukku* is traditionally used to make a refreshing cup of coffee and is a major ingredient in the Ayurveda medical system. It is also added to some puddings). The Cochin and Calicut varieties of dried ginger are reputed to be the best in the world. Ginger is considered a potent item in treating minor stomach and intestinal problems.

Jaggery

Jaggery (called *sharkkara* or *vellum* in Malayalam and *gur* in Hindi) is unrefined cane sugar in which the molasses are not separated. Ranging from golden brown to dark brown in colour, it is used in several traditional recipes in Kerala and across India. It is available in South Asian stores in large, rough chunks or in moulded cube forms. In Latin America, it goes by the name of *panela*.

Kokum (Garcinia Indica)

Kokum (Garcinia Indica) also belongs to the same Mangosteen family as the Kudampuli, but it is dark red to purple in colour. *Kokum* is used mostly in coastal Maharashtrian and Konkan cooking (and by the Bene Israelis).

Kudampuli/Gambooge

Kudampuli (scientific name: Garcinia cambogia) is also known as Gambooge or Malabar Tamarind and is the favoured souring agent in Cochini Jewish fish dishes. The fruit is yellow when ripe, but shrivels and blackens when dried in the sun. Rubbed with a mixture of salt and oil, the fruit can be preserved for a long time. The shrivelled bits are broken and soaked in water before adding both the water and the bits into fish dishes. *Kudampuli* is reputed to have digestive properties. It is sometimes mistaken for *Kokum*, although one cannot be substituted for the other.

Mustard seeds

Mustard seeds are small, round seeds from the mustard plant. In northern India, the plant is eaten as a vegetable, while in Kerala, it is the brown mustard seed that is used in practically every dish. When popped in coconut oil or ghee, it releases a delicious nutty flavor that complements ginger and other spices roasted in the same pan.

A 16th century mystic, Rabbi Moshe Cordovero of Safed, Israel, once compared the universe to the size of a mustard seed. "I am a mustard seed in the middle of the sphere of the moon, which itself is a mustard seed within the next sphere. So it is with that sphere and all it contains in relation to the next sphere. So it is with all the spheres - one inside the other

- and all of them are a mustard seed within the further expanses".[5] Jewish philosopher Nahmanides also mentions the mustard seed, saying that the universe "expanded from the time of its creation, in which it was the size of a mustard seed."[6]

NUTMEG & MACE

Nutmeg is a spice native to Indonesia. Nutmeg is the 'nut', of the *myristica* plant which also grows well in Kerala, while mace is the lacy covering of the nut. With a delicate and warm aroma, both spices are used in sweet and savoury dishes. In the Western world, nutmeg is necessary for making the béchamel sauces. Mace is best used when freshly ground.

PEPPER

The pepper plant or *piper nigrum* is native to Malabar and found in the compound of every home. The perennial vine yields the peppercorn berry. Black, white and red peppercorns come from the same plant; the colours depend on the way the berry is processed. Young green peppercorns, when dried in the sun, become black pepper; when they ripen on the plant they turn bright red to be sold as red peppercorns; when red peppercorns are soaked in water and skins removed, they become white peppercorns. The active ingredients in pepper are pungent alkaloids called *piperine* and *piperazine*. "Today, pepper is cultivated in many parts of the world ... Yet, the flavor of pepper, like many other spices, varies with the environment in which it grows, so Malabar pepper is still prized by chefs and gourmets."[7]

POPPY SEEDS

Although the poppy seeds come from the opium plant, the seeds do not contain any opiates. They are highly nutritious and the seeds

[5] Cited in website: http://learnkabbalah.com/the_meaning_of_god/

[6] Schroeder, Gerald Dr. Age of the Universe. http://www.aish.com/ci/sam/48951136.html. Nahminides was the name of Rabbi Moses ben Nahman Girondi, a Spanish scholar and kabbalist of the 13th century.

[7] Spudich, Annama, *Pepper rides the monsoon*, Cobblestone Publishing, 2006.

are added to meat gravies in Kerala, especially in the northern part of the state, to make them richer and thicker. In northern India, they are mixed with dough to make breads. Sometimes, they are substituted for sesame seeds.

SAFFRON

Saffron or *zafran* is an ancient spice derived from the flower of a plant known as *Crocus sativus*, the saffron crocus, which originated in Greece. Crocus is a genus in the *Iridaceae* plant family and the dried stalks and stigmas (which contain a carotenoid golden-yellow dye called *crocin*) are used as a seasoning and colouring agent. Saffron is one of the world's most expensive spices by weight. Iran produces almost 90 per cent of the world's saffron.

SESAME SEEDS

Sesame seeds are valued because of their heavy oil content and their ability to add texture and crunchiness to specific foods. Both sesame oil and sesame seeds are used widely in Keralan cooking, in savouries and sweet dishes. The seeds come from the *sesame indicum* plant, widely grown in India and which remains the world's largest producer and exporter. There is also a popular brittle in Kerala made with sesame seeds and jaggery called 'Ellunda' (*ellu* is sesame in Malayalam).

SHALLOTS

The name 'shallot' is said to have come from the ancient Philistine city of Ashkelon of Greek times (covering the areas of modern day Gaza, Ashkelon, Ashdod, Ekron and Gat). It is grown widely in India and is popular in southern Indian dishes, especially all-time favourite curries like the *sambhar and* in a variety of *chutneys* and dips. Shallots have a sweeter taste than the ordinary onion. Indian names for shallots include *kanda* or *gandana* or *pyaaz* and *kunjulli/cheriya ulli/chuvanna ulli* in Malayalam. Scallions or green onions and pearl onions can be substituted for shallots in many dishes.

TAMARIND

Tamarind is the reddish-brown pulp from the pod of the tamarind tree (*Tamarindus indica*). Believed to have originated in Sudan, the

Game-Changers In The Cochini Kitchen

tree is now grown throughout the tropical belt. In Kerala, almost every home boasts a tamarind tree.

Tamarind Sauce

Soak about 30 gms of dried tamarind in a cup of hot water for about 10 minutes. Allow to cool and squeeze pulp as dry as possible. The flavoured water is used in curries and when sweetened and thickened, it becomes a delicious dip.

Turmeric

Turmeric is a yellowish/orange root that gives colour to Cochin Jewish dishes. The root adds warmth, flavour and an attractive tinge to food and is grown in the foothills of Kerala. Also known as "Indian Saffron", turmeric finds many uses in traditional Indian medicine. Part of the ginger family, the turmeric root is dried and ground to a powder called *manjalpodi* (Malayalam - yellow powder), before it becomes an essential ingredient of the 'kari'.

• • • • •

The other magic ingredients in the Cochini Jewish kitchen include: yogurt, lemon juice, mint and allspice.

• • • • •

The Blends

When spices are blended together, they are known as *masalas*. The combination, the quantity of each ingredient and the roasting time contribute to the zest and aroma of the *masalas*; the cook must ensure that spices complement each other, not compete. *Masalas* can be either dry or wet.

Biryani Masala

(See recipe on page 99.)

2" cinnamon	1 tsp crushed cloves
4 tbsp coriander seeds	1 tsp cardamom powder
2 tbsp cumin seeds	2 tsp red chilli powder
2 tsp fennel seeds	1/3 tsp nutmeg
2 bay leaves	
1 tsp ground pepper	

Garam Masala

Stir fry all the spices in a dry, hot wok for about 3 to 4 minutes until fragrant and the ingredients start to brown. In a food processor, grind the spices into smooth powder. Use sparingly in chicken and other meat dishes.

Cochin Masala Marinade

2 tsp chilli powder	paste
1/2 tsp turmeric powder	Juice of 2 lemons (vinegar preferred for meat dishes)
3 tbsp coriander powder	10 tsp oil
1 tsp, pepper, crushed	Salt
2 tsp ginger and garlic	

Mix all ingredients in 1/3 cup cold water to make a smooth paste.

Sambhar Powder

The *sambhar* powder is also used in the making of *rasam*, a light, spicy broth made with lentils.

12 dry red chillies	1/2 tsp cumin seeds
1 tsp of whole black pepper	1/4 tsp fenugreek seeds
3 tbsp coriander seeds	1/2 tsp coconut oil

Heat the oil in a wok, on medium flame, and roast coriander seeds until fragrant. Add fenugreek seeds, cumin seeds, crumbled dry chillies and keep roasting until the coriander seeds turn a dark brown. Let cool and grind to a smooth powder in a food processor. In a different version, split yellow lentils, split chickpeas, turmeric powder and asafoetida are also added to the wok for roasting.

Dosa/Idli Powder

2" cinnamon	powder
4 tbsp coriander seeds	1 sprig curry leaves
2 tbsp cumin	Salt, as needed
3 tbsp black gram dhal	2 tsp fennel seeds
3 tbsp split chick peas	2 bay leaves
2 tbsp coriander powder	1 tsp ground pepper
2 tbsp rice	1 tsp crushed cloves
1 tbsp red chilli powder	1 tsp cardamom powder
1/4 tsp asafoetida	1 tsp red chilli powder
	1/3 tsp nutmeg

In a heated wok, roast the *dhal*, chickpeas and rice until the ingredients begin to brown. Add the coriander powder, chilli powder, chopped curry leaves, asafoetida and roast for another 3 minutes. Cool and grind to a coarse powder. When serving, drizzle a tsp of coconut oil or melted ghee over powder and serve with *dosas/idlis*.

BIBLIOGRAPHY

Banerji, Chitrita. *Eating India: Exploring a Nation's Cuisine*. New Delhi, Penguin, 2007.
Berkovitz , Gila. *The New Jewish Cuisine*, New York, Doubleday, 1986.
Buchanan , Claudius. *The Works of the Rev. Claudius Buchanan, Comprising his Christian Researches in Asia,* Whiting and Watson, New York, 1812.
Cassel's Dictionary of Cookery, Cassell Petter & Galpin, London, 1870.
Chawla, Singh Maina. *Being Indian, Being Israeli: Migration, Ethnicity and Gender in the Jewish Homeland*, Manohar, New Delhi, 2010.
Daniel, Ruby & Johnson, Barbara. *Ruby of Cochin. An Indian Jewish Woman Remembers*, Jewish Publication Society, Philadelphia, 2002.
Encyclopædia Britannica. http://www.britannica.com/
Fischel, Walter J. 'The Exploration of the Jewish Antiquities of Cochin on the Malabar Coast', *Journal of the American Oriental Society*, Vol. 87, No. 3 (Jul. - Sep., 1967), pp. 230-248 Published by: American Oriental Society. Stable URL: http://www.jstor.org/stable/597717. Accessed: 01/02/2011 23:09
Gamliel, Ophira. *Jewish Malayalam Women's Songs,* PhD dissertation, Hebrew University of Jerusalem, Jerusalem, 2009.
Johnson, Barbara C. *Shingly or Jewish Cranganore in the traditions of the Cochin Jews*, with an Appendix on the Cochin Jewish Chronicles. MA thesis, Smith College, 1975.
Johnson, Barbara C. *Our Community in Two Worlds: The Cochin Paradesi Jews in India and Israel*, PhD dissertation, University of Mass., 1985.
Johnson, Barbara & Zacharia, Scaria. *Oh, Lovely Parrot, Jewish Women's Songs from Kerala*, The Jewish Music Research Centre, Hebrew University of Jerusalem, Jerusalem, 2004.
Jussay, P.M. *The Jews of Kerala*, University of Calicut, Kozhikode, 2005.
Katz, Nathan & Goldberg, Ellen S. *Asceticism and Caste in the Passover Observances of the Cochin Jews*, Journal of the American Academy of Religion. LVII/l, Stable URL: http://www.jstor.org/stable/4467074. Accessed: 24/03/2010 15:08

——— *Kashrut, Caste, and Kabbalah:The Religious Life of the Jews of Cochin*, Manohar Publishers & Distributors, New Delhi, 2005.
——— *The Last Jews of Cochin: Jewish Identity in Hindu India*, Columbia, SC: University of South Carolina Press, 1993.
Lehman-Wilzig, Tami. *Passover Around The World,* Lerner Publishing (Kar-Ben), Minneapolis. US. 2007
Leonard, Leah W. *Jewish Cookery*, Crown Publishers, New York, 1949.
Mandelbaum. David G. *The Jewish Way of Life in Cochin,* Source: Jewish Social Studies, Vol. 1, No. 4 (Oct., 1939), pp. 423-460, Published by: Indiana University Press. Stable URL: http://www.jstor.org/stable/4464305.
Mendelssohn, Sidney. *The Jews of Asia, Especially in the Sixteenth and Seventeenth Centuries,* Kegan Paul, Trench, Trubner & Co., Ltd. New York : E. P. Dutton &Amp; Co., 1920.
Menon, Sreedhara A. *A Survey of Kerala History*, DC Books, Kottayam, 2008.
Montefiore, Cohen Judith. *The Jewish Manual*, London, 1846. The Project Gutenberg EBook #12327.
Nandi, Ashish. *Time Warps*, Rutgers University Press, New Brunswick, New Jersey, 2002.
Narayanan, M.G.S. *Cultural Symbiosis in Kerala*, Kerala Historical Society, Trivandrum, 1972.
Parker Grant. Reviewed work, *Ex Oriente Luxuria: Indian Commodities and Roman Experience,* Source: Journal of the Economic and Social History of the Orient, Vol. 45, No. 1 (2002), pp.40-95. BRILL Stable URL: http://www.jstor.org/stable/3632707. Accessed: 10/04/2012
Prange, Sebastin R. 'Where the Pepper Grows', *SaudiAramcoWorld*, Jan-Feb, 2008.
Roland, Joan G. *Jews in British India: Identity in a Colonial Era*, Hanover, NH: University Press of New England, 1989.
Roland, Joan G. *The Jews of India: Communal Survival or the End of a Sojourn?*, Jewish Social Studies, Vol. 42, No. 1 (Winter, 1980), pp. 75-90, Indiana University Press.
Rushdie Salman. *The Moor's Last Sigh,* London, Jonathan Cape, 1995).
Sahni Julie. *Indo-Jewish cuisine dates back 22 centuries*, The Gazette, Montreal, March 27, 1991. Syndicated -Los Angeles Times. http://proquest.umi.com.ezproxy.torontopubliclibrary.ca/pqdlink? did=165128271&Fmt=3&clientId=1525&RQT=309&VName=PQD
Segal, J. B. *A History of the Jews of Cochin*, London, Vallentine Mitchell, 1993.
Spudich, Annamma. *Pepper rides the monsoon.* Calliope. Cobblestone Publishing, a division of Carus Publishing Company. 2006. HighBeam Research. 29 Dec. 2009 <http://www.high beam.com>
The Scribe (Journal of Babylonian Jewry), London. Online archives.
Tsuji Shizuo. *Japanese Cooking, A Simple Art*, Kodansha USA, Inc. New York, 2011.
Ulyseas, Mark. 'Jews in God's Own Country'. Special Report, *Live Encounters*, September, 2011. - http://issuu.com/liveencounters/docs/september2011
Whitehouse, Thomas Rev. *Lingerings of Light in a Dark Land: Researches into the Syrian Church of Malabar*, William Brown & Co., London, 1873.

Index

SO, WHAT'S FOR BREAKFAST?
  Crepe with side dish,
    Polappam & Chikkiyathu , 34
  Everyday breakfast *dosa,* 31
  Fluffed, spiced semolina,
    Upma (Uppumavu), 36
  Masala *dosa,* 32
  Plain *(blintz) dosa,* 31
  Rice crepes,
    Palappam/Vellayappam, 29
  Rice fritters, *Appam,* 28
  Rice flour steamed in coconut shell,
    Cheratta puttu, 35
  Steamed appam,
    Pongiya appam, 30
  Steamed rice cakes, *Idlis,* 36
  Spicy crepes, *Pongalam,* 33
  String hoppers, *Idiyappam,* 28
  Toddy pancake, *Kallappam,* 37

BOUNTIES FROM THE NETS
  Cochin fish curry with *pomfret,* 42
  Cochin Jewish fish curry with
    coconut milk, 48
  Cochin Jewish fish kofta curry,
    Meen unda kari, 45
  Cochin Jewish green fish curry, 39
  Coconut-laced fish, *Meen peera,* 49
  Cochin tuna salad, 55

Dried Malabar sole curry,
  Nangu/Manthal kari, 57
Fish, eggplant & coconut milk
  casserole, 49
Fish patties/cutlets, *Meen undas,* 46
Fish fillets in vegetable sauce,
  Meen varuthu vechathu, 43
Fish salad with tomatoes
  & coconut milk, 48
Fish with coconut milk & shallots, 54
Fish with ginger, coconut & onion,
  Meen inji ulli, 53
Fried fish, *Meen varuthathu,* 50
Fried fish in coconut milk &
  tomato sauce, *Meen pollichathu,* 51
Fried, salted fish,
  Unakka meen varuthathu, 56
Green fish curry in coconut milk, 41
Pan-fried fish with shallots,
  Chuttulli meen, 44
Salmon miso, 52
Sardines & Chinese potatoes,
  Chaala & koorka salad, 47
Simple sardine curry, 53

POULTRY IN THE POT
  Capsicum chicken,
    Mulagirachi, 65
  Chicken in cashew nut sauce, 59

Index

Chicken in rich coconut sauce,
    Kozhi Varuthu Arachathu, 60
Chicken in thick gravy,
    Kozhi Pollichathu, 60
Chicken with Chinese potatoes,
    Kurkirachi, 64
Chicken with vegetables,
    Kozhi puzhungiathu, 63
Cochin chicken curry, 61
Cochin Jewish chicken soup,
    Marak oaf, 68
Cochin Jewish chicken roast, 58
Cochin spicy chicken, 63
Coriander fried chicken,
    Malli varutharacha kozhi, 67
Dry chilli chicken roast,
    Erachi olathiyathu, 66
Green chilli chicken, 66
Minty carrot chicken, 62

EGG
Eggs in rich onion sauce,
    Mutta kari, 68
Sweet egg yolk strings,
    Motta salada, 169

KUBBAH, YOU DELIGHTFUL DUMPLINGS!
Cochin *kofta* dumplings in gravy,
    Kubbah, 73
Fried *kofta* balls,
    Kubbah varuthathu, 72
Kofta soup, *Kubbah Hamidh,* 74

LURE OF THE PASTELS
Classic tuna *pastel,* 79
Cochin *pastel,* 77
Kadathala *pastel,* 76
Rachel Roby's baked
    cheese *burekas,* 79
Sarah Tovachi Elias's
    chicken *pastel,* 78

HERE'S THE BEEF, ALTHOUGH IT'S RARE!
Beef cutlets, 87
Beef fry/chilli beef roast,
    Beef olathiyathu, 86
Beef stewed in rich sauce, *Ispethi,* 82
Beef with Chinese potatoes,
    Kurkirachi, 87
Curry style beef stew,
    Ispethi kari-style, 82
Red beef curry, *Elaggal,* 85

LAMB/MUTTON
Cochin lamb chops,
    Attirachi varattiyathu, 91
Cochin lamb soup, 91
Fried lamb dish, *Chuttirachi,* 89
Lamb in coriander sauce,
    Malli aracha attirachi, 88
Lamb with vegetables,
    Attirachiyum pachakariyum, 90

RICE IS NICE!
Biryani, Arabic style, *Majboos,* 100
Cochin coconut rice,
    Thenga chor, 94
Cochin Jewish *biryani,* 98
Cochin Shabbat dish,
    Hamin/cholent, 102
Cochin spiced rice, 96
Coconut rice with coconut milk, 96
Coconut rice with shallots, fennel
    & fenugreek, 95
Rice with turmeric & coconut milk,
    Resaya pulav, 97
Rice porridge with beans,
    Kanji & payar, 103

THE BREAD BASKET
Classic *challah,* 106
Flaky flatbread, *Porotta,* 108
Fried flatbreads, *Puris,* 107
Matzah ball soup, 108
Matzah bread, 107
Shabbat bread, *Homotzi/rotti,* 105
Unleavened bread & drink,
    Indari appam & Pesaha paal, 110
Wheat flatbread, *Chappati,* 109

OUR VEGETABLE GARDEN
Classic lentils & shallots curry,
    Sambhar, 112
Cochin pineapple curry, 115

Cochin Jewish vegetable stew, 121
Cochin tapioca/cassava, 123
Curried lentils, *Paripppu,* 113
Devilled okra,
   Olathiya vendakkai, 118
Mango in coconut & yogurt sauce,
   Mambaza kaalan, 116
Melon in coconut milk sauce,
   Olan, 125
Mixed vegetables in rich coconut &
   yogurt sauce, *Avial,* 124
Okra in coconut milk, 118
Pineapple in yogurt sauce,
   Pineapple pachadi, 114
Spicy Cochin okra, 117
Stir-fried cabbage,
   Motakoose thoran, 120
Stir-fried Chinese potatoes,
   Koorka varatti, 118
Stir-fried string beans,
   Payaru thoran, 120
Stir-fried raw banana,
   Kaaya thoran, 121
Stir-fried vegetables,
   Unakki vevichathu, 119

BLEND OF SPICES
Biryani masala, 99
Cochin *masala* marinade, 201
Curry powder, 135
Dosa/Idli powder, 201
Garam masala, 201
Sambhar powder, 201

CHUTNEYS & SALADS
Cochin cabbage salad, 132
Cochin cucumber salad, 129
Cochin Jewish pineapple salad, 131
Cochin Jewish salad dressing, 135
Coconut & coriander chutney, 127
Coriander chutney (variant), 128
Cucumber salad, *Tarator,* 134
Date sauce, 136
Fruit salad, *Queenie Aunty's,* 134
Ginger & yogurt dip, *Inji Thairu,* 136
Ground coconut chutney,
   Thenga chamanthi, 128
Ground lentils chutney,
   *Parippu chamanthi,*136
Hulba dip for pastel, 77
Mango chutney,
   Manga chamanthi, 127
Native potato salad,
   Koorka sambola, 132
Onion salad with vinegar or yogurt,
   Ulli sarlas, 131
Plain salad, *Pulip,* 131
Plain *pulip* (variant), 132
Pomegranate salad, 133
Shallots chutney, *Ulli chamanthi,* 129
Spicy pineapple salad, 130
Toasted mango salad, 130
Yogurt & cucumber sauce, 135

PICKLES & PRESERVES
Etrog jam, 141
Etrog pickle, *Nerthanga achaar,* 141
Fish pickle, *Meen achaar,* 137
Guava jam, 142
Jack fruit jam,
   Chakka varattiyathu, 142
Lime pickle,
   Cherunaranga achaar, 140
Tamarind & ginger pickle, *Puli Inji,* 138
Tender mango pickle,
   Kannimanga achaar, 139

WINE & OTHER DRINKS
Ambrosia (pineapple & coconut), 148
Cochin pepper water, *Rasam,* 150
Coriander & fennel drink, *Mooli,* 152
Cumin water, *Jeeraka vellam,* 151
Ginger lime *sherbet,* 147
Ginger wine (spicy, sweet) 146
Ginger wine, 146
Kiddush wine & *Kosher Mai,* 144/145
Kokum sherbet, 149
Limeade Sarasaparilla, 149
Pineapple & banana cocktail, 149
Raisin vinegar,
   Chorka/vinaagri, 145
Spiced buttermilk,
   Sambhaaram, 152
Spiced jaggery water,
   Panakam, 151
Spiced tea, *Spice chaaya,* 153

Index

IN PLANTAIN/ BANANA COUNTRY
Banana fritters, *Pazham pori*, 155
Banana sautéed in butter/ghee, 156
Gingered plantain in cashew
   & coconut sauce, 155
Gingered plantain (variant), 156
Fried Nendran plantain chips,
   Kaaya varuthathu, 157
Jaggery-coated, fried plantain chips,
   Sharkkara upperi, 157
Steamed plantain, 156

THE COCHIN SAVOURIES
Cigar shaped snack,
   Coil appam/Kuzhalappam, 158
Cochini potato fritters,
   Aloo Bonda, 159
Crispy-fried spiced rice dough,
   Cheeda, 161
Crunchy rice spirals, *Murukku*, 162
Rice & semolina crisp,
   Kallu appam (Stone appam), 160
Semolina-coconut-sesame snack,
   Cheepappam, 160
Spicy, fried flour strings,
   Nula mala, 161

EATING BRICK & MORTAR - THE CHAROSET
Bernadette Baum's *charoset*, 164
Cochin *charoset*, Duwoo, 164
Cochin *charoset*, Mala version, 165
Rachel Roby's *charoset*, 166
Rebecca's *charoset*, 167
Spiced Ernakulam *charoset*, 167

OUR SWEETS ARE SUBLIME!
Apple confection, *Meruba*, 184
Cashew & coconut *halwa*,
   Kashuandi-Thenga halwa, 179
Cashewnut brittle,
   Kashuandi mittai, 176
Chewy fruit confection, *Meruba*, 184
Chocolate mousse, 174
Cochin Jewish coconut cake, 173
Cochin Hanukkah cake,
   Neyyappam, 173
Cochini Hanukkah fritters,
   Unniyappam, 171
Cochini holiday cookies, 172
Cochini Jewish spice cake, 181
Cochini sponge cake, *Burdoor*, 182
Coconut milk *halwa*, 180
Coconut rice pudding, 172
Crepe with coconut & jaggery,
   Churullappam, 185
Fried rice & coconut balls/powder,
   Avalose podi/unda, 187
Honey & sesame *halwa*, 179
Rice & coconut crisp,
   Arikarakal, 187
Rice *halwa* with coconut milk, 180
Rice pudding, *Payasam*, 177
Semolina sweet, *Sheera*, 170
Steamed rice & jaggery,
   Sharkkara ada, 183
Sweet, crispy rice rosettes,
   Achappam, 186
Sweet rice & sesame dumplings,
   Modakam, 177
Tiny, sugared rice & coconut balls,
   Chukunda, 188
Ural halwa, 175

www.ingramcontent.com/pod-product-compliance
Lightning Source LLC
Chambersburg PA
CBHW031142160426
43193CB00008B/221